ANNE L. ALSTOTT

No Exit

What Parents Owe Their Children

and What Society Owes Parents

OXFORD
UNIVERSITY PRESS

2004

OXFORD
UNIVERSITY PRESS

Oxford   New York
Auckland   Bangkok   Buenos Aires   Cape Town   Chennai
Dar es Salaam   Delhi   Hong Kong   Istanbul   Karachi   Kolkata
Kuala Lumpur   Madrid   Melbourne   Mexico City   Mumbai   Nairobi
São Paulo   Shanghai   Taipei   Tokyo   Toronto

Copyright © 2004 by Oxford University Press, Inc.

Published by Oxford University Press, Inc.
198 Madison Avenue, New York, New York 10016

www.oup.com

Oxford is a registered trademark of Oxford University Press

Library of Congress Cataloging-in-Publication Data
Alstott, Anne, 1963–
No exit : what parents owe their children and what society owes parents /
by Anne L. Alstott.
   p.   cm.
Includes bibliographical references and index.
ISBN   978-0-19530641-5
1. Parenting. 2. Parenthood. 3. Child rearing. 4. Parent and child. I. Title.
HQ755.8.A463 2004
649'.1—dc21   2003013060

Printed in the United States of America
on acid-free paper

For my father, David Alstott,

and my sons, John and David

Acknowledgments

I began to develop the ideas in this book in 1999, as I defended *The Stakeholder Society* (Ackerman and Alstott 1999) to my feminist friends. They objected that the social inheritance of $80,000 that Bruce Ackerman and I proposed would do too little to help women and might even harm them. Gender, they worried, would warp women's choices about how to spend their funds: too many women would withdraw from the labor force to care for children, deepening their own disadvantage in the process. Their thoughtful comments, and the birth of my twin sons in that same year, led me to revisit the feminist literature on paid work and care work. Although I was inspired by much that I read, I was not entirely satisfied with existing theories of care or with policy proposals for income support or family-friendly workplace accommodations. The search for an alternative policy led me to some basic normative questions. How should a liberal, egalitarian feminist think about equality for children and people who rear children? Is parenthood just one life plan among many, or is there something distinctive about it, something that justifies redistribution to parents? Is it possible to assist parents while also fighting gender subordination? Is the risk of subordination inherent in child-rearing work? Or can we imagine a free society in which some women and some men, perhaps in equal numbers and perhaps not, choose to rear children but without losing their status as autonomous equals capable of choosing and pursuing a life plan of their own?

In a bit of hellish irony, one of my children was struck with a serious illness while I was completing revisions to this book, and I learned first-hand the difficulties of caring for a child with special medical needs. Tony Kronman, the dean of the Yale Law School, responded to my situation with characteristic grace, and I am forever grateful to him. I am also indebted to my colleague Jed Rubenfeld, who agreed to take up the duties of the deputy deanship.

Many friends and colleagues generously offered their comments on various drafts of this book. Bruce Ackerman encouraged the project, interrogated my ideas, and read the manuscript more than once. I am always stunned by the quickness and accuracy of Bruce's perceptions—and grateful for his insights. More good friends on the Yale Law faculty—Vicki Schultz, Kenji Yoshino, Michael Graetz, and Daniel Markovits—graciously took the time to talk about these ideas at length or to read the manuscript. Scott Shapiro, visiting at Yale in 2002–2003, engaged my ideas about family law at a critical stage in my thinking; I am grateful for his perceptive and constructive comments. Amy Wax gave me extensive comments on a first draft; her intelligent challenge to my ideas at an early stage helped me refine my argument and refocus the book. I also benefited from comments offered at different stages by Christine Jolls, Michael Livingston, Dan Shaviro, David Bradford, Deborah Schenk, and participants in the Yale Law School Faculty Workshop and the NYU Colloquium on Tax Policy. Harvard's 2001 Workshop on Current Research on Taxation provided a helpful forum for what became Chapter 9; although the events of September 11 led to the cancellation of the conference, Julie Roin and Dan Halperin took the time to give me their excellent comments in writing.

I owe a great debt of thanks to Dedi Felman of Oxford University Press, who saw the best in a long and dustily academic first draft. Her engagement, enthusiasm, and intelligent suggestions helped bring out the manuscript's strengths through several rounds of revisions. She is truly one of the great editors in this business. Every comment she made helped sharpen the book's focus and expand its potential readership.

I am also grateful to the three anonymous reviewers who provided excellent comments on the initial manuscript. Their pointed but constructive questions helped motivate me to reframe the normative argument and to engage more directly with family law. I later learned that one of these reviewers was Beth Garrett, and I am pleased to be able to thank her, by name, for her searching, challenging, and constructive comments.

Five outstanding Yale students worked as research assistants on this book. Anne Joseph, a law student, helped me pull together research materials on the family-friendly workplace in 1999, during the early stages of my thinking about the topic. Another law student, Tyra Williams, provided a year of early research assistance, carefully searching for empirical sources on the division of labor and other topics. Grace Lee worked energetically during her second and third years of law school, providing thorough and precise research assistance on a variety of topics. I am grateful for her incisive comments on several drafts. Jane Gao, a graduate of Yale College, devoted a summer of hard and effective work to reading and researching a late draft of the book. And Lisa Mahle, another law student, gave me tough and insightful comments on a late draft.

Patricia Spiegelhalter, my assistant at Yale, is irreplaceable. She brings not only great efficiency and organization to her work but also a wonderful spirit of generosity and human concern. She always cares about how my family is doing, and her incredible almond cake has sustained me through more than one long evening at the hospital with my son.

I am grateful every day for Russ, John, and David. I sacrificed their time as well as my own to this project, and I appreciate their love and understanding. Russ keeps me going; without him, I could not do any of the things I do. My love for David and John defies expression.

I also want to thank Shannon Delaney and Amanda Abbott, whose affectionate and responsible care for our sons helped make my work possible. Finally, I want to express my gratitude to our pediatrician, Dr. Joseph Avni-Singer, who has been a model of generosity, patience, and sympathy during difficult days.

Contents

No Exit

Introduction

A child alters his parents' lives forever. Parenthood brings new experiences but also new responsibilities: a parent is no longer quite the author of her own life.[1] Parents must protect, nurture, and guide their child and remain at his side for 18 years—or more, if needed. Today, marriages may come and go, but parenthood endures for better and worse, for richer and poorer, and in sickness and in health.

It is an understatement to observe that parents find it difficult to combine child rearing with their own endeavors in the larger world. However good our day care provider, school, or babysitter may be, children need parental care in order to flourish. Today, more than ever before, parents do manage to care for their children and work outside the home too. But many of us feel a constant pull between the children's seemingly limitless need for our time and our own need to lead an independent life. For some parents, this tension is primarily psychological: we feel torn between competing desires, and we never seem to have the balance quite right, whatever decision we make. But for many parents, the conflict has a harder edge: we must work to make ends meet, and yet we also need time to meet our children's noneconomic needs—for closeness, for conversation, for recreation.

Parents take justifiable pride in meeting their responsibilities. Parenthood requires real moral and emotional growth. We learn to be more generous than we thought we could be to another human being. We feel newly mature; we are the grown-ups now. We give more of ourselves than ever before, knowing we are doing the right thing.

And yet, the tension between our own plans and our children's needs persists. Where does this tension come from? Many books document the balancing act that parenthood entails, but this book tackles a more fundamental question: Why should balance be so elusive? Is the tension we feel merely a product of our emotions or of moral strictures we place on ourselves? Could we, should we, simply *choose* to feel less conflicted? Or is there a deeper dilemma here?

This book aims to consider parenthood in social perspective. What role do—and should—parents play in a good society? Over time, our society's demands on parents have steeply increased, while the economic rewards of child rearing have diminished. At one time, children were an emotional *and* economic bonus, providing workers for the farm or factory and old-age security, too. For today's parents, in contrast, child rearing is a one-way obligation: parents spend time and money preparing their offspring for modern life, without expecting much other than love in return.

Today, society expects parents to do the intensive work of preparing children for modern life. We expect parents to invest in their children far more time and money than ever before; we rely on parents to give priority to their children's needs for nearly two decades; and we expect them to do so without much economic reward. Slowly, but surely, a combination of technological, social, and legal change has transformed modern parenthood into an extraordinarily demanding social role, and one that carries a built-in tension between meeting our children's needs and pursuing lives of our own.

Once we understand the source of the dilemma, we can begin to address it, to take steps to help parents give children what they need and also preserve for themselves the opportunity to shape an independent life.

"Do Not Exit"

Society expects—and needs—parents to provide their children with *continuity of care*, meaning the intensive, intimate care that human beings need to develop their intellectual, emotional, and moral capabilities. And society expects—and needs—parents to persist in their role for 18 years, or longer if needed. A variety of social and legal institutions convey a common message: do what it takes to give your children the continuing care that they need. Put even more simply: "Do Not Exit."

Continuity of care expresses the insight that children's development depends on a long-term, continuing relationship with at least one parent (or parent figure). Indeed, continuity of care helps define what a parent is. Both in folk wisdom and in family law, a parent is someone who cares for a child and who puts that child's interests first when need be. And who does so, not for a day or a year, but for the long term.

Why is *continuity* important as well as *care*? Child psychologists explain that healthy emotional development requires a close and enduring relationship with one or more parental figures. Parental continuity gives young children a stable foundation for their increasing interactions with the outside world. Consistency in parental praise and discipline helps children develop emotional control. Parents also provide lasting role models which older children can begin to identify with—and which teenagers can reject, safe in the knowledge that the parent will not leave. Of course, parents sometimes must exit their children's lives; illness, accident, or other calamities may cut short a parent-child relationship. But psychologists emphasize the importance of recreating continuity for these children as soon as possible.

Continuity of care serves a second function as well: parents who persist with their children for the long term can best represent children's interests in interactions with the health care system, the educational system, and other public bureaucracies. Parents with a close, and lasting, connection to their child tend to develop expertise in caring for that child and to identify with his or her fate. Public institutions rely on parents to act as children's protectors and advocates; when parents fail, our schools and other institutions for children perform badly.

To be sure, parents do not ordinarily perceive "Do Not Exit" as a command from the state. Good parents provide their children with continuity of care out of love and a sense of moral obligation to these vulnerable humans who are given to our charge for a time. They remain with their children for the long term and do their best to respond to their children's needs. For these parents, the state's role in child rearing is nearly invisible day to day. The state, it may seem, is a distant arbiter of the tragic cases that arise when parents abandon or neglect or abuse.

But if we take a closer look, we can see that the state plays a role even in successful families. In the United States today, individuals usually choose whether to be parents, but once the child arrives, every parent assumes a role whose rights and responsibilities are defined explicitly by the state through its laws. Parents who provide their children with continuity are granted wide authority over them. These parents scarcely feel the law's supervision, and this is as it should be: continuity of care implies a warm and intimate connection, not a cold legal calculus. But when parents fail to provide continuity of care, the state revokes or curtails their parental prerogatives.

Society's "Do Not Exit" command to parents is grounded in a deep and appropriate commitment to human dignity and equality. If every child is to have a fair start in life, we cannot authorize parents to act in any way they wish. A society that seeks to protect the life chances of every person cannot be indifferent to the conditions of child rearing. We understand that society owes every child the conditions he or she needs to flourish. Every child deserves a parent who will not exit.

But from a parent's perspective, "Do Not Exit" has a double edge. Parents can, and should, take pride in meeting their obligations to their children. Continuity of care is good for children and for society, too, because well-cared-for children can grow into autonomous adults. Yet, at the same time that the "Do Not Exit" command promotes children's interests, it also burdens parents' opportunities. We can acknowledge the moral and emotional satisfactions of parenthood while also recognizing that parents provide continuity to their children at considerable cost to themselves.

My complaint is not that parents must learn to work hard, give priority to their children's needs, and moderate their own dreams. That is just growing up. Instead, the point is that the No Exit obligation can severely limit the ordinary jobs, and ordinary lives, that parents can choose to live. Parents who meet their responsibilities to their children will find their personal opportunities more circumscribed than they would otherwise be. They may compromise in their choice of jobs and limit their geographic mobility. They may turn down better options that would require working the night shift, reliance on a questionable babysitter, or too much out-of-town travel.

For some parents, these economic adjustments mean a lower living standard and uncertain old-age security. For others, compromise brings real hardship. A low-income mother needs her job to pay the rent, but a lengthy commute, long workday, or rigid job schedule may make it difficult or impossible to give her children adequate supervision. Parents with a severely ill or disabled child may find it especially difficult to meet their child's need for extra care while keeping the family financially solvent.

These economic pressures will come as no surprise to most parents, and certainly to most mothers. Study after study confirms that mothers *in every income class* compromise their working lives in order to provide their children with continuity of care. Mothers work less, earn less, and achieve less than men and than childless women. Job interruptions take their toll on mothers' earning power. Even when mothers stay in the race and accumulate the same credentials as their childless counterparts, they still earn less. Over the long term, work disruptions and lower earnings take their toll. Mothers are terribly vulnerable at divorce and accumulate less financial security for old age.

Changing gender roles have not saved the day. Although more mothers hold jobs now, they still bear primary responsibility for child rearing. To be sure, attitudes have evolved, and fathers do more now than a generation ago, but the rate of change in actual behavior has been slow. On average, it is still the mother who manages the household, identifies the children's needs, and takes responsibility when children are sick, schools close, or the babysitter quits. But even if mothers' and fathers' roles could magically be equalized, the hard fact is that child rearing requires intensive emotional work and a large time commitment: 18 years or more.

Why Marriage Isn't the Answer

Traditionally, society has looked to marriage to provide the emotional and financial foundations for child rearing. In idealized form, marriage is a long-term partnership, and at one time, marriage was (at least in theory) a No Exit relationship. But today, Americans legally exit their marriages at high rates, and former spouses owe limited financial obligations to one another.

Society could try to make marital exit more difficult.[2] But legal reforms cannot easily reverse the underlying social trends that are making marriage marginal to many children's and parents' lives. Rates of divorce and nonmarriage remain high. A full one-third of American children are now born to unmarried parents. Black children and children of younger or less-educated mothers are least likely to spend time in a married family.[3]

Nor can the state readily improve parents' economic security by increasing child support or alimony obligations. Although enforcement of child support has improved in recent years, even so, in 1997, only 56 percent of custodial parents had a child support award, and of these, only 67 percent received any payment at all. Low-income single parents are least likely to receive child support payments, and the amounts they do receive are quite low.[4]

Even with better enforcement, the likely impact of child support and alimony reforms is blunted by economic reality. For poor and working-class families, the grim fact is that men's real wages have fallen over the long term, while women's wages remain low, leaving little surplus to divide between two households when parents divorce (or fail to marry). For middle-class couples, the long-term trend is that wealth is changing its form, with easily visible (and divisible) physical and financial capital being replaced by human capital—earning power—which, for reasons both principled and practical, is far more difficult to divide. The increasing number of stepfamilies and second families also limits the possibilities for wringing greater financial support out of absent parents.[5]

These realities suggest that it is both impractical and unwise to rely on marriage as the primary source of security for children and those who care for them. But what is the alternative?

Can We Do Better?

The status quo represents one path. Today, society tells parents "Do Not Exit" but disclaims any public responsibility to assist parents who provide continuity of care. It's their duty, we say. (The government's budget contains a few programs for parents, but they provide limited amounts and often assist only a subset of families.)[6] When confronted with evidence that parents, especially mothers, are faring badly in economic life, we shrug: that's life. After all, prospective parents have fair warning of what they are getting into.

But we can—and should—aspire to do more to assist parents. It is both unfair and counterproductive to pit children's need for care against parents' need for economic security and a life of their own. Instead, we should aim both to ensure continuity of care for every child and to reward and support those parents who provide it.

The key is to change the way we think about parents' obligations to children and society's obligations to parents. Parents make a private decision to have children, but when they do so, they also step into a public role. Children deserve the parental care they need to develop their autonomy and take their place in adult life, but parents deserve the chance to provide that care while leading lives of their own. A fair society should expect parents to care for their children and to sacrifice time and opportunity if necessary, but it should also help parents preserve a reasonable range of life options during and after their years of care.

Today, most parents, and especially most mothers, provide continuity of care to their children. In the process, too many drift toward the margins of economic life. But parents' present economic position reflects a failure of social policy and not a law of nature. It is both practical and affordable to create new programs to assist parents who live up to their obligation of care. Public policy can help ensure that these parents have the opportunity to combine child rearing with independent projects over a lifetime.

In this book, I propose two new programs designed to enhance parents' long-term opportunities. Both programs aim to serve parents in a wide range of economic circumstances. And both aim to respect parents' own judgments about how to combine paid work with child rearing.

The first program, *caretaker resource accounts,* would provide parents with financial resources to help remain in or reenter the mainstream of economic life. The program would give parents an annual grant of $5,000, which could be used for any of three purposes: child care, parents' own education, or parents' retirement. Each individual could choose how best to use the funds to further his or her own plans, but every option would improve parents' long-term prospects.

The second program, *life-planning insurance*, would offer extra help to the parents of children with serious illnesses or disabilities, in the form of job leave, income support, and supportive social services. The two programs work in tandem: caretaker resource accounts would provide a standard package to all parents, whereas life-planning insurance would offer more individualized assistance to those whose children suffer severe illness or disability.

The goal should not be to render child rearing costless. It would be impossible, as well as unwise, to attempt to erase any imprint of parenthood on parents' lives. Instead, the goal should be to lighten the burden. Child rearing should be a life stage, and not a life sentence.

One Family's Experience

As I completed this book, one of my children was struck with a serious illness. Our 3-year-old son has joined the millions of American children with asthma, and unfortunately, he has an especially severe form of the disease. Many children with asthma respond well to standard medications; our son does not. He has spent too many weeks in the hospital and far too many months taking medication with harmful side effects. His illness has puzzled several specialists, and he has undergone more invasive procedures than any small child should.

My son's uncontrolled and unpredictable illness has changed our family life. Several days a week, he needs careful treatment and monitoring. We use a stethoscope and an oxygen monitor, and we are alert for the physical signs that signal a respiratory crisis. Often, we must wake our little boy—and ourselves—every two, three, or four hours around the clock to give him the breathing treatments that keep his airways open. When the wheezing gets especially severe, we need one parent to take him to the emergency room and another parent (or babysitter) to take care of our other child.

My husband and I have reorganized our working lives so that we can care for our son. I resigned my administrative post at the law school where

I teach; although I still teach classes, a professor's schedule is more flexible and forgiving than is a deputy dean's. My husband also shoulders significant child care responsibilities.

What I have written has thus come home to me, quite literally. I feel the No Exit obligation that binds me to my sons: I love these children fiercely. I see how vulnerable they are and how much their very lives depend on our continuing care and love. The changes I have made in my working life feel relatively unimportant. Sometimes I miss the rhythms of being a dean; I liked having more responsibility and authority, and I liked solving day-to-day problems for students and other professors. Still, I know that I made the right decision.

Many parents in the United States have limited resources. They may find it difficult or impossible to provide their children with continuity of care without endangering their own economic prospects. Even healthy children can strain parents' resources. When illness or disability strikes, many families face economic crisis.

No Exit?

No Exit may seem a surprisingly unsentimental title for a book about parents and children. For some readers, the phrase will evoke Jean-Paul Sartre's one-act play about hell. Sartre imagines a hell without demons or physical torment. Instead, he presents us with an ordinary, even pleasant room, which holds three people. The twist is that the three strangers are locked together for eternity—there is no exit from the room—and they will torment each other endlessly through needling conversation that revisits their worst actions in life.

I do not imagine that family life is hell. And yet, the No Exit metaphor conveys the sense of being trapped that I think parents do feel. Many excellent books have documented the costs of motherhood.[7] But we have not quite faced the hard fact that we inevitably constrain parents' opportunities when we seek to promote children's. For children's sake, parents must remain in the locked room of parenthood for 18 years or more.

But this book has a hopeful message as well. Society can take productive steps to preserve parents' opportunities—to prop open the door to the room—and to allow parents greater autonomy during their child-rearing years and thereafter.

These ideas raise as many questions as they answer. Should parents resent the implication that they care for their children from a sense of obligation? Is the No Exit obligation really a legal duty, or a product of personal morality and social norms? If society does impose a No Exit obligation, why does it permit so many parents to freely exit their children's lives, at divorce, for instance?

More fundamentally, is it fair to tax the childless to lighten the economic costs of child rearing, when parents freely choose to have children, in full knowledge of the cost of doing so?

And how heavy *are* the costs of child rearing, really? Haven't we made enormous strides in recent decades enabling parents, especially mothers, to rear children *and* hold paid jobs? Given the enormous progress in gender equality in the last generation, why should we now create programs aimed largely at mothers? Isn't there a danger that rewarding parenthood will worsen women's situation by making traditional gender roles more appealing?

There are also a host of practical details that merit attention. How much would the proposed programs cost? Would they require expensive, and intrusive, new bureaucracies? Why aren't existing programs sufficient? And, given my commitment to assisting parents, why don't I embrace proposals for family-friendly workplace reforms that would guarantee parents access to flextime and part-time work?

This book addresses all of these questions, and more.

Part 1

Why Continuity of Care Is Important for Children and Costly for Parents

What Is Continuity of Care?

Joe and Jeannie Allen had very different attitudes toward their son Joshua's disability. Joshua was born deaf. Joe, Joshua's biological father, had a difficult time dealing with his son's condition and tended to take a passive, even fatalistic, outlook. Jeannie, Joshua's stepmother, took a more active approach. She learned sign language, helped teach Joshua how to sign, and insisted that her other children learn to sign, too, so that Joshua could participate in family conversations. Jeannie fought for, and won, a special one-on-one tutoring program at school. She believed that Joshua had unlimited potential.[1]

Jeannie truly treated Joshua as her child. When she married Joe, Joshua was already a toddler, but Jeannie took the time to really get to know him, to find out what he needed and what he could do. She rearranged the family's home life to make sure Joshua felt included, and she expected her other children to help him feel fully part of the family. Jeannie also looked outward, beyond the home, and acted as Joshua's advocate in the school system, securing an unprecedented level of services.

Not all children face the challenges that Joshua faced, but most parents can understand what motivated Jeannie. Being a parent means knowing your child better than anyone; it means making that child feel wanted and loved; and it means speaking for that child in the outside world, promoting his interests, and, if necessary, challenging conventional practices that do not meet his needs. A parent, more than anyone else, must come to identify with his child's needs and his interests.[2]

Jeannie's actions exemplify what *continuity of care* means. Jeannie cared for Joshua, intensively and loyally, and she committed to him for the long term. She entered Joshua's life as a stepmother, but her actions signaled a lasting dedication to his interests. Indeed, Jeannie's story is famous in legal circles because, when Jeannie and Joe divorced, Jeannie sought, and won, permanent custody of Joshua.[3]

Continuity of care requires a parent to take on a demanding, dual role. Put succinctly, parents must be both nurturers and advocates, just as Jeannie was, and they must continue in both roles until the child is grown.

This much will seem familiar and quite intuitive. It is obvious that children need nurturing, and a moment's reflection confirms the importance of advocacy, too; young children cannot speak for themselves, and even older children may not be able to identify and articulate what they need from schools and other institutions. But how does continuity come into the picture? What does *continuity* add to the idea of *care*? Why is it important that each parent continue in that role for the long term?

How Continuity Fosters Children's Development

The Yale law professor and psychoanalyst Joseph Goldstein offered a striking account of the importance of continuity of care for children. Writing with Anna Freud (Sigmund's daughter) and Albert Solnit, a specialist in child development, Goldstein emphasized the importance of continuing care provided by one (or more) "psychological parents."[4] The authors explained that every child needs "unbroken continuity of affectionate and stimulating relationships with an adult." The goal for society, they wrote, should be to ensure "each child a chance to be a member of a family where he feels wanted and where he will have the opportunity, on a continuing basis, not only to receive and return affection, but also to express anger and to learn to manage his aggression."[5]

I begin with Goldstein, Freud, and Solnit because their theory has become a classic in the academy and in the legal world, and because it explains, in an accessible and compact fashion, the developmental importance to children of continuity of care.

The heart of the Goldstein, Freud, and Solnit theory is the observation that children rely on their psychological parents to create a stable environment and set of close relationships in which the children can accomplish their developmental tasks. Good parents, for example, feed and soothe infants and begin to establish routines that help babies learn to "tolerate postponement of gratification and inevitable frustration." Later in the child's development, parents provide appropriate praise and discipline, laying "the first foundations for the child's own control of his drives and impulses, the lessening of his selfishness, and the beginning of consideration for others." Parents also provide role models for attitudes and values with which the child can identify. During the rebellions of adolescence, parents offer a stable relationship, permitting the child to experiment with rejection and distance without rejecting the child in return.[6]

Goldstein, Freud, and Solnit worry that adults systematically underrate the challenge of being a child:

> Physical, emotional, intellectual, social, and moral growth does not happen without causing the child inevitable internal difficulties. The instability of all mental processes during the period of development needs to be offset by stability and uninterrupted support from external sources. Smooth growth is arrested or disrupted when upheavals and changes in the external world are added to the internal ones.[7]

Throughout the child's development, stability is key: it is crucial that children be able to rely on a parent's continuing presence. Disruptions in continuity of care can inflict serious psychological trauma on children. Children, say the authors, are egocentric and have difficulty maintaining equilibrium when their environment and relationships are disrupted. They may experience disruption as a personal attack or rejection, and they "respond to any threat to their emotional security with fantastic anxieties, denial, or distortion of reality, reversal or displacement of feelings—reactions which are not helpful for coping, but rather put them at the mercy of events."[8]

Goldstein, Freud, and Solnit sought to build on their psychological account of children's development to offer prescriptions for social and legal reforms that, they argued, could better meet children's needs. Although some of their legal ideas have been contested over the years, the basics of their psychological theory of continuity have been widely accepted.[9] Even those who disagree with the authors' proposals for legal reform acknowledge that there is now near consensus on children's need for continuity of care.[10]

It is worth emphasizing that continuity of care does not rely on maternal bonding theories. These spring up from time to time in the popular media, urging that children must develop a close bond with their mother—and only their mother—in order to flourish. Maternal bonding theorists sometimes demand that mothers stay home for years and warn that working mothers are doing lasting damage to their children. But these extreme views are empirically questionable, and in any event they do not represent the views of Goldstein, Freud, and Solnit.[11] Nothing in the psychological parent theory requires parents to quit their jobs or devote every moment to their child. While continuity of care emphasizes a loving bond between parent and child, it also recognizes that children develop such attachments with more than one parent, and that appropriate use of a substitute caregiver will not disrupt the parent-child relationship.[12]

Continuity, then, is an integral part of nurture: children need a sense of stability and permanence that helps them navigate the challenges of growing up. But the psychological bond between parent and child serves a second function as well: it turns out that continuity helps parents act as effective representatives for their children in the wider world.

How Continuity Protects Children's Interests

Today, children must interact with a variety of large, impersonal institutions. The assumption that parents will faithfully represent their children's interests is ingrained in virtually all our public institutions for children's care. Public education and health care rely especially heavily on the parent's role as advocate for his or her child. Teachers and medical personnel can provide expert advice, but their diagnoses often rely on the parent's close observation of the child. Parents may seek special programs or treatments for a sick or disabled child, or they may actively contest a proposed course of therapy. One vivid example comes from special education. Although federal law requires public schools to provide a free and appropriate public education, parents' repeated experience is that they play a crucial role in asserting their children's rights and in ensuring that the schools provide adequate educational programs for special-needs children.[13]

Any parent who has had to deal with the health care system can attest to the importance of parental advocacy. For instance, our son has been hospitalized many times in the local children's hospital. For the most part, this is a highly professional operation, and we are grateful that the pediatricians and staff are (usually) very caring people. Even so, I have sometimes worried about hospital errors. Well-meaning doctors and nurses are overworked, and frequent shift changes mean that any given patient may have four to six nurses and two or three doctors (residents and interns) each day. In that setting, mistakes are only human, but they can also be quite serious. At various times, I have had to question emergency triage procedures and make repeated requests for medication. At a more mundane level, I have provided a great deal of my son's care myself. As a novice "hospital parent," I was puzzled by the curious absence of nursing staff, but I quickly learned that families simply cannot rely on the harried staff to wash, dress, feed, or even medicate the children in their care. Instead, the parent must be on duty twenty-four hours a day.

My point is not that we should expect parents to compensate for the nursing shortage or for flawed staffing procedures. Reforms in education and hospital practices should be a top priority. Instead, my point is that even good institutions cannot function without parental participation and advocacy. We will never be able to create impersonal care that mimics personal care; we will never train teachers who know our children as we do, or doctors and nurses who remember every detail of a child's medical history.

And, once again, continuity is a critical component of parental care. Parents are more likely to act with greater fidelity to children's interests if they bond to children over the long term. When parents have a close emotional tie to their children, they can promote the child's interests most effectively. When parents know that they are responsible for the child for the long term, they may feel a greater stake in the child's life. And parents who persist with their children develop expertise about them that neither the state nor shorter-term caretakers can match.[14]

Compare a parent's role with the role of other representatives for children. In different settings, various professionals may speak on children's behalf: teachers, doctors, caseworkers, even lawyers in a courtroom setting. These representatives bring special expertise, but they are most effective when they work *with* parents. Their formal training is not designed to substitute for the knowledge and intensity that a parent brings to the table. Parents' long-term, close, and continuing relationship with their children creates a depth of knowledge and personal identification that cannot be duplicated in shorter-term or more casual relationships.

Once we give continuity of care a name, it feels entirely familiar. Indeed, parental continuity is so bound up with our notions of good child rearing that it is hard to imagine how parents could act otherwise. Could we possibly call someone a good parent if he intended to commit to his child only for the short term? No matter how tenderly that person cared for his child day to day, it is unlikely that we would praise his conduct if he expressed a willingness to leave that child (for trivial or selfish reasons) at any time.

Having introduced continuity of care, I now step back and take a wider perspective. Continuity of care expresses an ideal for children's care. But what does continuity mean for *parents'* lives? How costly is it for parents to provide continuity of care in today's world?

The Cost of Continuity
for Parents' Lives

Laverne, a Brooklyn single mother of three, worked two jobs, as a school aide from 9 A.M. to 2 P.M., and for Blue Cross/Blue Shield from 4:30 to 11:00 P.M. For a while, all seemed well, but then things began to fall apart. A neighbor reported that Laverne, who was living in a hotel, was leaving her children unattended for long periods while she worked. (The children were then 10, 6, and almost 2.) Laverne had not otherwise neglected her children, but she agreed to place the children in foster care temporarily until she could get her finances in order and find better housing (as well as adequate child care). When a caseworker told Laverne she would need to find a three-bedroom apartment to get her children back, Laverne worked hard and found the apartment, even though the $500 monthly rent was terribly expensive on her salary of just $11,000 a year.

Then things went from bad to worse. Laverne's school job was eliminated, her mother died of cancer, and a new caseworker told her she would have to earn more or find a cheaper apartment to get her children back. Laverne, by then ill herself, snapped. She spent 11 months on the street before pulling herself together. During Laverne's legal battle to retrieve her children from foster care, the kids lived in four foster homes in seven years.[1]

The State of New York attempted to terminate Laverne's parental rights on the ground that she had permanently neglected the children because of her 11-month failure to communicate with them. But an appellate court disagreed:

> It cannot be too strongly emphasized that, to the extent that [Laverne] fell short of ideal standards for parenting, it was largely due to her economic condition and the despair to which she plummeted because of it. Indeed, it is to respondent's credit that, despite enormous difficulties, she has persisted in her attempts to regain the custody of her children.... It would appear that, throughout these difficult years, [Laverne was] the sole consistent parental figure these children have had.[2]

Laverne's case illustrates how difficult it can be even for motivated parents to provide their children with continuity of care. I do not suggest that Laverne was a model parent; indeed, the court counseled that she might have dealt more responsibly with her situation. And yet, Laverne was a very human parent, with good intentions and a drive to care for her children, who simply found it too difficult to care for them and make ends meet.

Laverne's case is dramatic, but her story is not terribly far removed from the day-to-day lives of other low-income single mothers. They face painful decisions: Pay the rent or the babysitter? Take a second job or spend more time supervising their children?[3]

Middle-class parents can avoid these harsh trade-offs, and yet they, too, experience the very real conflict between caring for their children and preserving their economic opportunities. The basic problem is obvious to any parent: child rearing is time-intensive work that interferes with one's ability to pursue other projects. Young children require care twenty-four hours a day, and though paid child care can absorb some of that care, some tasks cannot be delegated. A typical school day is six or seven hours, and a typical day care day is eight or nine. That leaves many hours of child care for parents during the day, as well as an extra load of housework at night to ensure that the family has meals, food, and clean clothing.

Studies confirm that child rearing takes up enormous amounts of parental time, especially mothers' time. Taking into account the hours spent on child care, housework, and paid work, mothers (especially employed mothers) work harder than any other group.[4] To compound the organizational problem, child rearing tends to be what sociologists call "low-schedule-control." This means that the pace and content of the work are driven by the child's needs and cannot always be scheduled by the parent in order to preserve time for outside projects. Some household tasks, such as mowing the lawn, can be scheduled at a convenient time; child care cannot. No one will be harmed if the lawn gets a little overgrown, but a child who is ill must be cared for right away.

In the following discussion, I show how costly it is for parents (especially mothers) at every income level to rearrange their working lives to meet children's needs. But before diving in, two caveats will clarify my argument.

First, existing data are imperfect for my purposes. I am most interested in the impact of child-rearing work on the economic opportunities of *caretakers*: that is, parents who persist for the long term in caring for a child. But most studies look at mothers, and not at caretakers. Although motherhood is a reasonable proxy for caretaker status, it is not perfect. On average, mothers take on a greater share of child-rearing work than fathers, and they are more likely than fathers to make adjustments in their work plans to accommodate children's needs. Still, data on mothers do not adequately convey the economic situation of fathers who participate as active caretakers or of mothers who eschew the traditional role.[5]

Second, although the data demonstrate that mothers fare worse in earnings and career achievement, I want to emphasize that I do not claim that the difference in outcomes is in itself an injustice. My goal is not absolute parity in earnings or promotions; we can imagine a fair society in which some parents chose a balance between work and child rearing that left them with lower wages or fewer promotions than the childless. My concern, instead, is that the extreme disproportion in outcomes and achievements flags a too-large gap in opportunities for choice. I am worried that child-rearing too dramatically contracts the options among which mothers can choose.

I recognize that statistics are no substitute for argument, and it will take another chapter (or two) to show why the present situation is unfair and deserves redress. For now, I simply want to set the stage for the fairness inquiry by demonstrating just how large the economic cost of child-rearing work currently is.

The Motherhood Gap in Wages, Achievement, and Economic Security

The data on mothers' workforce participation reveals the tension between child rearing and paid work. Men (including fathers) and childless women tend to work full time. In contrast, a high percentage of mothers either do not hold paid jobs or work part time, and mothers interrupt their paid employment at far higher rates than fathers. These job interruptions persist across class lines: in 2000, at least 20 to 35 percent of mothers of children over age 1 were at home in every income class. Mothers also report higher rates of job turnover and unemployment attributable to child-rearing responsibilities.[6]

The highest-tech measure of mothers' disadvantage is the "motherhood wage gap," which measures the difference between mothers' wages and childless women's wages. The advantage of this statistic is that it compares two groups of women, thus isolating the impact of child rearing while filtering out the impact of gender discrimination. Estimates suggest that the motherhood wage gap is 10 to 20 percentage points; that is, mothers earn about 70 percent of the mean wages of men, and childless women earn 80 to 90 percent.[7] The motherhood wage gap reflects, in part, mothers' interrupted working lives: people who drop in and out of the workforce earn less. But researchers have found that the gap persists even after controlling for age, education, and work experience. In other words, mothers earn less *even when they have the same education and on-the-job experience as childless women.* For example, in a study using longitudinal data and controlling for work experience and education, Waldfogel found a motherhood penalty of 4 percent for mothers of one child and 12 percent for mothers of two or more. Although the wage penalty diminishes when mothers return to work, some studies find that an interrupted career can take a long-term toll on mothers' earning capacity.[8]

A skeptic might object that perhaps mothers' lower earnings reflect some *other* difference between mothers and childless women. For example, suppose that less ambitious women choose motherhood, while more ambitious women remain childless. In that case, the women who became mothers would have earned less even if they had not had children. Put in the most provocative terms, the question is whether mothers' lack of success is caused by their child-rearing obligations or by their preexisting lack of commitment to the working world.

At first glance, this is a difficult objection to address, because it seems impossible for statisticians to quantify traits such as ambition and commitment. But clever researchers have developed proxy techniques. For example, some track the relative earnings of mothers and nonmothers with similar credentials *before* the first group has children. To take a simple example, if Susie and Shannon have the same credentials and experience and work in the same kind of job but Susie earns $5 more per hour, they predict that the wage gap would continue even if both women remain childless. If Shannon later has a baby and Susie does not, the first $5 of any wage gap between them would be attributed to "unobservables" and not to motherhood. This method is not perfect; it is impossible to know whether Susie's wage advantage might have widened to $7 or dropped to $3 over time. But it helps.

Studies that make such adjustments consistently find that the motherhood wage gap persists even after taking unobservable characteristics into account. A standard finding is that mothers earn about 5 percent less per child; thus, the motherhood wage gap is 5 percent for one child and 10 percent for two.[9] A recent study looked at class differentials and found that medium-skilled mothers—the large group that graduated from high school but does not have a four-year degree—bear the largest motherhood penalty.[10]

A few innovative studies use twin births as a "natural experiment" to isolate the impact of the workload of child rearing from other factors that might affect labor market outcomes. The logic is that because twin births are unplanned, their impact on mothers' work decisions cannot be explained by mothers' preexisting attitudes toward work and child rearing. Put another way, the control group is a group of mothers whose ambitions presumably are comparable to those of the twin mothers. These studies find that twin births do reduce mothers' labor force participation and wages relative to singleton births.[11] No surprise to any parent of twins, but a helpful twist for the statisticians.

Other studies confirm that mothers achieve less in the workplace than nonmothers do. For example, women who have had children are far less likely than childless women (or men) to hold high-status jobs in business, the professions, and politics.[12] Sociological studies confirm that mothers, including professionals like lawyers and doctors, make significant compromises in their paid work to meet their child care responsibilities.[13]

My own experience mirrors the large-scale studies. A surprising number of my law school friends and my husband's business school classmates have left the workforce to care for their children full time. Many of these at-home parents are mothers, but some are fathers. Each family's situation is different, and yet there is a common theme: even these highly paid professionals found it difficult to work full time while caring for their children in the way they wished. Before I had children, I was stunned that so many friends, who had competed so fiercely for so many years to earn their Yale and Stanford credentials, would walk away from jobs during their prime earning years. Now, older and wiser, I understand.

Child-rearing duties also shape gendered patterns of entrepreneurship. Self-employed men (on average) work harder and earn more than their counterparts in traditional jobs, whereas self-employed women work fewer hours and earn less, apparently choosing self-employment to buffer work-family conflicts rather than to earn more.[14] For instance, my best friend from college now is an Avon representative. She enjoys running her own business and prizes the opportunity to work flexible hours while still spending plenty of time with her children. She has built a successful venture that she is proud of, but still, it is very different from the career she thought she would have.

A less familiar fact is that so few women manage to combine motherhood with careers. Claudia Goldin studied the motherhood and work patterns of several cohorts of college students. Importantly, the Goldin study is longitudinal; it tracks the fortunes of the same group of women over time. The youngest cohort is the baby boom generation, and the study's findings are striking: by their late thirties and early forties, *fewer than 20 percent of these women had managed to have children and also achieve a career.* "Career," for purposes of the study, was defined fairly modestly as two years of paid work earning at or above the twenty-fifth percentile of the *male* college graduate wage distribution. In contrast, about 50 percent of childless women achieved a career by the same standard. Although Goldin recognizes that her definition of career is arbitrary, she finds that the results for mothers do not improve appreciably even when career achievement is defined even more humbly, for example, as three continuous years of full-time work at *any* wage.[15]

Mothers' disadvantage in paid work compounds over time. Relatively few homemakers reenter the workforce in midlife. Women's lower lifetime earnings and more frequent job interruptions reduce their private pensions as well as their Social Security coverage. Although many married women can claim a higher Social Security pension based on their husband's (higher) earnings, never-married women, and many divorcees, must rely on their own earnings history and are disproportionately likely to be poor at retirement.[16]

Some readers may wonder whether these facts reflect the last vestiges of outmoded gender roles. After all, women's and men's opportunities have changed remarkably since the previous generation; more mothers than ever before hold paid jobs, and fathers no longer feel exempt from child-rearing work. Looking forward, isn't it possible that gender progress will dramatically lighten mothers' load?

Why Gender Role Change Won't Eliminate the Problem

The answer is almost certainly no. Despite major shifts in patterns of paid employment, child rearing remains primarily mothers' responsibility. Since 1960, the proportion of employed, married mothers of young children has increased from less than 20 percent to more than 60 percent.[17] Yet, there has been relatively little change in the gender division of child-rearing work within the household. Although fathers in the current generation often participate in caretaking more actively than their own fathers did, there is still a considerable gender gap. Mothers typically shoulder the management burden of caring for the children and running the household. Even when both parents hold paid jobs, the mother usually bears the lion's share of the "second shift" of household work and, in addition, must arrange child care, take care of the children during nonwork hours, and take time off for children's frequent minor illnesses.[18]

Despite the increase in mothers' labor force participation over time, fathers still work substantially more than mothers. In 2000, 70 percent of mothers held jobs. But only 54 percent of mothers worked full time, and 27 percent were not in the labor force at all. Sixteen percent of mothers as a group, and 25 percent of the working mothers, worked part time.[19] In contrast, fathers overwhelmingly continue in the traditional "breadwinner" role. In 2000, 90 percent of fathers worked full time.[20]

Data on child rearing and housework confirm that mothers do substantially more than fathers. In the past thirty years, men have taken on a greater role in these areas, and women have reduced their hours at home somewhat as they have taken on a greater role in the labor market. But in absolute terms, mothers still do the bulk of child care and household work. Wives spend about three times as much time doing housework as their husbands do, and the pattern persists across ethnic groups and family structures. The gender gap closes only slightly when both the husband and wife are employed outside the home, and then primarily because women do less (not because men do more).[21]

Mothers take a primary role in child rearing that fathers (on average) simply do not match. One measure is simply time spent: how many hours per week Mom and Dad spend with the kids. The most recent studies of two-parent families find that fathers spend from 45 to 67 percent of the weekday time that mothers do. But that ratio somewhat overstates the typical father's contribution, because there are qualitative differentials in mothers' and fathers' roles. When fathers spend time with their children, they tend to play, watch TV, or do social activities, leaving the custodial care, homework, and errands to mothers. Fathers also spend relatively less time with younger children, who tend to require the most demanding custodial care. For instance, fathers spend about 46 percent as much time with infants and toddlers as mothers do, meaning that mothers do about two-thirds of total caregiving for the youngest children.[22]

Another crucial difference is that mothers in two-parent families tend to take on managerial responsibility in the household. Mothers define the tasks, including child care, that need to be done, and they take responsibility for seeing that the work gets done. Fathers tend to take a "helper" role: they help out when their wife asks, but they do not (by their own admission) set the agenda for the family, and they often do not act unless asked.[23] The gendered division of labor grows more pronounced the more fathers earn. All other things being equal, a man's higher earnings predict fewer hours of time with children; longer work hours (typical of high-earning fathers) also reduce paternal time with children.[24]

Mothers do even more in single-parent families, of course. More than 80 percent of single-parent households are headed by mothers, and more than two-thirds of children of divorced parents live primarily with their mother. Even joint physical custody arrangements often resemble mother-custody with father-visitation; only about half of joint custody decrees split the children's time equally between mother and father. There is also a well-known pattern of "paternal drift," meaning that fathers have a tendency to spend less and less time with their children in the years after the divorce.[25]

The facts on gender and child rearing are uncomfortable, even embarrassing. It is as if we are living in a slightly updated version of an old-fashioned sitcom. Dad is still in the easy chair watching TV and Mom is still in the kitchen. But now, Mom occasionally leaves the kids to lounge in front of the TV set with Dad, and sometimes she yells out, "Dear, could you change the baby's diaper?" instead of doing it herself. But more frequently than before, there is no dad in the easy chair to help at all.

However uncomfortable these gender patterns may be, they do not seem to be changing very quickly. Fathers with access to family-friendly workplace benefits, such as paternity leave and part-time work, tend not to use them. Sociological studies confirm that fathers aspire to be good providers and fear that devoting time to child rearing would put them at a disadvantage in the workplace.[26] There are signs of modest progress: some recent studies have detected increases in fathers' child-care participation, and a small but growing number of fathers stay at home to rear their children while their wife works.[27] Nevertheless, the gender gap in child-rearing roles remains substantial, and the rate of change is sluggish. Gender role equality will not magically save the day.

There is also a fundamental problem, which even lightning-fast gender role change could not erase: child rearing requires an irreducible minimum of hard work that cannot readily be delegated. The fact that so many mothers stay home or work part time or interrupt their working lives is not simply a product of gender bias. Gender surely plays a role in allocating the work between fathers and mothers, but child rearing requires hard work that *someone* must do.

And many parents believe that one or both parents should take time away from paid work to do so. These parents are motivated by religion, or tradition, or just the personal conviction that parental care is best, and they go to great lengths to accomplish their goal.[28] For example, in 1997, 27 percent of infants and toddlers whose mother worked were cared for by their father during the mother's working hours, with the parents typically working split shifts or odd hours to accomplish this.[29] Split shifts are a recipe for parental exhaustion, but the parents involved believe it is worth it. Some of these couples might be trying to save the cost of child care, but we know that many people strongly value parental care, especially for young children, and will arrange their lives to provide it.

It is telling that, at least anecdotally, there is a small trend among high-income couples for the mother to work while the father stays home.[30] In those cases, we cannot attribute their choice to gender tradition. Nor do these high-income couples lack access to high-quality paid child care. Instead, the dad-at-home arrangement confirms that child care is a matter of values as well as financial resources; even couples with the greatest range of options value having a parent at home.

Continuity of care imposes a heavy cost on parents', especially mothers', lives. In light of that fact, perhaps we should ask some deeper questions about the value of continuity. *Should* society place a high priority on continuity of care for children? Or should parents be granted leeway to set their own priorities, and even to compromise continuity if they judge it important to do so?

Part 2

Why Society Imposes the

No Exit Obligation and

What Society Owes Parents

as a Result

3

Should Society Expect Parents to Provide Continuity of Care?

Harold's wife and baby daughter died in a car crash, leaving Harold and his 5-year-old son, Mark, to pick up the pieces of their lives. Harold decided to leave Mark with his grandparents in Iowa for a while. Mark had a rocky time at first; he was aggressive toward smaller kids and disliked by his peers. But he grew to love his grandparents, the Bannisters, and to depend on them. Although Mark remained somewhat anxious in personality, he ultimately developed a closer and more secure relationship with Grandpa than he had had with Harold.

Harold returned after an absence of 15 months. He had remarried and found a house in California, and he was eager to bring Mark along to make a fresh start with his new family. But Mark's grandparents objected; they worried that Mark could regress if he left the environment in which he was (by then) thriving.[1]

What was best for this family? Harold had his heart set on taking Mark back, and he considered his son's stay with the Bannisters a temporary measure, nothing more. But from Mark's perspective, the question is harder. Fifteen months can be a long time in the life of a small boy, and during that time Mark made an important emotional adjustment; he came to feel secure in the Bannister family. If Mark found it too disruptive to leave the Bannisters, he could suffer lasting psychological harm. But if Mark stayed with his grandparents, he could give up the chance to form a satisfying relationship with his father.

Most of us have conflicting intuitions about this hard case.[2] Harold's exit is a very human reaction to tragedy; imagine how devastating it would be to lose a beloved partner and a child in a car accident. It seems cruel to dismiss Harold's pain or to expect him not to act out in some fashion. Some people respond to catastrophe with fortitude, but others become depressed or need to leave the scene for a while, as Harold did.

Still, even as we sympathize with Harold, we can question whether he did the right thing. If Harold was in pain, imagine what 5-year-old Mark must have felt. He lost his mother and sister and then, for more than a year, his father too. It was the Bannisters, who must have been feeling considerable pain themselves (Mark's mother was their daughter), who stepped up to recreate continuity for Mark, to provide him with a "family where he feels wanted."[3] When Harold reappears with a new wife, it may be too much to expect Mark to leave the Bannisters and make yet another transition.

Harold's story demonstrates the potential conflict between parents' needs and children's needs: Harold needed to leave, but Mark needed him to stay. Even in less dramatic circumstances, parents encounter these conflicts all the time. Parents may want, or need, to take (or leave) a job, to marry (or to leave a marriage), or simply to change a way of life they have come to dislike. But their children need something else. Perhaps the family needs the money that the hated job brings in. Or perhaps the children need so much care that a challenging job can no longer be managed. Perhaps a fiancé demands a geographic move or other changes that would too seriously disrupt the children's sense of stability. Just as in Harold's case, we may have conflicting intuitions about how parents should act in these cases. We want parents to do what is best for the children. But parents also deserve to have a life of their own.

How should we think about these conflicts? Is it fair to expect parents to provide continuity of care to their children when doing so requires serious compromises in the life parents wish to live?

Children and the Conditions of Autonomy

These are deep questions about the nature of child rearing in a fair society. One way to approach these questions is to consult the underlying principles that guide the organization of our society. Individual autonomy is one such value; many of our laws and institutions seek to make it possible for every person to live a life that is autonomous, a life that is meaningfully of one's own choosing.[4] In a society that prizes individual autonomy, a central function of the state is to create institutions that ensure to every person the conditions of autonomy: the chance to develop the capabilities that one needs to formulate, choose, and pursue a vision of the good life. Often termed "liberal egalitarianism," this view asserts that society has an obligation to help every individual develop the capabilities he or she needs to be truly free. Although libertarians view people as "free" if they can act without state interference, liberal egalitarian theory defines freedom in a more demanding way. People are free only if they have the capability to make deliberate, informed choices among different visions of the good life.

(Whether these egalitarian precepts lead to "liberal" or "conservative" results in politics depends on the context and on the interpretation we give to the twin principles of freedom and equality. Liberal egalitarians often endorse wealth redistribution in the service of equal opportunity, but they also tend to favor free markets and to reject the economic centralization associated with traditional socialism.)

If we are committed to the ideal of autonomy for everyone, we should create institutions to provide the conditions of autonomy to every child: the material, intellectual, and emotional preconditions that permit human beings to develop the capacity to be self-governing. For instance, a fair society should provide universal education, including not only skills training but also the chance to explore diverse visions of the good. Although conventional liberal theory has somewhat less to say about the role of family life in children's development, most theorists seem to agree that children deserve parental time and attention sufficient to cultivate their capabilities.[5]

My point is that continuity of care should be an integral part of this ideal of child rearing. Although theorists debate precisely what capabilities each individual may need, continuity of care represents a minimal, threshold requirement, a foundation for building *whatever* additional capabilities children may need.

Children need continuity of care to flourish; outside science fiction, there simply is no acceptable substitute for parental care. Of course, the law cannot prevent all disruptions in continuity; death, divorce, illness, and other calamities will always occur. Children can recover from these traumas, but they do so most effectively when a new family (or custody arrangement) recreates continuity of care. Continuity can be recreated, though not easily or without pain, but some degree of continuity is essential. In the rare cases in which children are deprived of continuity for long periods or during formative stages, they suffer serious and lasting emotional problems.[6]

Why Society Should Give Priority to Continuity of Care

The conditions of autonomy for children are so central to a fair society that they merit some degree of priority (how much, I discuss below) over parents' (and other adults') competing claims to autonomy and privacy. Imagine a group of people gathered together in what John Rawls, a leading liberal egalitarian theorist, calls the "original position": a hypothetical assembly charged with creating institutions for a fair society. To ensure that everyone's interests are represented, the assembly includes adults from the present generation as well as children who will not be born for some time yet. And to guarantee impartiality, the participants do not know to which generation they belong. What guidelines would these representatives adopt for children's care? How would they balance children's need for care against parents' wish to exercise their autonomy?

Contractarian hypotheticals of this type often produce indeterminate results, because it is difficult to determine, from abstract premises, the terms of the agreement that such representatives would reach. Would most people prefer institutions that promise greater freedom or greater security? An economy that produces more consumer goods or more leisure time?

But when the question is what kind of care society should expect parents to give their children, the answer is clearer. It follows from the structure of a society committed to equality and autonomy, and not from a contingent prediction about individual tastes. Suppose, as Rawls suggests, that the representatives would choose a society that would seek to provide individuals with a meaningful chance to choose and to pursue their own vision of the good life.[7] That kind of society is possible only if children have developmentally sound conditions for their upbringing. Only autonomous people can participate (meaningfully) in choosing a vision of the good life, and continuity of care is at least necessary, although probably not sufficient, for the development of children's autonomy.

Because children are human beings, they deserve developmental conditions that give them a chance to develop the capabilities that let them define and choose a vision of the good. At a minimum, then, each child should have a parent (or parent figure) committed to providing continuity of care, because only such a caretaker will give children a good chance to develop the capabilities they need to participate in society.

Some liberal egalitarian theorists have imagined something close to an ideal of continuity of care, without quite hitting the mark. Rawls, for example, assumes that families will exist and that they will provide children with early moral instruction. In a brief passage on child rearing intended to illustrate how family life instructs children in moral authority, he seems to be reaching for continuity of care as he emphasizes parents' intimate relationship with their child and the importance of the stability of that relationship over time.[8] Ackerman emphasizes that the task of public education is to liberate children from their parents' views and social context—to give children a sense of the wider possibilities for life in a pluralist society. Still, he concedes, the family has a constructive role to play: children rely on their parents to give them "cultural coherence" that acts as a foundation for ventures into the wider world.[9] Continuity of care is one way of understanding just how families do this.

We can imagine an objection to the contractarian hypothetical. Suppose that an adult representative stands up and asserts, "I do not particularly value the development of children's autonomy, and I do not want to squander my time or society's resources on continuity of care. I would far rather spend my resources, and have our society spend its resources, on more important matters. Thus, I am perfectly willing to forgo continuity of care as a child in return for greater freedom to rear my own children as I choose once *I* am an adult."

This objection is plausible at first, but a closer look reveals that the speaker is improperly asserting that her values—her wish to devote her resources to other pursuits—are more important than children's claim to continuity of care. Children are human beings in their own right, and their claim to the conditions of autonomy follows from their equal worth as individuals. Continuity of care is in this sense part of the bedrock of egalitarian society, and not an optional pursuit that can readily be traded off against other possible uses of society's resources. The question is not whether society should subsidize modern art, or build a space station, or engage in some other optional endeavor that a fair society might or might not endorse. Instead, child rearing implicates a foundational question: whether every child should be entitled to the conditions of autonomy (as we understand them, today, in this society).

Continuity of care cannot be an elective value in an egalitarian society. It cannot be up to parents to decide whether they endorse continuity or instead would prefer to spend their time and money on other things. Instead, continuity of care is part of the basic package that individuals ought to have if they are to grow up to be full participants in an egalitarian society.

This rationale implies that the state should expect parents to give priority in their lives to continuity of care for their children.[10] I hasten to add that parents need not be slaves to their children in order to provide them with continuity. In the ordinary case, it is acceptable, even desirable, for caretakers to pursue independent activities and relationships. The psychological and social functions of continuity can all be satisfied by parents who hold jobs (or not), who are married (or not), and who hold diverse views about how to accomplish the day-to-day work of child rearing. Parents may be strict or lenient, anxious or casual, conventional or idiosyncratic. What *is* essential to continuity is "direct, intimate, and continuous" care by one or more parents who persist in the work of child rearing over time.[11]

Thus, although parents should have considerable freedom to organize their lives as they choose, when continuity itself is at stake, a parent's own wishes should yield to the child's needs. Ordinarily, for instance, a child should not be deprived of his or her parents for periods that are unacceptably long given the child's developmental stage, so that the child experiences a serious disruption in continuity of care. A parent who is severely emotionally troubled for long periods may also disrupt continuity. And, of course, continuity is incompatible with parental neglect or abuse.

This simple formulation does not begin to address every hard case. For instance, what about a parent who is very ill: Should the child's care take priority over the parent's needs then? Or what about a parent who has several children, some of whom have greater needs than others: Is it ever acceptable to compromise continuity for some in order to provide it to others? I will not attempt to answer these questions fully here; my aim is to explain and justify the priority of continuity of care for the majority of parents in ordinary situations, rather than to craft rules suited to extraordinary cases. Still, continuity of care suggests some relevant considerations. Depending on the circumstances, parents who cannot meet their child's needs should be expected to make arrangements for the child to be cared for by others, temporarily or permanently. Continuity puts a premium on maintaining the parent-child relationship if possible, but if that relationship is severely disrupted for a long period, it may be better to take steps to recreate continuity with another family. (This, of course, is the ongoing dilemma that the foster care system faces: when to preserve a troubled or stressed family for the sake of the preexisting relationship, and when to place children with new families.)[12]

What if parents object to the priority rule? Perhaps a parent simply doesn't wish to make continuity a priority in her life and prefers to keep her (exit) options open. Or perhaps a parent holds religious or personal views that reject continuity. The answer is that such parents should not be permitted to rear children. This conclusion may seem harsh at first, but if we keep in mind the importance of continuity for children's development, it is easier to see why parents should be expected to provide it. Just as the law denies custody of children to people who beat, starve, or neglect them, so it should (at least in theory) deny custody to people who do not intend to provide continuity of care, even if those people are biological parents. Biological parenthood may fairly give parents a "first right" to step up to the duties of caretaking, but it should not be a license for parents to use children to their own ends, which is what a refusal to provide continuity of care amounts to. In practice, society cannot detect every parent who shirks his responsibilities. In principle, however, the law should expect parents to provide children with meaningful emotional and physical care for the long term.

A more sympathetic objection comes from the parent who is willing to provide continuity of care under ordinary circumstances, but whose child, by reason of serious illness or disability, requires extraordinary amounts of care, time, and effort. Child rearing is usually an 18-year obligation, ending when the child reaches maturity. But some children with chronic illnesses or mental or physical disabilities may require longer-term and more intensive care.[13]

How, then, should we respond to parents who understandably feel that they did not sign up for this kind of heavy responsibility? Providing care for children with disabilities can be physically and emotionally draining. As sympathetic as the parents in such cases are, however, we should also take into account the child's interests. While the parents suffer by being made a party to their child's misfortune, the child will suffer doubly if the disability is compounded by parental abandonment.

I do not mean to imply that society should deal harshly with parents who cannot cope; it would be intolerably smug as well as counterproductive to punish them or hold them up for censure. Instead, we should try to recreate continuity for those children whose parents do exit, and we should try harder to assist those parents who are willing to remain with their children but need extra help to do so.[14]

A skeptic might point out that the family does not always play a hero's role in an egalitarian society. Theorists have worried that families may perpetuate inequality, because some families do better than others in preparing their children for success in the wider world. Some families provide better developmental conditions than others; some emphasize reading and send their children to preschool, for instance, and others do not. And some families have greater wealth, human capital, and social capital, all of which help provide their offspring with greater material opportunities than children of families of more modest means.[15]

But the potential conflict between family inequality and children's life chances does not undermine the claim that the law ought to encourage *every* family to provide continuity of care. Continuity should be understood as necessary, though not sufficient, for equality. The law may wish to take other measures to "level up" developmental conditions for some children; universal, public preschool, for instance, might be a good start.[16] But virtually no one has advocated "leveling down" by denying some children continuity of care. Although families are diverse in their resources, interests, and capabilities, the great majority of them are capable of providing continuity of care—and indeed, already do so.

Parenthood in Social Context

These abstract principles find expression in our real-world institutions. Our society expects parents to provide continuity of care to their children and to sacrifice their own opportunities, if need be. Society uses both carrots and sticks to encourage parents to provide continuity of care. Using the coercive power of law, the state rewards parents who persist and punishes parents who exit.

Begin with the carrots. When parents persist with their children, the state rewards them with a sphere of privacy that is protected from state intervention. What lawyers call the doctrine of parental authority grants parents wide latitude to rear their children as they choose. Parental decisions can only rarely be challenged by the state, third parties, or even the children involved. Very generally, the state has the legal authority to challenge parents' actions only if they threaten serious harm to the child. The state intervenes in child rearing only in cases of abuse and neglect, and only when these conditions become apparent to outsiders: teachers, medical personnel, or neighbors who report the situation to child welfare authorities.

It may at first seem odd that the state grants parents so much authority. Although most parents act responsibly, some do not. If the goal is to protect children, wouldn't some children be better off if the state took a more active role in monitoring parents? But parental authority is a social institution deliberately structured to protect and promote continuity of care. The underlying judgment is that most children are best served when the state gives parents heavy responsibility accompanied by considerable control.[17] Step back a moment and consider the state's twofold dilemma when it seeks to ensure continuity of care for children. First, the state cannot monitor parents' actions too closely without putting continuity at risk. Clumsy intervention by bureaucrats could disrupt family bonds and children's perceptions of their parents as authoritative and powerful. (Imagine how intrusive and upsetting it would be if a state-appointed "family counselor" made weekly home visits to your house, correcting your disciplinary techniques, soliciting complaints from your child about you, or pointing out the mess in your kitchen.)

The second dilemma is equally serious. The state cannot easily recreate continuity of care in a substitute family. Even if the state discovers a mildly suboptimal situation—for example, a parent who is loving but sometimes emotionally immature—the state will find it difficult to predict whether the child might do better in another household. Removing the child from such a parent might do harm, for children become deeply attached even to flawed parents.

When the state does intervene, it will have predictable difficulty arranging a new placement that will be superior to the first one. Ideally, the state would create a deep pool of thoroughly screened foster parents and adoptive parents. But even in theory, it may be difficult to forecast how a particular caretaker will interact with a particular child, especially in the difficult situation in which the child has been removed from parental care. In the real world, the state has even more limited competence to provide adequate substitute care, as the dismal state of foster care suggests.[18]

Faced with these deficits in information, expertise, and administrative capacity, the state relies on parental authority to promote continuity of care. Because the state can monitor only *formal* continuity (i.e., the physical presence of a parent), it adopts that minimal standard as a proxy for substantive continuity of care, unless further evidence comes to light showing that parental conduct is harming the child. The state declines to second-guess parental decisions, except in cases where the harm to the child is clear and the risk of disrupting continuity of care is warranted by the certainty (or high risk) of abuse or neglect.[19]

This regime is not perfect. It leaves some children to live with parents who may not care for them as assiduously, or take their interests as seriously, as society would ideally like. Still, parental authority, as imperfect as it is, is likely to do better at protecting continuity of care than any alternative regime of active state intervention. Parental authority not only protects continuity of care by good parents but may even improve parental care by marginal parents. When parents know that their decisions will not be second-guessed by the state, they may act with a greater sense of commitment. And when parents are confident that they have a lasting relationship with their children, one that is not likely to be interrupted by state intervention, they may identify their children's interests more closely with their own and act more faithfully to represent their interests.[20]

It is important to bear in mind that the state does not grant parents absolute authority over their children. The law does set minimal standards for children's care, and it limits parental authority when necessary to protect children from harm. Generally speaking, parents must vaccinate their children and seek appropriate medical care; parents must send children to school; and parents must not permit children to drive, to go to work at too early an age, or to act harmfully toward others.[21]

The state's grant of authority to parents is the "carrot"; parents who provide continuity of care to their children are, for the most part, left free to live their family life as they choose. But the state also uses a "stick": parents who violate continuity of care may lose their opportunity to be parents at all.

We have already seen that when parents abandon their children or neglect or abuse them, the state grants custody of the children to a relative or places the child in foster care. Depending on the circumstances, these parents may lose their legal status as parents ("parental rights"), and the child may be adopted by others.

But even parents who are not obviously abusive may lose their opportunity to be parents if they exit their children's lives. To illustrate, return to Harold's case, which opens this chapter. When Harold returned from California to claim his son, Mark, the grandparents objected, and the case came to the Iowa Supreme Court as *Painter v. Bannister*.[22] The court decided that Mark should stay with his grandparents. In reaching its decision, the court relied heavily on the testimony of a child psychologist, who testified that Mark's grandfather had replaced his father as the primary father figure in the child's life. The psychologist emphasized the importance of stability and continuity for Mark, and he worried that Mark's more tenuous relationship with Harold would be insufficient to sustain the child through the stress of another family transition.

Painter v. Bannister is a wrenching case for any parent. Harold had a very understandable reaction to the death of his wife and daughter, and, to his credit, he placed Mark with grandparents who could care for him. But in the end, Harold paid a high price for his exit. He lost the opportunity to be a parent, to live with his child and to share with Mark the values and pursuits that he, Harold, held dear. The law's message to the next parent who finds himself in Harold's situation is quite clear: Do Not Exit.

Although Harold's case is especially dramatic, it illustrates how the law rewards parents (or grandparents) who provide continuity and how it sanctions those who do not. In a variety of circumstances, people who persist with their children for the long term are granted a strong preference to remain parents, whereas parents who exit or participate only intermittently in their children's lives may well lose the chance to be parents at all.[23] This is society's stick: parents who violate society's No Exit command risk losing their parental authority altogether.

Why Does Society Permit Parents to Exit?

Still, there is a puzzle here. My account shows that society depends on parents to provide continuity of care and encourages them to do so. When they exit, the law may deny them the right to be parents at all. But society does not absolutely oblige parents to remain with their children; it permits exit for people who simply no longer wish to be parents.

Many parents do exit their children's lives, leaving the day-to-day rights and obligations of parenthood to the child's other parent, or perhaps to a grandparent. Most commonly, one parent exits in the context of a divorce or a romantic breakup. Typically, it is the father who exits and the mother who remains as the child's only, or primary, parent. Today, nearly 33 percent of American children live with just one parent, usually their mother.[24] About 4 percent of children live in a household without any parent at all, and half of these live with a grandparent.[25] Although many children in single-parent (or no-parent) families have warm relationships with their noncustodial parent(s), many do not; it is not uncommon for visits, especially by fathers, to diminish after a year or two.[26]

Parental exit clearly is not beneficial from children's point of view: for children, the more adults who are committed to them, the better. Many children form strong and beneficial attachments to their mother and father when both are present in daily life, bonds that are severed if one parent exits permanently. In an ideal world, marital and romantic breakups would not lead to *parental* exits; ideally, all of the important adults in a child's life should persist in their relationship with the child, even after divorce or parental separation.[27]

But society has only limited means at its disposal to secure continuity. Our laws and institutions can encourage continuity, but they cannot compel the intimacy and care that are its foundation.

It is no coincidence that most parents who exit do so in the context of a marital breakup (or a split in a nonmarital relationship). When parents become hostile or simply can no longer cooperate with each other, it may be difficult or impossible for them both to remain in a close relationship with their child. Family experts and legal authorities have worked hard over the years to create joint custody options that preserve the parent-child relationship even when the parent-parent relationship dissolves. However, although joint custody has had notable success in some cases, it has drawbacks, too.

The hard, and unresolved, question about divorce is whether preserving continuity of care with just one parent is sometimes better for children than attempting to preserve continuity with both. Some legal theorists, notably the trio of Goldstein, Freud, and Solnit introduced in Chapter 1, advocate sole custody for one parent.[28] Their idea is that the law best serves children by recreating in one parent the parental authority that characterizes the "intact" family. Goldstein and his coauthors did not imagine that sole custody was ideal; they acknowledged the value of having continuity with both parents. But the authors' prescription reflected their deep skepticism about the law's capacity to compel hostile parties to cooperate in a shared-parenting arrangement.[29]

In contrast, joint custody advocates typically believe that joint custody *can* preserve continuity of care with both parents.[30] Although strict

50-50 joint custody is a difficult logistical prescription for many families, some legal actors, including the august American Law Institute (ALI), have suggested compromise arrangements, which can preserve the child's relationships with both parents but without expecting a strictly equal splitting of time.[31]

But while the legal experts continue the debate, most parents quietly resolve the issue on their own—and they typically choose sole custody. Nearly 80 percent of custody cases are uncontested, and in the great majority of these, the mother takes physical custody and major responsibility for the children's day-to-day care.[32] Joint physical custody remains relatively rare, at 10 to 30 percent of cases, with California at the high end.

My point is that the *fact* of parental exit in divorce does not reflect any societal lack of interest in the *value* of continuity of care for children. Rather, it reflects the difficulty of creating family structures that can preserve both continuity for children and a marital exit option for parents. It may be that we need to try harder. Perhaps we could do more to create support structures for joint custody, offering intensive counseling and other services to help parents cooperate after divorce. We might even restrict marital exit, as some experts advise.[33] But, to date, our society has not managed to deflect parents from breaking up or from exiting their children's lives.

The problem of divorce illustrates the more general point that society cannot compel parents to care for one another or for their children. The state does not literally prohibit parental exit—and for good reason. In most states, parents may technically renounce their parental rights and responsibilities at any time.[34] To be sure, there are procedural hurdles to be surmounted, and parents who abandon their children without following the legal process can be prosecuted. But a parent determined to sever her relationship with her child may do so. This does not mean that the state is indifferent to parental exit, only that it is a bad idea to stop parents from exiting when they really wish to do so. Any parent who genuinely wishes to abandon her child forever probably should be able to do so—for the child's sake.[35]

Still, the state accommodates parental exit only because it cannot absolutely prevent it. The state cannot coerce the intimacy and loyalty that characterize true continuity of care. It would be counterproductive to put exiting parents in jail. And it would be ineffectual, and most likely harmful to children, for the police to drag exiting parents back into their children's lives, kicking and screaming.

We can put the point another way. Society expects parents to provide their children with continuity of care, and it depends on them to do so. *Whether or not* an individual wishes to remain a parent, he *ought* to do so, and the law depends on him to do so. Parents should understand themselves as having a duty not to exit their children's lives, because society could not function if most parents exited. All of society's institutions for child rearing depend on parental persistence. When parents exit, children's care suffers greatly; education, health care, and children's basic emotional and social well-being are put at risk.

Society does offer escape hatches, which some parents use to exit an intolerable relationship with an ex-spouse or to disclaim responsibilities that they simply cannot meet. But the existence of these safety valves does not imply that society endorses parental exit. In a society that aspires to autonomy for all its citizens, parents should understand themselves as bound to their children: they have an obligation not to exit.

Today, most parents, especially most mothers, provide continuity of care to their children. Parental exit does happen, too frequently perhaps, but still we achieve a high degree of continuity for most children. Ninety-six percent of American children live with at least one parent, and two-thirds live with two parents. Somehow, the combination of parental love, social norms, and society's carrots and sticks induces most parents to do the right thing, most of the time.

This book is about the parents who stay. For this group, the social problem is not so much an incentive issue as a matter of distributional fairness. The difficulty is not how to get them to provide continuity of care to their children; they are already doing that. Instead, the question is whether the terms of modern parenthood are fair. Are the rules of the game equitable to those parents who meet their responsibilities?

That is the question for the next chapter.

4

No Exit and Parental Autonomy

It is time to confront the hardest questions. Why is the cost of continuity for parents a social problem rather than a matter for individual responsibility? Isn't it unfair to expect the childless to help out parents who have simply made different life choices?

After all, we usually think of parenthood as a mix of blessings and burdens. Parents have less freedom than nonparents in some important ways, but most parents love their children and accept their duty to them. And in the United States today, almost everyone can decide whether or not to be a parent. Parents do have special responsibilities, but it is easy enough to avoid the duties of parenthood: just don't have kids.

When we portray parenthood this way, it is difficult to see why society owes parents any extra help. Some people choose to have children, others choose not to. There is less and less social pressure to have children, and the ranks of happy, childless people are large and growing. We can infer that parents must feel that the economic costs of child rearing are worth it. Perhaps parents end up with less financial security but greater emotional satisfaction.

But the picture changes if we step back and consider the parental role in a larger context. Society strongly regulates the content of parenthood, and it demands more of parents than ever before. Individuals can choose whether or not to be parents, but society fixes the terms of that choice. In effect, society tells parents "Do Not Exit": it expects parents to persist with their children for the long term, to give priority to their children's needs, and to sacrifice their own plans, wishes, and opportunities, if need be.

From this analytic distance, we can frame some larger questions. Has society structured the parental role fairly? When society expects parents not to exit their children's lives, should society, in return, give any special consideration to the consequences for parents' lives?

Has Parenthood Become a One-Way Obligation?

Over the generations, the nature of American parenthood has changed radically. In the not-so-distant past, children were a pretty good economic bargain. Society did expect parents to feed, clothe, and manage their children, but not much more, and in exchange, parents received the value of child labor. Even young children were expected to be productive, and by 10 or 12 most worked hard on the farm or in a factory. Children also represented the only available means to "retirement planning." Most people had little wealth, and those who did held their assets in land, not in money. Modern financial intermediaries simply did not exist in anything like their current form. Families had plenty of children, not only because birth control was unavailable, but also because children represented one of the biggest financial assets a family might have.

In contrast, today's children cost their parents plenty and give back relatively little, in purely economic terms.[1] Parents make big and little sacrifices to spend time with their children and to give them the education they need to make their way in the world. While we hope that children will love their parents, we no longer expect them to be the main source of financial support in disability or old age.

Put another way, we now see children as an emotional asset but a financial liability. Our society's standards of care for children have increased substantially. We expect parents to keep their children in school until age 18 and to provide them with extensive, and expensive, medical care and social and emotional support. We recognize an increasing array of children's medical conditions and special needs, which entail therapies that require even more parental attention. At the same time, child labor (for the majority of Americans) has faded into the past; our laws forbid parents from sending children under 14 to work. At the same time, society's sense of what children owe their parents has weakened as well. We expect adults to save for their own retirement. Through Social Security, Medicare, employer pensions, and a variety of tax breaks, we send the clear message that retirement provision has become an individual and a public responsibility—not a matter of filial obligation.

The direction of change is clear. Over time, parenthood seems to have shifted from a two-way bargain between parents and children to a one-way obligation from parents to children. But our social and legal institutions have not kept pace with these big changes. We continue to think of parenthood as its own reward, and we continue to suppose that each family ought to be economically self-sufficient.

This chapter questions whether we ought to endorse this notion of parenthood as a one-way obligation. Should children have some obligation to give something back—to ensure that child rearing does not too heavily compromise parents' lifetime opportunities? I am not proposing a return to the days of strict filial obligation. It would be impossible and unwise, at this late date, to repeal Social Security and require every child to care for her own parents. Parents *and* children have come to value their own independence too highly for that, and families have become too loose-knit to enforce affective ties across generations. But, in a looser sense, we can imagine a social compact in which we accept an obligation to help all parents provide continuity of care without unduly sacrificing their own lives. We cannot travel back in time and help our own parents.[2] But each person could fulfill his obligation by sharing in the cost of providing the conditions of autonomy for the next generation.[3] Every one of us was once a child, and for the sake of what we received, we might share an obligation to ensure that today's children receive the care they need.

So far, this is just speculation. We *could* imagine a social understanding of this type. But why *should* we? Why should society ask all its members, including childless adults, to assist parents? And what, exactly, should society assist parents in doing? The key, I argue, is to recognize the No Exit obligation that is the defining feature of modern parenthood.

The No Exit Obligation

No Exit is the flip side of continuity of care. We have seen that society expects parents to provide continuity, and it depends on them to do so. But when parents commit to continuity of care for their children, they limit their own capacity to exit, in two senses. Most obviously, parents undertake to stay with their children for the long term and not to leave them. But in addition, continuity of care requires parents to reshuffle their priorities: parents must strive to meet their children's material and emotional needs, and they must, if need be, limit their own aspirations and forgo opportunities to do so.

Thus, the No Exit obligation for parents represents not merely the duty not to abandon one's children by the roadside, but also the much harder, more intensive, and crucially important duty to create the intimacy, stability, and loyalty that Goldstein, Freud, and Solnit describe. Continuity in its fullest sense requires parents deeply committed to the enterprise of child rearing—so committed that they consult their children's interests as much as their own in setting their life's priorities.[4]

In a sense, the No Exit obligation is thoroughly familiar; it is deeply embedded in the social and legal institutions that define parenthood. Chapter 3 explored those institutions and demonstrated that a parent who acts as the state wishes her to do should generally persist as the child's caretaker until the child reaches adulthood and no longer relies on continuing care for the development of his capabilities. That is not a terribly controversial proposition; indeed, it expresses at least part of what most people would say good parenting is. But if we look beyond parenthood to the wider social world, we can gain some perspective on how extraordinary the No Exit obligation really is.

Exit occupies a central place in most conceptions of individual autonomy. Although theories differ, most liberal egalitarian accounts imagine that an autonomous individual should be capable of choosing a life plan that seems good to her, and of modifying that life plan as her values change over time. To be the "author of one's own life," one should be permitted to choose among a variety of meaningful options.[5] Central to the notion of choice is the ability to alter one's decisions—to define and redefine one's projects and relationships over time.[6] A person who cannot exit her chosen life plan is less able to govern her life than a person who can exit, even if everyone knows about the constraint ahead of time.

We have already seen how this abstract proposition becomes concrete in parents' lives. Parents commonly find their economic options limited by their child-rearing responsibilities. And parents' noneconomic options may also contract. Parents may marry, decline to marry, or exit a marriage for their children's sake. They may reject other relationships that they might have pursued were they childless. They may stay in a community or leave it based on their children's needs rather than their own. Most parents continually make smaller sacrifices as well, adjusting expectations and ambitions downward, a little or a lot, for the sake of the children.

What is less obvious is that the No Exit obligation represents an extraordinary command from society to parents. The state ordinarily seeks to permit every citizen to choose a vision of the good life and to shape a life according to that vision. But the No Exit obligation erases some life-planning options on the menu presented to parents. Child rearing requires parents to give reasonable priority to the child's care, sacrificing, if need be, their own projects and plans. No matter what new and exciting opportunities come along, no matter how appealing or socially productive a new project, the parent's duty to the child should come first. If the new opportunity or relationship cannot be reconciled with the child's need for continuity, it should be declined.

Does this account overstate society's role in defining the obligations of parenthood? After all, many parents would surely endorse the No Exit obligation as part of their own values. Most parents probably feel that their sense of obligation to their children comes from within.

It is certainly true that society relies on parents' natural affection for their children and their strong sense of duty. Indeed, society tries to foster the conditions that permit love and responsibility to flourish: think of the doctrine of parental authority introduced in Chapter 3, which preserves privacy and personal space for child rearing. And the law counts on parental love when it threatens to punish harmful or irresponsible parents by withdrawing their parental rights.

Still, parental obligation is a social creation as well as a natural phenomenon. The historical record reveals that it is a mistake to suppose that parents naturally act responsibly toward their children even in a different social climate. A vivid study by John Boswell notes that child abandonment has a long history in Europe, ending surprisingly recently. Romans frequently "exposed" unwanted children, leaving them literally by the roadside to die or to be enslaved by anyone who picked them up. In the Middle Ages, parents continued to expose children and to sell them. In the eighteenth century, in urban France and Italy, from 10 to 40 percent of children were abandoned, including children born in prosperous neighborhoods. It was not only the hard-pressed poor who gave up their children, but also better-off people who found them inconvenient. A significant percentage of children even in wealthy districts were sent to foundling homes, where many died from disease and neglect.[7]

It is not particularly surprising that parents perceive the No Exit obligation as a matter of personal values rather than a social command. The No Exit duty is so intertwined with parental emotion and social custom that parents may not be aware of the social and legal institutions that support and reward their persistence. But parents' felt experience should not be the gauge of whether the No Exit obligation constrains their lives. It is impossible to disentangle parents' presocial values from their values as shaped by society. Indeed, it is one measure of our society's success in securing continuity of care for children that (most) parents have come to internalize the No Exit obligation, to incorporate it into their own morality.

But how does the No Exit duty create any collective obligation to parents? Doesn't society regulate people's conduct all the time? Why should we consider No Exit such an extraordinary burden that it merits special remedial action?

No Exit as an Extraordinary Regulation

The No Exit obligation curtails the exercise of two capabilities that citizens of a free society ordinarily take for granted: the capacity to set one's own priorities among competing projects or values, and the capacity to revise one's priorities and projects over time. The No Exit obligation requires parents to give reasonable precedence to children's needs, and it mandates parental persistence for the long term, even if parents' values and aspirations change during that time. Without the No Exit obligation, parents might more easily take and change jobs and begin and end relationships. They could more thoroughly exercise their freedom, because they could live only (or primarily) for themselves, concentrating more fully on the task of self-authorship.

A free society ordinarily views No Exit rules with suspicion. It cuts against the liberal egalitarian grain to use the power of the state to require individuals to persist in a particular way of life. The law professor Jed Rubenfeld frames an argument for abortion rights in just this way. Denying women the opportunity to have abortions, he argues, would amount to requiring them to live a life of the state's choosing.[8] Put another way, banning abortions would be like imposing a No Exit obligation on pregnant women. As long as we do not understand the fetus to be a child entitled to continuity of care, such a No Exit obligation would be an intolerable and unnecessary burden on women's capability to determine for themselves the way of life they wish to pursue.

Similarly, the modern trend in marriage law disfavors No Exit obligations. At one time in Western societies, marriages were No Exit relationships, at least in theory, because divorce was illegal. (In practice, some married individuals did abandon their relationships, but they could not abandon, at least without fraud, their legal status as married persons.) Today, U.S. divorce laws are relatively liberal, permitting either spouse to exit. Most legal theorists approve this trend, precisely because no-fault divorce permits autonomous adults to revise their lives. Although some critics worry that modern divorce rules fail to protect the interests of women and children, for the most part these reformers advocate greater financial awards and the revision of child custody standards rather than prohibitions on divorce.

One might object that parents freely choose to bear (or adopt) children. No one coerces them into doing so. But voluntary entry into parenthood cannot justify unlimited regulation of parents' lives. Society should not be able to harshly regulate fundamental life activities and then excuse its action on the ground that individuals can avoid that way of life. An abortion ban, for example, could not be dismissed as a trivial restriction simply because women could avoid the ban by not having sex. When society commands parents to persist, it is denying to some people a course of life they might otherwise wish to pursue: the option to capture the satisfactions of rearing children while also preserving the opportunity to exit, or to reshuffle one's priorities if it becomes attractive or meaningful to do so.

It is a mistake to dismiss the problem by imagining that only immature parents would want an exit option, or that anyone whose values change over time must be lacking in personal discipline. The disapproval that informs these stereotypes illustrates just how strong the social prohibition against parental exit is. Suppose that a person committed to social justice came to believe it to be his calling to leave his children in order to work in an impoverished country to improve conditions there. We might disapprove his choice, but we could not easily label it shallow or self-indulgent.

Parents limit their plans in more ordinary ways all the time. A father may decline a better job that would require mandatory overtime. A mother may reject a job that requires night-shift work or unpredictable hours. Parents with a sick child may put their own education and career aspirations on hold—for a time or forever. Parents are constantly living on less, curtailing their ambitions, and making hard choices for the sake of their children.

Parents may not resent these choices. They may make them without a second thought, or even with a sense of pride that their priorities are in the right place. My point is not that parents *feel* burdened, but that they *are* burdened—relative to the baseline of what childless people may do. A childless person might take the new job, work the night shift, or stay in college. The parent may not.

A Libertarian Mistake?

It may seem that this line of argument incorporates a libertarian mistake: I seem to be treating individual parents as if they have some "natural" right to exit their children's care when they wish, a right that society has foreclosed through the No Exit obligation. If I were making this argument, it would indeed be an error. To see the subtle, but crucial, difference, it is worth taking a few paragraphs to define the problem more precisely.

Liberal egalitarians normally reject the idea that there is some meaningful state of nature, or prelegal state of affairs, that defines a baseline for measuring individuals' autonomy (and state infringements of it). Egalitarians theorize that the institutions of a fair society set the autonomy baseline by defining what individuals should and should not be permitted to do. Accordingly, liberal egalitarians ordinarily do not suppose that (legitimate) state regulations infringe individual autonomy. Take two commonplace examples. If I want to buy a dog, I assume a legal obligation to keep it on a leash. If I want to operate a gas station, I must abide by environmental regulations and the labor laws. These regulations enjoin me to refrain from taking actions that I might wish to take: I may not let my dog run loose in the park, I may not discharge gasoline fumes into the air, and I may not require workers to work long hours without overtime pay. True, some or all of these rules constrain the freedom I would enjoy in the state of nature. But egalitarians reject the idea that I have a natural right to endanger my fellow citizens' safety, or to pollute their air or require them to work under inhumane conditions. Put more abstractly, we treat such regulations as defining the scope of individual autonomy rather than limiting it.

So why isn't the No Exit obligation just another regulation of this thoroughly familiar type? It seems to serve one of the most widely accepted rationales for state regulation: the prevention of harm to others. My own argument emphasizes that parents who exit do lasting harm to their children. Accordingly, it would seem entirely fair for the state to enjoin parents not to exit. No Exit prevents parents from harming or exploiting their children, just as the leash laws and environmental laws prevent harm to neighbors and the labor laws prevent exploitation of workers.

But I am not arguing that the No Exit rule is inappropriate, that a fair society should reject it. (Indeed, in Chapter 3, I went to some lengths to defend the No Exit duty.) The subtler insight that I am advancing is this: *not every regulation with a legitimate purpose imposes a fair burden on those individuals who pursue the regulated activity.* The No Exit rule implements the state's legitimate interest in continuity of care for children but simultaneously imposes an extraordinary restriction on parental autonomy.

Thus, the paradox is that society's No Exit command both expresses the state's legitimate interest in continuity of care for children and restricts the exercise of parents' autonomy. We can recognize that "Do Not Exit" is an appropriate command without pretending that its consequences for parents are trivial or morally untroubling.[9]

Society's Obligation to Parents

Still, the central question remains: Why should the *childless* help pay to protect parents' autonomy? After all, the childless have lives of their own to live. If they must pay taxes to create programs for parents, they will suffer some diminution in the opportunities they might have pursued. Why is that fair?

To set the stage, recall the normative argument for continuity of care that I introduced in Chapter 3. There, I began with the ideal of a fair society that sought to recognize and foster the autonomy of every person. In such a society, I argued, every child would be entitled to the conditions of autonomy, including continuity of care and a parent subject to the No Exit rule.

This chapter adds a second insight: such a society should act with due regard for the impact of its child-rearing practices on *parents'* autonomy, too. The underlying value is that each citizen should have some ongoing capacity to participate in the enterprise of defining and pursuing a life of his or her own choosing. But if that is true, then the state should not be indifferent to how it secures the conditions of autonomy for children. If the ideal is that everyone should enjoy the lifelong capacity to form, refine, and pursue a vision of the good, then it is insufficient to focus on children alone: we owe some consideration as well to the conditions of autonomy for adults.

There are many different accounts of society's obligation to safeguard adults' autonomy. Consider two that seem especially apt for my purposes. First, an egalitarian society commonly takes measures to preserve individual autonomy against its citizens' predictable failure to do so. Put another way, society often expects some adults to help preserve other adults from choices that may ultimately damage their life chances. The conceptual problem is that life planning is a difficult enterprise because it requires one's younger self to empathize with an older self in different circumstances. In theory, we could hold each individual strictly responsible for planning for old age, unemployment, and bad health, but because it is so pervasively difficult for people to imagine themselves in difficult circumstances, we rely on mandatory, public social insurance to protect people who suffer predictable, but serious, injuries to their life chances, for instance, the elderly, the unemployed, and the sick.[10]

Public old-age insurance can be understood in exactly this way: we provide Social Security and Medicare for the elderly because we know that many people will underestimate the financial and medical needs of old age. We could dismiss the plight of the elderly by insisting they *chose* not to save (or chose to lead financially imprudent or unhealthy lives). Instead, we understand that there is a very human difficulty in planning so far ahead. How many 21-year-olds can really empathize with the frailties of the 80-year-olds they may become?

It might seem that it is far easier for people to anticipate parenthood. Most parents are relatively young, in their twenties or thirties, and most of them know plenty of other parents. But many new parents find, to their horror, that they really didn't understand what they were getting into. Anticipating a new baby to love is one thing; facing the day-to-day and year-to-year dilemmas of parenthood is quite different. The analogy to old age isn't perfect, but it has some resonance. After all, we all know plenty of old people, but many of us don't begin to empathize until the first pains and small disabilities of middle age, or a first spell of unemployment, give us a hint of what it will be like to feel ill and financially vulnerable beyond our working years.

Parents' economic situation also resembles the plight of what policy wonks call "displaced" workers, that is, workers who chose one occupation, only to find that globalization or technological changes have made their skills obsolete. Skilled factory workers, telephone operators, and others have found themselves in middle age with skills no longer needed in a high-tech, information-based economy. Society might dismiss their situation; after all, they *chose* their jobs. But, instead, we have made some public provision for unemployment insurance and retraining assistance to help them retool for the new economy. Parents' situation is a bit different. On one hand, it isn't technological change that has unexpectedly shrunk their opportunities, but the predictable demands of child rearing in a society that demands No Exit. On the other hand, workers have greater flexibility than parents to adjust: technological change isn't instantaneous, and telephone operators and factory workers could have exited sooner for different jobs, whereas parents cannot.

The philosopher Seana Shiffrin offers a second, and more general, account of when a society might act to buffer some adults from the autonomy consequences of their life choices.[11] She points out that our society does not call its citizens strictly to account for the full costs of their actions. We do not require smokers, drinkers, or motorcycle enthusiasts to pay the full cost of their health care, even though their choices contribute to their higher rates of illness and injury. Nonreligious employers may be required by law to permit religious people not to work on their Sabbath. Workers who care for children or elderly parents have a right to take job leave without penalty. And so on.

All these practices, Shiffrin points out, involve a collective effort to make some choices less costly than they would otherwise be, *even though* smokers choose to smoke, Sabbatarians choose to be religious, and parents choose to have children. Why do we do this? There are many possible explanations, but Shiffrin suggests that too strict cost accounting would chill people's capacity to deliberate about the lives they wish to lead.

For some readers, these accounts of collective obligation will be sufficient to justify the obligations of the childless to help lighten parents' load. Parenthood is one among many "costly choices" that people make—and that society protects their ability to make.

But other readers may object. In theory, at least, the state need not tax the childless to protect parents; the law might require parents themselves to set aside resources to counter the burden of the No Exit obligation. Perhaps every person should be required to contribute to a special savings account to draw on if he or she ever became a parent. (Those who remained childless would receive refunds.) That kind of regime would ensure that parents paid the full cost of child rearing, not only the direct costs of feeding and clothing the children but also the cost of "rehabilitating" their own opportunities.

Call this the *private project objection.* This view insists that every adult should bear the costs of his or her own actions. According to this way of thinking, parents bring children into the world and should take full responsibility for the costs of rearing them. After all, if it weren't for the (biological) parents, there wouldn't be any children who could lay claim to society's resources for their upbringing.[12]

But this account of causation is far too simple. True, parents choose to have children, and children require costly care. In addition, parents have latitude in deciding how expensively and intensively to rear their children. At the same time, however, society regulates child rearing with a heavy hand. Children are people, not projects, and parents cannot entirely rear their children as they choose. The No Exit story attempts to draw out this second strand, to highlight society's role in shaping care, that most intimate and basic of parental functions.

In principle, causation cannot resolve the question. The private project objection emphasizes parents' role in creating children. But we could just as easily emphasize society's role in subjecting parents to the No Exit duty. We could even highlight children's role in the matter. Why should parents have to pay for the conditions of autonomy for other people (their children)? Why shouldn't children themselves (once grown to adulthood) be obliged to repay the cost of their own upbringing?

None of these three "theories" of causation reaches the bedrock issues here. In fact, the causal claim ("Parents cause children to exist") isn't really about causation at all. Instead, it is a shorthand for a deeper judgment about the appropriate baseline distribution of society's resources. Implicitly, the claim is that every adult deserves an equal share of resources, *ex ante*, and thereafter no one may claim more (or be required to take less) based on his or her choices about how to live. That thesis has a respectable lineage in liberal egalitarian theories. But a closer look suggests that the classical account of resource equality does not fully come to terms with society's role in making parenthood a No Exit obligation.

Is Child Rearing an Expensive Taste?

B egin with a little theoretical background. Liberal egalitarian theorists typically endorse the principle of resource equality, the idea that every person should enjoy an equal share of society's wealth. Individuals may dispose of their share as they see fit, but they should accept the consequences of their choices and they generally should not expect others to give them extra resources if they choose an expensive way of life.[13] The classic example is that it would be unfair to redistribute from the beer drinker to the champagne connoisseur. By hypothesis, both the beer drinker and the champagne drinker had an equal endowment of resources and an equal capacity to make choices about how to live. If the champagne drinker chooses the more expensive beverage, she should not be able to complain that she can buy fewer bottles than her beer-drinking peer.

By analogy, the parent and the nonparent both begin with equal opportunities and (at least in theory) equal resources ex ante. If the parent, like the champagne drinker, chooses to indulge a taste that is expensive—in terms of time or money—he will simply have fewer resources left for other pursuits. His choice cannot authorize him to claim greater resources than his childless peer because the parent could just as well have chosen a "cheaper" way of life, just as the champagne drinker might select a cheaper libation.

A familiar (and important) reply is that, in the real world, one's parental role is not entirely freely chosen. In particular, gender unfairly allocates a disproportionate share of child-rearing work to *women*. I incorporate gender into the policies I consider in later chapters; as we move from ideal theory to real-world implementation, it will be crucial to recognize the linkage between gender inequality and child rearing. But at this point, I want to bracket the gender question. Even today, there is some element of choice involved in child rearing. Some women choose not to rear children, and some men choose to do so. It is one thing to believe (as I do) that the conditions for choice are not presently fair; it is another to suppose that caretaking is so involuntary a choice that women should bear no responsibility for it.

Instead of going down that road, I want to address the problem at a higher level of abstraction: *even if* all parents freely choose their project, they *still* should not bear alone the autonomy burden of the No Exit obligation. Even in a gender-free society, the No Exit obligation would render caretaking quite unlike the usual beer-and-champagne examples. Child rearing is expensive not because of the operation of market competition among equally endowed individuals but because society must subject parents to the No Exit obligation in order to promote continuity of care for children.

The usual context for the expensive tastes debate is this: in liberal theory, markets that operate against a background of fair distribution are themselves fair. If we all enter the marketplace with strictly equal resources, then none of us should complain about the prices that result from bidding. If champagne is expensive and beer cheap, the pricing reflects the opportunity cost of the resources involved to our fellow citizens. I should not be able to buy champagne at $1 per bottle if the growers value the alternative uses of the land and labor higher than that. My wish for cheap champagne would be, in effect, a claim to conscript others' resources and opportunities.

But the No Exit obligation does not "price" parenthood based on a fair auction process in which individuals compete for resources. Instead, it represents a deliberate and necessary social regulation of parents' lives—in effect, a conscription of their time. The fact of regulation is not, of course, unusual. Many life projects are legitimately the subject of state regulation that renders them more expensive than otherwise. But the No Exit obligation represents an extraordinary limitation of parents' capacity to revise their conception of the good. Although the restriction is justified by the collective aim of promoting children's development, society as a whole should take part in ameliorating the consequences for parental autonomy.

Put another way, parenthood is a private project and an expensive taste only if you accept the premise that strict equality of resources, ex ante, is appropriate. The No Exit argument challenges that premise. My claim is that when society so heavily regulates just one social role, and in a way that fundamentally compromises the autonomy of individuals who choose that role, society may owe such people something *more* than their initial, ex ante, equal share of resources. The No Exit theory challenges the implicit assumption that underlies the objection that childless people are unfairly being taxed to "subsidize" parents.

Still, the expensive taste objection has greater force when we consider costs of parenthood beyond the No Exit obligation itself. Parents have considerable latitude in meeting the demands of the No Exit obligation, and parents differ in their tastes and ambitions. Parenthood will be relatively cheap (in autonomy terms) for those whose plans are extremely flexible, whose child-rearing style is casual, and whose life projects can flourish despite interruption. It will be far more expensive for those whose child-rearing style is intensive and whose projects can be easily derailed by interruption. Nothing in the No Exit argument seeks to justify greater compensation to the latter group.

It may be best to think of child rearing as an endeavor with both public and private costs. Parents should be responsible for costs that reflect their "private" taste for resource consumption (in lifestyle and style of child rearing), but the childless should bear some responsibility for ensuring that each child has access to the (publicly defined) conditions of autonomy, especially when the public mandate imposes heavy costs on parents.

The No Exit obligation is one example of a pubic directive of this type. Education is probably another. It would be prohibitively costly for most ordinary families to pay the full cost of adequate schooling for their children. We do not expect parents to do so; instead, we provide public schools. Although the childless (and those whose children are grown) sometimes protest that they are overtaxed to pay for the schools, we generally understand that schools represent a *collective* obligation to the next generation of children. Interestingly, even some theorists who take the position that parents should bear the costs of child rearing acknowledge that the public should fund children's education.[14]

I recognize that this is only a beginning, and not a full-fledged theory of how society and parents should share the costs of child rearing. When should we consider public mandates for child rearing to be extraordinarily burdensome for parents' lives? How would the theory apply to children's health care? To college education? My present aim is to start by showing that even continuity of care, that very private and intimate aspect of parenthood, has a public aspect as well, and that there is a plausible rationale for collective measures to assist parents who provide continuity to their children.

Does Society Owe Parents Compensation?

Out of all this, a picture begins to emerge of what society might aspire to help parents do. One model for assistance is compensatory. Initially, it is tempting to say that the state has "taken" parents' private opportunities for public use and so (on familiar constitutional principles) owes them restitution.[15] But the norm of compensation is not quite apt here; it implies that we could know what parents would have done had they not been subject to the No Exit obligation, and that we could measure the incremental loss of opportunity that the No Exit obligation imposes. This is, of course, impossible. The burden of the No Exit obligation will vary depending on each parent's values. A parent with a casual philosophy of child rearing or one whose life projects are easily integrated with parental duties will experience fewer conflicts than one who prefers a more intense style of parenting or whose career conflicts strongly with the parental role. Variations in parents' values render compensation both indeterminate as an empirical matter and undesirable as a normative matter; parents should bear some responsibility for their style of child rearing and for their alternative projects.

We should not conceive of the problem as if parents owned a stock of 100 autonomy units, 20 of which have been "misappropriated" by the state. Society has burdened parents' autonomy, but it has done so to promote a legitimate objective: continuity of care for children. The line to be drawn between fair and unfair burdens is not a precise one, and the task should not be to make parents whole but to define the parental role in a fair way. In seeking to protect children's care, a fair society should not leave parents to bear a No Exit obligation so burdensome that they become a caste of second-class citizens.

Equality requires that every citizen have a meaningful opportunity to form and to revise a vision of the good, and to act on it. When we adopt a No Exit obligation that strongly restricts such opportunities for parents, we risk excluding them from the community of autonomous individuals. Today, the law slights the No Exit obligation and treats parents as if they enjoy the same range of opportunities as any other citizen. Instead, the law should attempt to preserve for parents a fair range of life options while also securing continuity of care for children.

It will take some time to develop these abstract ideals into a practical program for action; beginning this process is the task for the remainder of this book. But even at this early stage, we should bear in mind that assistance for parents can help children as well. Although most parents already provide continuity of care, additional support could help them persist when children's care is especially difficult or when parents are so severely stressed that continuity has been put at risk. (We shall see a concrete example in Chapter 7, which considers care for children with severe disabilities or illnesses.) It is difficult to predict the extent to which parents might do better by their children if their own future were more secure. Still, we can anticipate that supportive measures could help lessen the tension parents now feel (however guiltily) between caring for their children and protecting their own prospects.

What about people who have large numbers of children? Does society have an unlimited obligation to protect the autonomy of people who burden society, as well as their own life, with large families? This is a serious issue, but one that is only tangential to the question of redistribution to parents. The prospect of introducing children into society raises two distinct questions: Should each individual be entitled to bring (an unlimited number of) children into the world, and What does society owe individuals who care for children once they arrive? Procreation raises fundamental questions of intergenerational justice: because each child should be entitled to a fair share of society's resources, a society should have only as many children as it can provide for in a just fashion. Overpopulation may strain a society's resources in other ways as well; pollution, poverty, crime, and other potential side effects may be taken into account as part of population policy. It is thus possible that a fair society might in some way restrict one's ability to bring children into the world.[16]

But the opportunity to procreate is quite separate from the obligations we owe children (and their parents) once they exist. In principle, there is no necessary relationship between parenthood and procreation. It is easy to elide the two, because most parents are biological parents. But a state might limit procreation (through coercion or incentives) yet still recognize our obligations to children and to their parents once they come into being.

Public Goods and Public Obligations

It may seem that the preceding sections labor too hard to craft a distinctive justification for redistribution to parents when there is an easier one at hand. Many theorists and policymakers have argued that children benefit society as a whole and that, therefore, every member of society has an obligation to help defray the costs of child rearing.[17] The logic is that children improve the society: they generate new cultural and economic opportunities that in some sense enrich us all. Thus, the argument concludes, the childless benefit from children's care, too, and so they should help fund it.

But the public goods theory has characteristic weak points. The classic critique is that the childless should not be obliged to help pay the costs of child rearing even if children do benefit them, because the childless have not asked for (or consented to) the benefits they receive. The logic is that children are not strictly necessary to society. We could imagine a fair society in which everyone decided to remain childless. That society would crumble, which might be unfortunate, but it would not be unfair. Anyone who objected should have children of his own; he should not demand that others do so.[18] According to this line of argument, it is beside the point that present institutions—the economy or the Social Security system— presume that younger workers will step up to support older ones. The current generation has no right to the higher living standard that an ongoing economy will produce. Because the benefits of children to third parties are unasked for, the argument concludes, parents should not expect state compensation for the costs of child rearing. Although the childless may benefit from parents' work, those parents undertook their work voluntarily and without promise of any extra reward.[19]

In contrast, the No Exit theory centers on mutual *obligation* instead of (as public goods theories do) mutual *benefit*. The claim is that every child has a right to claim developmental resources from society and that every adult has an obligation to help secure such resources for the next generation of children. The duty follows from the social compact that guarantees each person the conditions of autonomy and not from the benefit that children provide to their elders.

The argument from obligation is not vulnerable to the involuntary benefits critique, at least not in quite the same form. Society's obligation to parents does not arise because children benefit the rest of us (perhaps they do, perhaps they do not) but because an egalitarian society must accord dignified treatment to every human being: we owe each new generation continuity of care even if we will not benefit from their presence.

Some theorists justify a social obligation to parents by proposing that children are necessary for society.[20] My argument is agnostic on that score. Instead, my point is that when children do come into being, parents and the larger society must undertake to secure them the conditions of autonomy. It is children's (and parents') value as human beings, and not their economic or social contribution to collective life, that justifies society's obligation.

The public goods argument can evade the involuntary benefit objection only by making a move that brings an empirical objection to the fore. An advocate of the public goods theory might posit that even if children are not strictly necessary to society, many childless people would likely pay *something* to keep the economy going and the culture flourishing in their old age. Like any public good, children (and children's care) may be underprovided unless the state provides extra compensation to align parents' incentives with the collective interest.[21] Collective action problems probably would prevent those people from organizing to pay would-be parents, and so the state should step in and act on their behalf. Those citizens who would willingly retire in a cave to chew acorns and read moldy books by the light of the last few candles will feel themselves overtaxed. The rest of us (let us suppose) would endorse some level of taxation for the benefit of children and their parents in order to keep the lights on and Social Security solvent.

But it is not obvious, as an empirical matter, that the childless would be willing to pay much for the *net* benefits that children generate. Although it would be impossible to calculate a definite sum, it is not even clear that the net payment would be positive. Children create negative as well as positive externalities. Overpopulation, urban crowding, clogged highways, and overburdened public utilities and parks come to mind on the negative side. Younger people in general are more likely to engage in crime, violence, and risky behavior that harms others (driving too fast, for example). Advocates of child-free living also note the intrusion of children into adult social life, in restaurants, housing, and so on.[22]

The public goods theory also has troubling implications for the distribution of resources among parents. On a strict interpretation, the goal should be to produce children who are well-socialized, law-abiding, economically productive, or culturally interesting. But not all parents are equally good at rearing such children, and there is no reason to suppose that financial redistribution would improve their capabilities. Parents might be taught to perform better—by attending child-rearing classes, for example—but that kind of redistribution would not do much for parents' own life-planning opportunities. Alternatively, the public goods rationale may support institutions that improve children's well-being while circumventing parents. The state could deploy resources for day care, preschools, and health clinics to enhance children's development without making judgments about the merits of different parents.

The No Exit theory is subtly, but importantly, different. It aims to capture more directly the state's obligation to each individual parent, an obligation that cannot be satisfied either by selective redistribution to "good" parents or by the creation of schools and other resources that benefit only children. The No Exit obligation both defines parents' duties and binds society to take measures to alleviate its impact on parents' lives.

"No Exit" and Care for Adults

Thus far, I have not addressed the situation of individuals who care for adults with physical or mental illness or disabilities. Care for adults may burden caretakers' autonomy; some may persist in their care work for the long term, and many take on a burden of physical and emotional work that is comparable to or even heavier than the work of rearing a typical child to maturity. Think of the mother caring for an adult child with a development disability, or the husband caring for a wife with Alzheimer's, or the father caring for an adult child rendered paraplegic in a car accident. Does it follow, then, that adults' caretakers should be understood to be subject to a No Exit obligation—and eligible for redistributive measures to lighten the burden they bear?

Continuity of care is a less certain guide here than in the case of children. Adults with serious illnesses or disabilities do need care, and it may be in society's interest to create institutions that respond both to their needs and to their caretakers' situation. Yet, there are significant differences between children's and adults' needs for care. Children's development is a relatively transparent process. We have some idea of what it means to bring an infant from its helpless, newborn state to competent adulthood, and we know that it takes about 18 years to do it. We know the kind of capabilities most children can develop, and we know that continuity of care is crucial to healthy development. We also know that children are unable to participate in their own care. They cannot meaningfully indicate preferences about who should care for them or how, nor can they express views about how to allocate resources over the course of their life.

Adults' need for care is more variable and less transparent. Some adults will be childlike in the relevant ways: they will be unable to make meaningful choices about their own care, and they will need persistent, long-term care by the same person or persons to protect and facilitate their capabilities. But other adults will not be remotely childlike. Most people with physical disabilities, and many with mental disabilities, will be able to participate in making choices about how to live and who should care for them. Others will have been able to make such choices in the past, even if they cannot now make them (think of the Alzheimer's patient).

Thus, the continuity of care standard should probably apply only to certain adults who need care. The standard should be whether the psychological, emotional, and intellectual development of the person needing care depend on continuity of care by a particular caretaker (or caretakers). Every *child's* caretaker meets this standard; if a child's parent exits, there is no ready substitute. The same cannot be said of the caretaker for a person who became disabled or ill as an adult, with faculties and identity already in place. Imagine someone whose only disability is that she cannot walk. She will need some assistance in the tasks of daily living, and she may prefer to be cared for by a parent, child, or spouse rather than by paid surrogates. But she is already a fully developed person, and her caretaker's exit will not (by hypothesis) do fundamental damage to her psychological development.

For adults who are not childlike in this sense, there are harder questions about whether caretakers should be subject to a No Exit obligation. Today, caring relationships between adults are generally conceived as being relationships of equality, with each party able to exit at will. Should we expect more, or are there good reasons to decline to extend the No Exit obligation? I worry that we overlook too many important considerations when we equate care for adults with care for children. Although I understand (and applaud) the impulse to guarantee care to vulnerable people, it is not readily obvious that the state should respond in the same way to all needs for care that individuals assert.

These questions do not imply that a fair society should treat with indifference adults' need for care. Both fairness and practicality may command the state to ensure that people who suffer illness and disability are treated with respect and offered a decent menu of life options. Indeed, there is a flourishing literature in the liberal egalitarian tradition that seeks to define just what kinds of social insurance a fair society ought to provide, and what, and when, adults ought to contribute to the funding of such insurance.[23] My point here is more limited: we should be cautious in extending the continuity of care model beyond child rearing because it may be inappropriate to extend the No Exit obligation to adults' caretakers. It is one thing if an adult chooses to care for an ill spouse or a disabled adult child; it is quite another to propose that society should bind that person to do so and to persist for the long term.

The topic of care for adults goes well beyond the agenda for this book, and so I do not attempt to offer more detailed analysis or prescriptions for social welfare policy toward adults' caretakers. Still, one lesson of this book is that an appropriate program of health and disability insurance for adults should at least consider the autonomy burden that their care may impose on a caretaker. We should be attuned to the possibility that one person's disability or illness may also have serious implications for his caretaker's life.

In this chapter, I have sought to highlight an aspect of parenthood that we sometimes do not see or talk about: the No Exit obligation. Most parents do not feel especially burdened; we feel that we get (at least) as much as we give. But that is the way continuity of care ought to work: we are supposed to integrate our love for our children with our sense of duty toward them. We can, at the same time, recognize that the parental role imposes extraordinary restrictions on individual autonomy. Because of the No Exit obligation, parents who do their duty will almost always make some significant sacrifice of their own long-range prospects.

The next task is a practical one. How might we adjust the demands and rewards of the parental role, making it (more) possible for parents to provide continuity of care to their children while preserving good long-run options for themselves? The next chapters turn from theory to practice.

Part 3

New Programs to Assist Parents

5

Caretaker Resource Accounts

aretaker resource accounts would give the parent of every child under age 13 an annual grant of $5,000, which could be used to pay for child care, education, or retirement savings in the current year or in any future year. All three uses would, in some way, improve parents' future options. The hallmarks of the program are that each individual would receive an equal grant each year, and that each would decide for himself or herself how to deploy the funds over time. The program would direct resources not only to parents who remain in the paid workforce continuously but also to "sequencers," who leave their jobs (or take part-time positions) for a time and return to the full-time workforce later on. It would be up to each individual to decide how best to plan for the future.

The new program would offer annual grants not only to biological and adoptive parents but also to children's guardians or relatives who serve as parent figures. I use the term "caretaker" to describe the target group for the program: the goal is to assist individuals who take responsibility for providing continuity of care to a child, and who sacrifice their own opportunities in doing so. Many parents are caretakers, but as we have seen, some parents do exit. At the same time, some people who are not "parents" may assume the parental role: grandparents, aunts and uncles, and nonrelatives may take primary responsibility for a child's well-being over the long term. Caretaker resource accounts aim to expand economic options for people who are doing the substantive work of parenthood, whether or not they are technically "parents."

Not all parents will use their caretaker resource account in the same way, but that is the point.

For example, suppose that Abigail is the caretaker of a new baby. The government would establish an account in her name, on the books of a government agency or a private financial institution, and would deposit $5,000 once a year.[1] (In Chapter 10, I explain the justification for the $5,000 figure and document its budgetary cost.) Abigail's account would receive annual deposits as long as she remained the child's caretaker, until the child reached age 13. Each year, Abigail could spend up to $5,000 on child care or on tuition for herself or she could make a deposit of $5,000 into a retirement account in her own name. She could split her $5,000 among different uses or spend it all on one item. If she spent less than $5,000 in any year, the unspent funds would accumulate with interest to be used in a future year.[2] Abigail could not, however, withdraw cash or spend the money on other items (e.g., living expenses for her family or school tuition for her child).

Abigail might use her $5,000 each year to pay for child care while she holds a paid job. If she is out of the workforce or working part time, she might save all or part of her $5,000 for several years, earning interest in the meantime, to go back to school when her child is older. If she doesn't want either education or child care, she can supplement her retirement savings. Abigail might select different options as her plans evolve over time, choosing a child care voucher during heavy work years, some education to qualify for a new job or win a promotion in a transitional year, or extra retirement contributions to make up for time spent out of the workforce or in jobs with few benefits.

The rules of the caretaker resource program would require Abigail to use her funds for future-oriented endeavors and encourage her to make considered choices. In each year, and over time, Abigail must plan how to allocate her resources. If she claims a child care voucher of $5,000 this year, she cannot use the same $5,000 to beef up her retirement savings (although she might use future years' grants that way). To ensure that Abigail uses her funds to expand her own opportunities, the accounts would not permit her to use her $5,000 to pay day-to-day expenses for herself or her family. Although this restriction is sensible given the aims of this program, it does mean that caretaker resource accounts could supplement, but could not replace, antipoverty measures.

The child care subsidy would be especially valuable to moderate- and lower-income parents. For these hard-pressed caretakers, child care costs are often high relative to earnings, and yet child care is an important determinant of mothers' ability to work. A child care subsidy of $5,000 may seem modest to an upper-middle-class family used to the price of nanny care or high-end day care. But in fact, the $5,000 annual grant exceeds the average annual cost of child care purchased by full-time workers, workers with small children, and middle-class families.[3]

The $5,000 voucher is significantly more generous than existing child care subsidies in several respects. Most obviously, the dollar amount is larger. For example, the dependent care tax credit provides at most $1,500 to $1,800 per year. (And that program assists only a subset of families: two-earner couples and single parents who purchase paid child care and earn well above the poverty line.)[4] Caretaker resource accounts also provide the same dollar amount to each caretaker. In contrast, existing subsidies vary by family income, sometimes in arbitrary ways. Working-class families can find that they earn too much to qualify for low-income child care subsidies, yet earn too little to benefit much from tax subsidies for child care.[5] In addition, my proposal would defray the first dollar of child care costs, a feature that is especially valuable to families of modest means. In contrast, traditional child care subsidies contain a copay requirement; the dependent care tax credit, for instance, reimburses at most 30 percent of child care costs.

Caretaker resource accounts would also assist parents with low and moderate incomes in other ways. It may initially seem that such caretakers would use every dollar for child care while working. But parents' need for child care assistance depends on the child's age and the family's circumstances. Strikingly, only about half of two-earner families with children under age 13 purchase any paid child care at all.[6] School-age children require less child care than infants and toddlers. And in every income class, a substantial fraction of mothers do not hold paid jobs or work only part time, meaning they need less paid child care. Some workers have cheaper sources of child care; it is common for families to use relative care, or for husbands and wives to split shifts and purchase little or no paid care.[7]

Parents who did not spend all their funds on child care could use the remainder of their $5,000 to supplement their retirement savings. That option would be especially valuable to low- and moderate-income caretakers, who are most likely to work in jobs with no private pension benefits. It would also improve old-age security for the significant percentage of mothers who spend time out of the workforce or in part-time work. In contrast, existing tax incentives for retirement savings are far less functional for caretakers, especially those of modest means. These subsidies typically are available only to paid workers; they confer the greatest tax savings on higher-income workers; and they require workers or employers to make (in effect) a matching contribution.[8]

Caretaker resource accounts would also provide funds for education—an option especially valuable to low- and moderate-income caretakers, who often have less education to begin with and less disposable wealth for paying tuition. Most conventional student aid for higher education takes the form of loans rather than grants; existing grant programs tend to provide small dollar amounts targeted to poor recipients. The caretaker resource account would supplement, not replace, existing student aid, making existing grants more effective and decreasing students' need to take out loans. The education voucher would not be restricted to college but would be available for GED programs, vocational and technical training, and community colleges. College may not be the best option for everyone, but educational credentials in some form can enhance long-term earning power.

This brief description raises many questions. Why shouldn't caretakers be able to use their funds for living expenses? Why should the government direct funds to individuals, rather than to institutions? Could the same money be better spent on education programs or flexible workplace policies for parents? Should caretakers be eligible for $5,000 grants regardless of their income level, or should the program be income-tested? I will turn to these questions, but before I take the program to pieces, I would like to present it as a whole, in order to suggest what it could mean for caretakers' lives.

Three Anecdotes

To imagine caretaker resource accounts in action, consider three short, hypothetical scenarios. (Later, in Chapter 6, I draw on economic studies to make more systematic predictions about the program's impact.)

Beth has worked as a hairstylist since she was 19 and loves her job, even though the income is variable and the benefits nonexistent. She has a good chance to win a promotion to assistant salon manager in the next year. Her husband, Bob, works on a factory assembly line. The union wage is pretty good, Bob knows, but he dislikes the repetitive tasks, and the commute is more than an hour each way.

When Beth and Bob have a baby, Ben, they share responsibility for his care. During the day, Ben stays with a neighbor, who also cares for a few other children. Beth continues to work full time, but because she works nearby, she is more likely than Bob to take time off when Ben is sick or needs to go to the doctor. Both spouses agree that the caretaker resource account funds are best used to help defray the costs of day care.

When Ben is 3, the couple has a second child, and the family's world changes. Beth and Bob feel increasingly harried as they attempt to care for a toddler and a baby, getting kids to day care and parents to work by 8 each morning. They worry that their day care arrangement is not stimulating enough for Ben, who is now the oldest of the children the neighbor looks after. Bob and Beth would like to send Ben to preschool, but they can afford only a half-day program and can't pick him up in the middle of the day. Their babysitter can't help out; she can't drive Ben to and from preschool while also looking after the other children in her care. The daily routine is also beginning to wear on the parents. Bob's long commute means that he leaves the house early and returns late, leaving Beth to drop off and pick up the children and make dinner too, most nights. The baby has chronic ear infections, and both Bob and Beth have nearly used up their sick leave. The last straw is a bout of flu that leaves everyone in the family exhausted. Something has to give.

After careful and anguished discussion, Bob and Beth decide that one of them should cut back his working hours for the next couple of years. Beth has just won her promotion and hates to give it up, while Bob has been more and more dissatisfied with his job. Although money is tight, the couple decide that they could manage if Bob takes a lower-paying sales job at the nearby mall, which offers variable hours and evening hours. With Bob at home several days a week, the couple can save money on child care and send Ben to preschool a couple of mornings per week. Bob spends more time with the kids; the kids spend less time in day care; and everyone is a little less tired.

After three more years, Ben is in first grade, the baby has out-grown her ear infections, and Bob is itching to find a better job. Bob uses the accumulated balance in the caretaker resource account (as much as $15,000) to begin training as an electrician, taking classes at the local vocational and technical school. Going forward, Bob and Beth plan to use their caretaker account to pay for day care for the younger child and afterschool care for Ben. When the younger child goes to first grade, the couple's child care expenses will fall, and they can use the extra funds to sup-plement their retirement savings.

The caretaker resource account functions like a flexible benefits pro-gram, offering tuition assistance, child care, and retirement contribu-tions that supplement any benefits that employers provide. Caretaker accounts also can provide different benefits as family needs change. When Bob and Beth begin to work staggered shifts, so that they no longer need paid child care (as 20 to 30 percent of working couples do),[9] they can benefit from tuition assistance. Importantly, caretaker accounts (unlike conventional fringe benefits) are portable across jobs: Bob still has access to the caretaker account even though he has left his union job for part-time work. Caretaker accounts also support partners as they shift roles over time, as in this example, when Beth and Bob take turns as the primary caretaker.

In the hypothetical, Bob and Beth are neither particularly well-off nor terribly poor. But their place on the economic ladder is not crucial; a Bob and Beth with similar concerns might be higher in the middle class, with Beth working to make partner at her accounting firm and Bob leaving advertising for journalism. Or they might be far poorer, two high school dropouts working at low-skilled jobs and hoping to earn their GEDs. In any of these situations, caretaker resource accounts would improve their options regarding education, child care, and pension savings. The child-rearing years tend to be financially hard-pressed even for middle-class families, because consumption needs are also high. Even middle-class families typically have little wealth until late middle age, and then their wealth tends to be illiquid, tied up in pensions and equity stakes in cars and houses.[10] Poor and working-class families often have zero or negative net wealth, even later in life.[11] Child care costs tend to be high relative to income for all these groups, and experts predict that child care subsidies could improve employment opportunities and opportunities to purchase paid child care.[12] Many jobs have minimal or no private pension benefits; this situation is almost universal for low-paid jobs but also common for some higher-paying jobs.[13]

One characteristic, but perhaps initially puzzling, feature of caretaker resource accounts is that they give Beth and Bob a fixed sum of $5,000 and require them to make trade-offs. If they use their funds for child care, they cannot also spend the money on tuition or retirement. That structure may at first seem restrictive: Wouldn't Beth and Bob be better off if they could simultaneously claim government assistance for child care, tuition, *and* retirement?

The answer is that caretaker resource accounts reflect a normative judgment about the fair allocation of resources among caretakers. To see the point, suppose that there are 1,000 eligible caretakers and a fixed budget of $5 million. Caretaker resource accounts have three features: they divide the funds equally among individual caretakers; they permit each caretaker to choose how to allocate the funds among child care, education, and retirement; and they allow caretakers to defer unspent amounts across years. In contrast, traditional subsidies reject one or all three of these features. They allocate funds to different purposes in a centralized fashion (devoting, say, one-third of the budget to child care programs, one-third to education, and one-third to retirement funding). They may also adopt a use-it-or-lose-it structure: individuals who do not claim their subsidy in one year cannot ask for twice as much the next year. And conventional programs often ration resources unequally among claimants: only those who apply receive funds, and energetic applicants who seek multiple subsidies may claim more than their more passive peers.

Caretaker resources are thus egalitarian, individualistic, and decentralized; the program divides total funding equally among individuals, and it allocates resources to child care, education, and retirement according to individual rather than government preferences. I defer until later in this chapter a defense of these normative commitments. For now, I simply want to foreshadow that the choices implicit in the program design are deliberate and not arbitrary.

Beth and Bob in the anecdote use their resources cooperatively, planning together how to use the caretaker resource account. Not all couples will do so, however, and one serious question of program design involves how (and whether) to divide the caretaker account funds between parents when both live with their child. Should the program identify one parent as "primary," or split the caretaker account equally between parents? It turns out that there is no simple way to direct resources to caretakers who bear the greatest autonomy burdens while also fully recognizing the diversity of caretaking arrangements that exist. Because this issue requires a lengthy and slightly technical discussion of alternative rules, I defer it until Chapter 10.

> Carla left her secretarial job after the birth of her child. Although the loss of one paycheck meant a tight budget for Carla and her husband, they decided it was worth it to have one parent at home during the preschool years. Carla ended up taking five years out of the workforce, working intermittently at part-time jobs during the Christmas season or in the evenings to supplement her husband's paycheck. Each year, Carla deferred all the balance in her caretaker resource account.
>
> Carla's marriage broke up when the youngest child was just 5. In the divorce settlement, she received sole custody of the chil-

dren and modest monthly child support payments. Carla decided to upgrade her skills to qualify for a better job. She used the accumulated balance in her caretaker resource account ($25,000 plus interest) to fund a two-year degree program in human resources management at the local state college. The caretaker resource account funded tuition, books, and child care while she attended classes.[14]

Carla and her kids lived in a small apartment during those two years, making ends meet on child support payments from her ex-husband and the wages from part-time jobs. But at age 35, she has just accepted an entry-level job as a manager in the HR department of a large firm.

Carla's interrupted work path is typical of a significant percentage of mothers. Even after children leave infancy, 35 to 45 percent of mothers in every income class are at-home mothers or part-time workers. Because caretaker resource accounts do not depend on parents' paid-work status, they provide benefits that workplace programs do not: Carla's time out of the workforce leaves her without access to conventional employee benefits, but the caretaker resource account remains available to any parent, whether employed full-time, part-time, or not at all. In Carla's case, she can save her grant for five years because she needs little or no paid child care; later on, she can reenter the workforce with a new degree. The program does not, of course, erase the effects of Carla's years out of the workforce; at age 35, she is an entry-level worker, in contrast to Beth, who remained in continuous, full-time work, and has already been promoted. (In Chapter 8, I consider whether this situation is fair, or whether we should devote *additional* resources to improve the paid-work possibilities for sequencers like Carla.)

When Carla divorces, the caretaker resource account becomes especially valuable. The account funds would be segregated in her name and exempt from property division in the event of a divorce. The caretaker grant should also be excluded in calculating alimony and child support awards.[15] Caretaker resources would provide a guaranteed capital grant that a divorced parent could count on to supplement her retirement wealth or to support her efforts to return to work.

As a single parent of two children, Danielle needs steady work but also time to take care of the children when they're sick or to get them to doctor's appointments and afterschool activities. Most recently, Danielle has worked in a commission sales job with flexible hours but variable income. In a good year, when sales are high, Danielle manages to save something. In other years, when the economy is depressed or the kids are having a tough time, she earns less, and sometimes her working hours drop to part time.

Danielle uses the caretaker resource account in different ways. For a few years, her cousin watched the kids during the workday. During those years, the caretaker resource account built up a significant balance. Later, when Danielle's cousin got sick, the child care voucher eased the family budget a bit. When Danielle's hours drop to part time, child care costs also drop and the balance builds up again. Over time, Danielle has deferred about half the annual grant each year and intends to use the funds for retirement savings—a welcome boost, because the sales job has no pension benefits.

Danielle's situation demonstrates the adaptability of the caretaker resource account to changing circumstances. When she has a relative to provide child care or her hours drop to part time, the caretaker grant can be used for retirement savings instead. Her benefits are also independent of the hours she works: she does not lose caretaker benefits when her hours drop to part time.

Caretaker resource accounts could make a dramatic impact on the economic situation of single mothers. Whether divorced or never married, single mothers cluster at the lower end of the economic spectrum: in 1999, for example, 50 percent of single mothers had incomes of $24,000 or less.[16]

Danielle also illustrates a situation that is particularly common in less well-off families: she uses relative care rather than paid child care. In general, poorer workers tend to use less expensive child care than middle-class workers and are more likely to have their children cared for by a relative than by a stranger. This group could use caretaker resource accounts in one of two ways. Parents who are using cheaper or relative care out of financial hardship could use the child care voucher to purchase child care in the marketplace, if they wish. But relative care is not always the option of last resort; studies suggest that many parents affirmatively *prefer* relative care to commercial care, especially for very young children.[17] For example, in 1997, 54 percent of infants and toddlers were cared for by a relative while their mothers worked.[18]

These hypotheticals begin to suggest the dynamic impact of caretaker resource accounts. In Chapter 6, I take a closer look at the program's likely effect on parents' work behavior and educational attainment, and at possible effects on dynamics within the family. At this early stage, however, I want to pause and take a closer look at the program's two defining features: the restriction of caretakers' choices to child care, education, and retirement and the award of equal grants to every caretaker.

Planning for the Future

At first glance, caretaker resource accounts may appear to provide an oddly limited menu of options. Why should caretakers be required to choose among just three options? Even if some limitations are appropriate, why are these three uses—child care, education, and retirement— the right ones? What could be wrong with letting caretakers use the money for more down-to-earth purposes, such as paying the rent or the grocery bill?

In fact, the restrictions on the use of caretaker resource accounts are less arbitrary than they may first appear; the principle is that individuals ought to use their grants to enhance their long-range opportunities. A closer look suggests that all three options support future-oriented activities. Child care assists caretakers who wish to preserve their skills and opportunities by holding paid jobs. Education helps caretakers improve or maintain their skills. Retirement assistance is obviously linked to the long term, assisting those who, in the shorter run, work for low wages, no benefits, or not at all.

In more abstract terms, caretaker resource accounts represent a (mildly) paternalistic initiative rather than the unconditional "social inheritance" some academics and policymakers advocate.[19] The objective is not simply to give parents cash to spend. Instead, the program responds to the burden of the No Exit obligation by enhancing parents' long-term economic opportunities.

The caretaker resource grant is paid year by year, rather than in one lump sum, for similar reasons. Recall that the program would pay $5,000 into each individual's account for every year he or she remains a caretaker. Thus, the more years a caretaker actually spends, the greater the resources he should receive. With each year of child rearing, his situation merits additional life-planning assistance. Paying the caretaker grants over time also provides some safety net for a change in plans; a parent will have a fresh resource grant each year, so that if he decides that an old plan no longer works, he can start in a new direction. A child's illness, a family move, a divorce, or simply a change in life objectives could motivate a change in plans. Paying the grant year by year protects future caretakers, too. It would be inappropriate (and would invite strategic behavior) if a parent could grab 18 years' worth of resources, leaving nothing for a later caretaker if the first one exits.

The program's focus on long-term life planning also explains why caretakers should not be permitted to use their grants for ordinary living expenses or even for more altruistic forms of consumption.

> Emily is passionate about environmental protection. More than anything else, she would like to donate the $5,000 in her care-taker resource account to the Sierra Club. Given the choice, she would happily cash in her caretaker grant and devote the funds to this important cause.

Emily's wishes are thwarted by the structure of the program, but appropriately so. Caretaker resources should not underwrite current consumption or even altruistic projects unless they directly advance the care-taker's own long-term fortunes. Emily could use her tuition voucher to attend a degree program in environmental studies. She could even take a volunteer job with the Sierra Club; if she devotes sufficient time to that job, she should be able to use her child care funds just as she would if she held a paid job.[20] The distinction should not be between paid and unpaid jobs, but between endeavors that build experience and future earning potential and those that represent current consumption with no future payoff in terms of opportunities.

Although the three options—child care, education, and retirement—should generally operate to support future-oriented activities, they inevitably support some life projects (e.g., plans that involve paid work and formal skills training) more effectively. Some parents may find that their grants cannot be used to support their preferred life plans, even though they have the requisite future orientation.

> Frank is a real estate agent who would like to start his own business. He is sure that he could charge clients lower fees than his current employer does and still turn a profit. But Frank has been unable to save the kind of capital he needs to get started, and he cannot qualify for a loan on such a speculative project. If Frank could count on an extra $5,000 every year to supplement his income, he could more confidently quit his job and take the plunge into self-employment.

Frank should be denied the ability to cash out his caretaker account, not as a matter of principle, but because of a problem of administration. In cases like Frank's, it is difficult to distinguish life planning from misuse. Caretaker resource accounts should support only forward-looking activity, with some prospect of preserving or expanding long-term opportunities. It is difficult to monitor whether Frank's plan meets that criterion. His stated aspirations are appealing: he'd like to run his own business. But will he really use his $5,000 to motivate his business effort, or will he use the extra cash in some other way? It will be difficult for the government to know whether Frank is setting up a new business or just sitting in his pajamas watching reruns all day. In the latter case, he will have used up his $5,000 with nothing to show for it.[21] This is why caretaker resource accounts do not offer cash. Although some parents, like Frank, might use an income supplement to underwrite life projects with a long-term payoff, others, like Emily, would use their funds to benefit others or in ways that would not protect their long-term opportunities.

One caveat is important here. Like any in-kind or voucher program, caretaker resource accounts are vulnerable to the phenomenon of *cash equivalence.*[22] Nominally, caretaker resource accounts grant $5,000 to every caretaker and require him or her to use the money for child care, education, or retirement. But it is fairly obvious that any parent who, in the absence of the program, would buy one of the three services will find that caretaker resources free up extra funds in her general budget. For example, suppose that Gabriela would work full time and buy at least $5,000 of child care each year even without a caretaker resource account. If she withdraws her annual grant as a child care voucher, she will find herself with an extra $5,000 in her (regular) budget. She might use some of the extra cash to increase her child care spending, but she is also free to put the money toward a vacation or a higher car payment.

Cash equivalence affects subsidy programs of many kinds; a subsidy targeted to one good (say, retirement savings or child care or education) may not increase net purchases, if consumers already buy that good and simply substitute the subsidy for their own funds. In that case, the subsidy redistributes wealth but does not change the consumption bundle. Empirical studies find some substitution in the case of subsidies for child care and higher education but conclude that, on net, subsidy programs do increase purchases of child care and enrollment in higher education.[23]

In contrast, studies find that conventional retirement subsidies produce significant substitution; instead of increasing net savings, such programs tend to reward individuals for earmarking existing savings for retirement.[24] But there is good reason to predict that the dynamics will be different in the case of caretaker resource grants. Present-law retirement subsidies provide tax benefits most valuable to (and, in fact, mostly used by) relatively wealthy individuals. In contrast, caretaker accounts extend education and retirement savings opportunities to a younger, less affluent, and lower-earning group. Although some parents may substitute caretaker grants for amounts they would have saved anyway, others who would have saved nothing may now save something.

The bigger point is this: although cash equivalence dilutes the net impact of caretaker resource accounts, it does not fundamentally undermine the program. Caretaker resource accounts will meet the objective of ensuring that parents spend *at least $5,000* on future-oriented investments, even if some, like Gabriela, find that they also have extra money in their general budget. In principle, the program should not transfer $5,000 to Gabriela, but "windfalls" of just this sort are ubiquitous in targeted sub-sidies.[25] It would be impossible to monitor household expenditures in order to deny caretaker resources to those who spent their own money on child care, education, or retirement. Families would quickly learn to hide or avoid such expenditures to collect their grants. A broad-based, universal program also has considerable symbolic and persuasive force: the care-taker grant encourages Gabriela to continue to invest in her own fugure prospects, even if the family budget contracts.

Caretaker resource accounts would encourage individuals to take steps to improve their future opportunities, but they cannot guarantee success, of course. Henry may pursue an associate's degree in nursing, only to find that he hates working amid the understaffing and paperwork has-sles that managed care creates. Izzy may invest her retirement savings at the height of a bull market, only to see their value plummet as the reces-sion hits. Janele may devote 10 years to a job as a telephone operator, only to find it a dead end, with no prospects for promotion and a heavy risk of layoffs as machines replace live voices.

"Human Capital" and Life Planning

Caretaker resource accounts may seem to be a program for enhanc-ing what economists term parents' "human capital"—that is, their long-term earning capacity. Indeed, for many parents, the program will operate in precisely that way. Some mothers will earn more over the long term because they remain in the paid workforce, using their child-care voucher to defray the present costs of working. Others will use the educa-tion voucher to return to school and reenter the workforce in higher-pay-ing jobs.

But one might worry that workforce participation and education may not enhance human capital for all parents. Many low-wage workers lack opportunities for advancement. Of course, low-wage workers are hetero-geneous—some may start out as hamburger flippers and end up in middle management. But many people who answer phones or wash dishes may find that remaining in the workforce doesn't do much to enhance their long-term earning power. Education may also have small financial payoffs for some people; although higher education enhances earnings for the average person, sending additional people to school may not produce big payoffs at the margin.

This is a useful challenge to caretaker resource accounts because it requires clarification of what kinds of "future-oriented" projects the program ought to support. If we intend only to underwrite efforts to improve parents' earnings over time, then work and education are not always "good investments" for everyone. In purely financial terms, some parents would be better off saving their caretaker grants for retirement: they ought to invest in the capital markets rather than in human capital.

But this is too narrow an account of what caretaker resource accounts ought to aim to accomplish. The No Exit obligation certainly burdens parents' financial prospects, but it also burdens parents' capacity to pursue ways of life they find meaningful. In principle, then, society should aim to help parents make a broader range of future-oriented investments. Even if the financial payoff is small, the personal payoff, in terms of identity formation and the good life, may be large.

So, for instance, some low-wage workers may work because the work is part of their identity; even if the job itself is not uplifting, they may feel it important to be *workers*. Others may pursue low-wage endeavors with a small financial payoff but a significant personal meaning. Meaningful work in this sense is not solely the province of the well-off: imagine someone who chooses to work as a church secretary rather than in a corporate setting, albeit for a lower wage, because it is important to her to support the religious mission of the church. Or imagine someone who works as a cook in a soup kitchen instead of a restaurant becuase he finds it more meaningful, even though the work is harder.

In purely financial terms, these people may not be building up their human capital: the secretary and the cook may not earn much more 10 or 20 years from now, because (like many low-wage workers) they do not have many opportunities for advancement. But does that imply that caretaker resource accounts have simply been wasted on them? No. The point of the program is not necessarily to make parents richer than they otherwise would be but to enable them to pursue projects they find significant.

To be sure, the program does not extend quite the same opportunity to someone whose primary life project is simply child rearing. Imagine someone who simply wants to stay at home with the children and in doing so gives up her market wage. Nothing in the program mitigates the immediate financial burden of this life project. That person will not need paid child care; she will have to use her caretaker resource account funds for education or retirement, even if she'd prefer to draw on them for present financial support. Is this unfair? Does it violate the principle that all parents should be treated equally, whether or not they choose to hold paid jobs?

To answer this challenge, we have to keep a firm grip on a basic idea. Caretaker resource accounts do not represent an unconditional grant of the "social inheritance" type. Nor do they aim to pay parents a "wage" for child rearing. Instead, the program responds to the fact that the No Exit obligation compromises parents' capacity to combine child rearing with independent projects over time. The goal is to preserve for parents a broader array of life options than present market arrangements provide.

Almost every parent has values and commitments that orient them to life projects in addition to child rearing. These people will make considered choices in deciding how to deploy funds for child care, education, and retirement in ways that support their life projects. But even for parents who (hypothetically) value only child rearing, the program addresses one long-term deficit inherent in that particular way of life: caretaker resources provide funds for retirement, to improve parents' ability to be self-supporting once the children are grown and labor-market options are few.

An Equal Grant for Every Caretaker

Parents are, of course, a diverse lot. Some are rich, others are poor; some have children with special needs; some enjoy good luck, others suffer terrible misfortune. Why, then, should every caretaker receive the same annual grant? Wouldn't it be far more effective to target greater resources to those who really need assistance?

These are important questions that merit a thorough discussion, even though, in the end, my answer is no. It is useful to identify two distinct issues. First, should caretaker resources offer a standard grant to every parent, ex ante, or should we instead wait and see which parents succeed and which fail, ex post? Second, even if we decide to grant extra resources to parents, shouldn't we at least income-test the program to target greater financial assistance to those who begin with the fewest financial resources? I address the first question now and turn to the second in the next section.

Ex Ante versus Ex Post Assistance to Parents

Caretaker resource accounts give each individual an ex ante endowment: the program anticipates the economic burden of child rearing and gives parents extra resources to counteract it. By design, the program operates *before* caretakers become marginalized; it aims to improve caretakers' choices from the moment the No Exit rule affects them and to encourage them to think about the future and plan for it.

But there is a serious question whether prevention is the right approach, or whether remediation might be the better strategy. Ex ante resource grants have strong roots in the liberal egalitarian ideal, which emphasizes the equal dignity of every person and the equal importance of every individual's life chances.[26] Here, however, the aim is to protect economically vulnerable parents. Why should resource equality be a guiding principle?

More concretely, we know that some parents would succeed even *without* caretaker resource accounts, and that others will fail even *with* them. For that reason, it may seem that the program's purposes would be most effectively served by waiting to see who swims and who sinks and then targeting aid to the latter group. Perhaps the government should provide, in effect, "caretaker rescue," instead of caretaker resources.

I readily concede that there is something to this intuition, and that ex post measures have a role to play in caretaker justice. But instead of conceiving of caretaker resources as entirely a matter for ex post intervention, we should think in richer and more creative ways about how to ameliorate the burden of parenthood. I propose a dual approach. Caretaker resource accounts would anticipate (and alleviate) the *ordinary* autonomy burden of the No Exit obligation. At the same time, we should create supplemental programs that target greater, ex post assistance to caretakers in special circumstances, particularly those whose children suffer serious illness, disabilities, and other calamities. I defer until Chapter 7 the rationale for the latter programs; here, I want to explain why the ex ante approach is best for the basic program of caretaker assistance.

Ex ante grants respond to the autonomy burden of the No Exit obligation in a straightforward way. The problem is that child rearing creates a predictable burden on parents' opportunities, and so the response should be to lighten that burden by giving them resources to take preventive measures. Instead of waiting for caretakers to encounter obstacles to life planning, as many predictably will, caretaker grants attempt to lower some of those barriers. Prevention has the important advantage of not catering to individuals' risk preferences: it does not devote more resources to those who pursue risky life plans, and fail more often. Instead, the program gives each caretaker a chance to deploy her resources as she chooses, and it requires her to take some responsibility for the consequences of those choices.

This ex ante structure implies that caretakers who suffer bad outcomes ex post should be treated like other citizens in similar situations. Caretakers and noncaretakers alike may find themselves in middle age with severely restricted opportunity sets. Henry (the nursing graduate), Izzy (the bear market investor), and Janele (the telephone operator) have counterparts who are not parents but have suffered the same bad luck. A decent society should not permit any of them to languish on the margins of society. But there is no obvious reason to grant Henry, Izzy, and Janele greater ex post security against unfortunate choices.

One might still object that the ex ante approach seems indifferent to suffering. Some parents will take greater economic risks than others, and some of these will fail badly. Other caretakers may mismanage their affairs. Although many parents are organized, far-seeing, and careful, others are disorganized, short-sighted, and sloppy. And caretakers differ in other attitudes and aptitudes. An ex post approach would by definition do a better job of targeting assistance to those who suffer most.

There are two principled motivations for this line of argument. A welfarist would claim that *suffering*, not autonomy burden, is the proper metric for redistribution to caretakers. On this view, careless life-planners should receive more than careful ones, to make up the resulting gap in well-being, and parents whose risky choices or expensive tastes leave them in severe distress should be granted more assistance than those who choose low-risk pursuits and moderate tastes. But liberalism gives primacy to individual choice and responsibility instead; the ideal is to guarantee the *conditions of autonomy* to each individual and to guarantee equal opportunity, not equal happiness. The No Exit argument for redistribution to parents is entirely in this spirit: it is the autonomy burden of child rearing that is problematic, not the welfare burden. Whether the autonomy burden is heavy or light will depend, in part, on individual tastes and ambitions. But it should not be the function of redistributive programs to reward some tastes or some life plans over others.

The second form of the objection is more sympathetic: What if bad luck, rather than deliberate choice, compromises the life-planning options available to some caretakers? At this point, it is useful to foreshadow how caretaker resource accounts and my second proposal, life-planning insurance, would fit together. Caretaker resource accounts serve as a preventative program for parents in ordinary situations, whereas life-planning insurance addresses caretakers in extraordinary circumstances. Life-planning insurance would supplement caretaker grants by providing tailored, ex post assistance to parents whose long-term life options are severely limited by reason of their children's misfortune. Life-planning insurance would offer extra aid to caretakers whose children suffer dire illness, injury, or other crises, with the aim of improving (or preserving) the parents' economic opportunities.

To this point, I have argued for an ex ante approach on grounds of principle, but there is also a practical advantage. Ex ante resource grants can avoid some of the moral hazard problems that plague ex post approaches. Whenever public programs attempt to measure distress, they create incentives for individuals to risk failure (or to feign it). Although the magnitude of these disincentives are sometimes exaggerated in public debates, the ex ante approach helps circumvent the moral hazard problem. Ex ante resource grants also have a dignitarian advantage, because they do not invite public scrutiny and blame directed at the vulnerable people who are targeted as especially needing aid.

But even if one prefers prevention to remediation, one might still question whether the program should pay equal grants to every parent, or whether, instead, it ought to provide greater resources to caretakers who begin, ex ante, with fewer opportunities.

The Question of Income Testing

Nearly all universal programs face the income testing objection: Shouldn't the program target greater assistance to lower-income individuals? The concern is that universal programs accomplish less than they might. Universal grants to parents might seem to have little impact on the opportunities of the privileged, while at the same time devoting too few resources to addressing the dire economic situation of parents who live in poverty.

For a vivid example, consider Candice Carpenter Olson, the co-founder and chief executive of iVillage, who retired with an independent fortune in her forties to become an at-home mother.[27] She probably would not find her lifetime opportunities enhanced meaningfully by a caretaker resource account. Olson is not only wealthy but has already achieved an exceptional degree of career success. In contrast, a single mother struggling to get by on modest earnings might benefit greatly if her grant were *doubled* to $10,000. Isn't it obvious that funds should be reallocated from the Olsons of the world to their poorer peers?

Actually, no. Despite its intuitive appeal, I think the argument for income testing is weaker than it first appears, for three reasons. First, income testing presumes that family income is a reliabale proxy for something quite different: parents' long-term economic opportunities. In principle, caretaker resource accounts *should* be "opportunity-tested." A perfect program would monitor each individual's opportunity set: parents whose opportunities never fell below some benchmark should receive nothing, and those whose opportunity set dipped to low levels because of the No Exit obligation should receive additional resources. But unfortunately, human beings do not come with autonomy gauges. Even if they did, no simple measure could tell us whether an opportunity deficit stemmed from the No Exit obligation or some other source.

Income testing is a troublesome substitute for opportunity testing because a caretaker's income does not always convey accurate information about her autonomy. Not everyone with low income is opportunity-poor. The classic examples are the professional-school student who has low cash income and the highly educated artist who has chosen a limited income in return for greater psychic satisfactions.

At the same time, not everyone with a high *family* income has adequate *individual* opportunities. Income tests generally measure family income, for both technical and principled reasons. It is difficult in practice to allocate income to each member of a household, and usually unnecessary, because most income-tested programs aim to boost family consumption. But family income may overstate the resources to which an individual caretaker has access. Consider a hypothetical at-home mother of a wealthy family, a woman who has sacrificed her own career prospects to raise the children. She may live in luxury and yet have limited control over the family's savings and no opportunity to invest money to expand her own options.

Economic class is not a reliable metric for the autonomy burden of child rearing, especially for mothers. Studies of household expenditures and marital dynamics suggest that middle- and upper-middle-class mothers may have limited power to direct resources to their own use.[28] Because mothers tend to sacrifice paid work opportunities, the caretaker role itself tends to reduce women's control over household assets and to reduce their power to bargain for a change in their role over time. Gender attitudes compound the problem; when caretaking is deemed women's work or the appropriate female role, mothers may suffer economic constraints that belie their material prosperity. In a highly traditional marriage, for example, a mother may live in a comfortable house, drive a late-model car, and take nice vacations but lack financial independence. Women like Candice Olson, who are *independently* wealthy because of successful business careers, are rare even in upper-income households. Typically, in high-income families, fathers earn more but also work long hours and do less child care. The economics of divorce underscore the point: a formerly affluent mother can find herself with limited financial options when the marriage dissolves.

A universal program best expresses the judgment that the No Exit obligation creates a unique autonomy burden. Caretakers *at every income level* have fewer options than noncaretakers at the same income level. Part of the autonomy burden is the persistent uncertainty that attends the parental role. Even a caretaker who is doing well today, through his own earnings or a spouse's or partner's, must anticipate that No Exit constraints will persist even if his circumstances take a turn for the worse: the loss of a job or the death of a spouse.

A second drawback of income testing is purely practical: income-tested programs are expensive to administer, error-prone, and make planning difficult for individuals. Measuring family or individual income requires a significant bureaucracy and introduces possibilities for error on the part of both claimants and the government.[29]

Income testing also has a troubling tendency to undermine programs' capacity to direct resources in a timely and predictable fashion. Income tests may deny resources to needy people because of lags in income measurement. When, as is likely in a program of this size, income is measured on a lagged basis (e.g., based on last year's tax return), a caretaker who is poor in Year 1 must wait until Year 2 for her grant. It would also be difficult for many parents to know (until year-end) whether they will meet the income requirements for next year's grant. In contrast, a universal program has the advantage of providing a reliable grant each year, so that the caretaker not only receives immediate resources but also can plan ahead, counting on the grant as he thinks about how to deploy his resources next year.

Income-tested programs also have a characteristic structural flaw: they tend to compound the problem of high marginal "tax" rates on low earners. This phenomenon arises because as a worker earns more, she loses some percentage of her benefits. Suppose, for example, that caretaker resource accounts provided $5,000 to parents earning up to $25,000 and then phased out benefits gradually, with no grant at all payable to those earning over $50,000. That structure would impose, in effect, a 20 percent marginal "tax" on each dollar of additional earnings over $25,000. This "tax" is not an actual income tax, but simply an effect of using a sliding scale to withdraw benefits; the caretaker loses twenty cents of benefits for every dollar of extra earnings.[30] Although 20 percent may initially seem a small price to pay, consider that taxpayers in this income range already pay marginal tax rates in the range of 45 percent.[31]

These prudential considerations suggest that, if employed at all, an income test should be modest in its aims. For example, the program might offer every caretaker a substantial amount, say $3,500, but then offer somewhat more, perhaps a total of $5,000, to lower-earners on a sliding scale. This structure would be an obvious and rather inelegant compromise, but it would guarantee every caretaker a minimum grant, while providing extra resources to caretakers considered more in need.

A third and final problem with income testing is that it reflects a common mistake about the relationship between taxation and spending. The usual argument is that a fixed amount of funds can be spent most progressively, and most effectively, by targeting expenditures on low-income recipients. For example, I estimate (in Chapter 10) that caretaker resource accounts of $5,000 would cost $100 billion without an income test. It is tempting to infer that *with* an income test, the same budget would fund grants of $15,000 targeted to the neediest one-third of care-takers. Alternatively, we could spend just one-third as much while giving $5,000 to the neediest one-third of caretakers. But this line of thinking assumes that there is a fixed budget for the program and a fixed tax structure for raising the funds. Once we relax those two assumptions, the logic of "target efficiency" no longer holds. Politics determines the size of the budget, and a universal program may be more popular, and disproportionately better-funded, than an income-tested one. The familiar, if cynical, saying is "Programs for the poor are poor programs." Moreover, a universal program can be just as progressive (as between rich and poor taxpayers) as an income-tested one. A universal program of caretaker accounts funded by a progressive income tax could be highly redistributive, while ensuring that, *at every income level,* caretakers receive more than noncaretakers.

By this point, we have seen how caretaker resource accounts could help parents in a wide range of circumstances. But there are still important questions yet to be answered. The program may seem like a nice idea, but would it *really* make much of a difference in parents' lives? How well do caretaker resource accounts do when we evaluate them in comparison to other initiatives to help parents? More sharply, shouldn't we consider a direct attack on the gendered division of labor in the household? And why do caretaker resource accounts take as given the structure of paid employment? Could we do more by directing our efforts to create family-friendly jobs for parents? The next chapter takes up some of these questions, and Part 4 considers workplace reform.

A Closer Look at Caretaker Resource Accounts

Five thousand dollars for child care or education or retirement every year. Some readers will think that's a nice chunk of cash, which might make a real difference in a parent's life. But others may worry that $5,000 is too little, or too late. In this chapter, I want to evaluate the impact of caretaker resource accounts from two perspectives. I first ask how individuals are likely to respond to the program. Will mothers change their work habits? Might the program alter family dynamics? Consulting economic studies, we can make some educated predictions.

I then compare caretaker resource accounts with alternative programs. There are a variety of proposals that might help at least some parents, ranging from welfare to family allowances to job leave to part-time jobs. The hard question is which of these initiatives best responds to the distinctive costs of parenthood. This is, of course, a normative question and not a technical one. A comparative analysis can articulate more fully the advantages of caretaker resources, a project that I continue into Part 3, which addresses the merits and limitations of family-friendly workplace reforms.

Later on, in Chapter 10, I return to some less fundamental, but still important, practical questions. How much would the program cost each year? Why should the program identify caretakers rather than pay benefits to any parent? How can the government prevent fraud and ensure that funds are spent properly?

Predictions

Caretaker resource accounts expand opportunities in a financial sense: a parent with an extra $5,000 has more dollars to spend. But would extra dollars meaningfully improve individuals' life options? One fear may be that caretaker grants are too small to make a difference in individuals' lives; perhaps $5,000 will have only a trivial impact. Alternatively, perhaps caretaker accounts will do too much; an important feminist concern is that programs to support child rearing may reinforce gender roles, making mothers more comfortable in the short term but less independent in the long term. Some worry that caretaker programs would encourage mothers to drop out of the paid workforce, leaving them vulnerable to divorce, and too likely to remain in a bad marriage or to have too many children.

But it is crucial to keep in mind that this criticism has been directed primarily at welfare programs, which provide income support but (typically) do not help mothers preserve or expand their future economic opportunities. In contrast, caretaker resource accounts would improve mothers' position in the paid workplace and in the family as well.

Before we launch into the evidence, one caveat is important. Just as in Chapter 2, there is a mismatch between the *opportunity* question (Would caretaker resources improve opportunities?) and conventional studies, which measure *outcomes*. Although I use predictions of outcomes as a rough proxy for changes in opportunity, it is important to keep in mind the distinction. Caretaker resource accounts should not stand or fall on whether they raise caretakers' wages relative to those of noncaretakers, although they may well do so. Nor does the program aim to increase the number of full-time workers—or at-home mothers or men acting as caretakers—although, once again, it may do so. The program's objective is, instead, to enhance caretakers' ability to pursue a richer array of life plans. Caretaker resource accounts should be counted a success if they offer more parents the ability to rear their children in the way that seems best to them, while still preserving reasonable economic options for the future.

Will Caretakers Work More or Less?

conomic theory and empirical studies predict that individuals will respond in diverse ways to caretaker resource accounts. Some parents will increase their labor supply; others may cut back. Although it is difficult to adapt simple models and empirical studies to a program as complex as caretaker resource accounts, the best prediction is that mothers as a group will increase their commitment to paid work, some in the short run and some in the longer run.

Begin with the simplest question. Will caretakers work more or less in response to caretaker resource accounts? Because mothers are most likely to be caretakers (and because there is little data on fathers who compromise their working lives to focus on child rearing), we can reframe the question in gendered terms: Will *mothers* work more or less? In economic theory, the answer is "both." Caretaker accounts can make work more attractive by lowering the costs of holding a job (child care) and by reducing the costs of education for better and higher-paying jobs. Accordingly, some mothers will increase their commitment to paid work, either by working continuously instead of intermittently or by working longer hours than they otherwise would. For these mothers, caretaker resource accounts operate like a family-friendly workplace policy, offering child care assistance, education assistance, and retirement supplements. At the same time, however, caretaker resource accounts will permit other mothers to work less. These mothers experience what economists term an "income effect"; because caretaker resource accounts expand their future options, they feel less pressure to work now, and they feel freer to take time away from the paid workforce. How many mothers will fall into each group? The answer depends on the structure of their preferences.

The theoretical ambiguity can only be resolved by empirical evidence. But here, the task becomes more difficult, because the labor supply literature has typically studied programs that differ significantly from caretaker resource accounts. At one extreme, there are welfare programs: small cash grants intended to supplement family consumption. At the other extreme, there are programs that provide resources only to support paid workers; conventional child care subsidies fall into this camp, as do work subsidies like the EITC.

Caretaker resource accounts fall somewhere in the middle. Unlike cash income transfers, caretaker resource accounts do not directly support time away from work: one cannot use one's account to pay the grocery bill. But unlike work-support programs, they do enhance caretakers' nonwork options, and they improve caretakers' ability to change the timing of their paid work participation. For example, a parent who chooses to save her grant for retirement might feel somewhat less pressure to take a paid job for long-term financial security. Similarly, the education option might lead some parents to defer their return to work longer than they otherwise would; they may count on their improved education to help make up for lost earnings.

Because caretaker resource accounts permit choice, both in the current period and over time, their aggregate effects are hard to predict. There are no existing precedents that can reliably predict how many caretakers will choose each option, and how their decisions will influence their paid work behavior. The best we can do is to use studies of cash grants, on the one hand, and child care subsidies, on the other, to create a *very* general approximation of what the middle route might look like.

Begin with the evidence on cash grants. Empirical studies of pre-1996 welfare programs found that recipients worked less, although reductions in work effort were relatively small.[1] These studies, as I suggested, are likely to exaggerate the negative labor supply effects of caretaker resource accounts. One crucial difference is that caretakers must deploy their grants in some future-oriented way. Moreover, they do not face income testing, which tends to discourage work effort in traditional welfare programs.

Now compare the impact of programs that support paid work. One well-known finding of the economics literature is that mothers' labor supply is highly "elastic" or responsive to changes in work incentives. Both married women and single mothers tend to increase their paid work participation in response to programs that increase their after-tax wage.[2] The EITC, for example, seems to increase mothers' labor supply. Child care subsidies also have substantial positive effects on both single and married mothers' labor supply.[3] Although individuals respond in diverse ways, the aggregate effect of these programs is to increase mothers' labor force attachment.

Some mothers will experience caretaker resource accounts as a work subsidy. They will choose the child care voucher and will (re)enter the labor force or increase their hours of work. To the degree that caretakers respond in this way, the program should increase caretakers' paid work effort, compared to the status quo. But, as I suggested earlier, caretaker resource accounts permit individuals to make complex choices among different options and over time, and these may increase *or* reduce the labor supply impact. Every caretaker can choose to consume $5,000 in child care or education this year, *or* $10,000 (plus interest) in child care or education next year, *or* some larger sum in the distant future if she saves her funds for retirement. In contrast, the programs that have been studied are relatively straightforward and do not permit intertemporal trade-offs of this complexity. The EITC, for example, is an annual wage subsidy conditional on paid work. The opportunity for choice, which is the normative hallmark of caretaker resource accounts, could reduce the impact of the program on caretakers' first-year labor supply, compared to a subsidy that could be used only for paid work and only in the current year.

At the same time, the opportunity for choice over time enhances the options for those who do not respond in the short term to do so in the longer term. Compared to conventional programs, like the EITC, caretaker resource accounts offer greater opportunity for "sequencing" child rearing and paid work. Some mothers will reenter the labor force sooner than otherwise (even if not immediately) or will acquire education and reenter at a higher level than they would have done in the absence of the program. In this way, caretaker resource accounts should encourage greater reentry of caretakers into the paid workforce and higher education in midlife than we see today. The program may also support more varied life patterns than we see today, when early education and job experience tend to set the tone for the long term.

Whether increases (and dynamic changes) in mothers' labor supply will improve their wages is a complicated matter. Increasing human capital, in the form of job experience (and education, as I discuss in the next section), should increase wages. But the overall effect depends on market forces and industry and occupational structures. For example, a large increase in the supply of workers in a heavily female sector (teaching, say) could drive down wages in that sector. But this complexity confronts any program that operates by increasing women's work participation.

How would caretaker resource accounts affect discrimination against women (or mothers) in the workplace? "Statistical" discrimination occurs when employers make employment decisions based on assumptions about the average behavior of a group of employees based on their gender or their caretaker status. Employers may believe that women and mothers, for example, quit more often than men or fathers. How might caretaker grants change these perceptions?

This is an important issue, and it merits a full discussion when I turn to workplace restructuring in Chapter 8. Briefly, I conclude that despite some uncertainty, it seems likely that caretaker resource accounts would not worsen discrimination compared to the status quo. As I have suggested here, the net impact on caretakers' labor supply is ambiguous, but there is no reason to suppose it will cause a large drop in persistence. At the same time, the program should improve education opportunities and permit mothers to reenter the labor market sooner or at higher levels. Thus, caretaker resource accounts should improve employers' predictions about mothers' prospects as workers, although it may take time for employers to update their perceptions.

In thinking about mothers and work, it is crucial to keep the bigger picture in mind. Caretaker resource accounts do not aim to maximize mothers' labor supply or wages. Instead, they aim to expand parents' opportunities to lead fulfilling lives and to do so in ways that accord with their own values. Accordingly, it should be counted as a success rather than a failure if some parents happily use their new resources to work less or to combine paid work and child rearing in sequence, while others recommit themselves to paid work.

Can Caretaker Resource Accounts Improve Family Dynamics?

Caretaker resource accounts may also improve mothers' position within the family, although predictions in this sphere are always speculative. Studies of marital decision making suggest that spouses' relative earning power is one factor in determining whose opinion counts and who has control over (or some input in) family spending and other economic decisions.[4] By implication, caretaker resource accounts should improve mothers' bargaining power within marriage, to the extent mothers use their accounts in ways that increase their employment, earnings, and education.

Caretaker resource accounts could also improve mothers' bargaining power regardless of whether they are used to increase paid work participation. Existing studies treat *earnings* as the key variable but have little to say about other kinds of wealth, for the simple reason that most couples have very little of the latter. But caretaker resource accounts create a new form of "independent wealth," improving mothers' ability to make—and follow through on—a credible threat to exit the relationship. The magnitude of this effect is uncertain, because money endowments interact with gender attitudes and marital psychology in complex ways. But to see the point, consider this example: with a caretaker grant of $5,000 per year, the at-home mother of a 5-year-old would have more than $25,000 at her disposal for education, child care, or retirement. That sum is not a fortune, but it is large considering that the median family under age 35 has net wealth of just $27,000, with most of that tied up in cars and home equity. The caretaker resource account represents substantial wealth even for slightly older families, age 35–44, with median wealth of $42,000.[5]

Predictions about family dynamics are inevitably contingent, however, and we can imagine less rosy outcomes if family decision makers attempt to dilute the initial gains to caretaker parents within the family. To take a stylized, and probably extreme, example: imagine an employed father who currently sets aside $5,000 per year in savings for retirement for his wife, who is an at-home mother. That man might stop doing so once the caretaker resource account is adopted, using the funds instead for leisure or his own pursuits. In that case, the husband, rather than the caretaker-mother, is better off than before.

That scenario is probably unduly grim; it supposes that the couple already has ample financial resources, that the husband can make a one-to-one adjustment in response to caretaker resource accounts, and that the new funds in the family budget will be used solely for the husband. There is also a broader point: even if some families adjusted their saving and spending patterns in response to caretaker resource accounts, the program would guarantee the caretaker's entitlement to resources. Without the program, the hypothetical employed father might decide at any time to stop saving for his wife's retirement. The caretaker resource account guarantees her a minimum grant.

More positively (but even more speculatively), caretaker resource accounts could change the life cycle patterns of caretakers in ways that may catalyze further change in the family, in higher education, and in the workplace. Today, mothers and fathers tend to follow a relatively narrow set of predictable roles. Education occurs relatively early in life; career tracks are set early on; and child rearing requires a lasting sacrifice of job options—and life options. Caretaker resource accounts could help shake up those patterns, enabling midlife transitions and making education later in life a frequent rather than rare occurrence. As these new possibilities take hold, family dynamics may change, too, as mothers make a planned transition to greater earning power. Colleges, community colleges, and vocational schools will undoubtedly make a play for the new educational dollars, encouraging parents to return to school. And employment dynamics may change, as employers take advantage of a new pool of older entry-level workers with up-to-date education and mature work habits.

Although these are exciting scenarios, I offer them as possibilities, not certainties. It is always difficult to predict how social policy will affect gendered attitudes and patterns of life. It may be that caretaker resource accounts will operate only at the margin, improving motheers' human capital and life chances, but within a cultural setting that remains heavily gendered. Even that impact, however, would represent an improvement over the status quo.

Alternative Programs

Caretaker resource accounts represent one effort to improve parents' life options, but there are a host of appealing alternatives, including family allowances and policies to encourage fathers to share child-rearing work. What is novel in caretaker resource accounts? And should caretaker grants supplement, or supplant, these other programs?

The Uses and Misuses of Individual Accounts

Caretaker resource accounts make use of a device that is growing in popularity in policy circles: individual accounts funded (or subsidized) by the government. Although accounts for *parents* have not (yet) taken center stage, policy wonks have debated several applications of the account idea. Individual development accounts, which are government-subsidized savings accounts for poor people, have gained considerable attention. Some have endorsed "human capital" accounts for young people. Children's savings accounts, in one guise or another, have won advocates in government and the academy, notably, British Prime Minister Tony Blair, whose "baby bond" program would endow every Briton at birth with a government-funded savings account.[6]

These proposals are different, and yet they share a common appeal. They address different constituencies—parents, poor people, young people—and they provide funds to be used in different ways. But each program endows an *individual* with a sum of money and permits him or her to exercise some significant choice in how the money is used. Each initiative aims to minimize bureaucracy, affirm the dignity and equality of every person, and help individuals plan a life of their own choosing.

Of course, individual accounts are not a panacea for social policy. The strengths of individual accounts can become weaknesses if the device is ill-suited to the aim of the policy.[7]

And sometimes the language of private accounts is used to mean something quite different: a *lessening* of government's commitments to citizens. Privatization proposals for Social Security often fall into this camp. The idea is to convert Social Security from a defined benefit program, which promises each citizen a certain payout, to a defined contribution program. Proponents envision Social Security operating as a kind of 401(k) plan, which allows individuals to make their own investment decisions and requires them to bear the consequences of bad or unlucky investments. In that context, private accounts could radically reduce the government's obligation to the elderly and would shift to the elderly a new class of risks. But *nothing in the private account device requires this regressive outcome*: caretaker resource accounts, individual development accounts, and children's savings accounts, by contrast, all represent efforts to improve the prospects of vulnerable citizens.

Income Transfers

Proposals for income support for parents have lost political ground in the United States in the past decade, but they retain a distinguished constituency among those who wish to reward or protect child-rearing work. For example, some scholars endorse a basic income, or an annual cash grant paid to every adult, as a way of improving the economic fortunes of those who rear children (and of others who opt out of market pursuits). Others propose cash allowances targeted specifically to parents, along the lines of the family allowances found in some European countries.[8]

Caretaker resource accounts share deep normative roots with caretaker income support.[9] Both seek to improve individuals' options while preserving room for independence and choice. Both would enhance parents' opportunities in the broadest sense, and without restricting assistance to those engaged in paid work.

But I have come to believe that caretaker resource accounts better serve the cause of justice for parents. The crucial difference is that income support tends to improve *family* consumption options, whereas caretaker resource accounts concentrate funds on *caretakers'* life-planning opportunities. Income support may still have an important role to play in a fair society. Most important, family allowances could help combat child (and adult) poverty. Parents whose earning capacity is low find it nearly impossible to make ends meet and to care adequately for their children without income support. Laverne's story (which opens Chapter 2) is a case in point; there are many low-income mothers who simply cannot earn enough to keep their families together.[10]

But although income support may be essential for a subset of families, my focus in this book is broader: How can we protect parents' ability to define, and refine, the life they wish to live and with a degree of independence? Here, income support falls short of the mark. It may seem that income support solves several social problems at once, addressing child and adult poverty as well as parents' economic insecurity. But one-size-fits-all may not fit anyone very well. Caretaker resource accounts address the No Exit obligation that burdens all parents; they do not attempt to attack the causes of poverty, which are multiple and complex. Put another way, not all parents who shoulder an autonomy burden are poor, and not all those laboring under the burden of poverty are parents.

But income support is not the only alternative to caretaker resource accounts. What about programs that look to a more traditional institution—the family—to improve caretakers' situation?

The Egalitarian Family

The equal division of child-rearing work between parents has become a central tenet of feminist thinking about gender equality and family justice. Most famously, Susan Okin argues that the gendered division of labor unfairly subordinates women.[11] Consigned to the maternal role, she explains, women sacrifice job opportunities and the capacity to participate in public life, as well as bargaining power within marriage. She also fears that the gendered division of labor reproduces gender bias in the next generation, as boys and girls reared by women come to identify child rearing as a feminine task. The just solution, Okin concludes, is to encourage mothers and fathers to participate equally in both child rearing and paid work. The ideal of a gender-free society, she concludes, requires an *egalitarian* family, in which fathers and mothers take equal responsibility for child rearing and market work.

Okin is entirely right to insist that the family be governed by principles of justice, but I am less certain that equal sharing of child-rearing work is either strictly necessary or practically achievable. To begin with, the egalitarian family ideal fits uneasily with the realities of modern marriage. *If* we imagine marriage as a long-lasting partnership that creates a mutual duty of life-long support, it is easy to suppose that the parties to a marriage could be, and should be, true partners in child rearing and economic life. The contributions of one should be matched by contributions by the other, whether in child rearing or in the marketplace. But this rosy picture of marriage has lost what authenticity it had.[12]

The ideal of the egalitarian family seems to require a marriage, or at least a quasi-marital relationship, between parents who share child rearing equally and share paychecks as well. This kind of partnership, however, would require society to reverse long-term trends toward divorce, non-marriage, remarriage, second families, and alternative families. A large percentage of children now live with just one parent or in a stepfamily. This situation raises serious questions about the possibility of sharing child rearing equally when an unmarried parent may live far away from her child, be hostile or uncommunicative to her ex-spouse, or be involved with a second family. Joint physical custody is far from a majority practice, and even formal joint custody arrangements rarely implement truly equal sharing of child rearing by divorced spouses.

Even in two-parent families, the egalitarian family would require enormous changes in present gender roles. Legal reforms might nudge partners toward greater role equality; parental leave incentives for fathers represent one possible initiative.[13] But it is difficult, in practice, to use social policy to alter behavior, especially men's working habits. Studies consistently find that prime-age married men do not respond to incentives (whether deliberate or unintended) to work less; their labor supply elasticity is near zero. Even countries with the most extensive and gender-neutral parental leave programs have had difficulty encouraging men to take time away from paid work. In Sweden, for example, the average mother takes a lengthy, paid job leave and then returns to work on a part-time schedule, whereas the average father takes little leave. In the United States, although a significant percentage of men express a willingness to take parental leave, very few do so.[14] It is possible that social policy initiatives, including care-taker resource accounts, could increase men's participation in child rearing. But there is no simple way to enact egalitarian gender roles.

These are practical objections, but they lead to a problem of principle: Why should parents be obliged to follow strictly equal roles within the family, if their genuine preferences lead them to another pattern? Okin offers the egalitarian family as a model for changing gender roles, as a way to shake up the traditional division of household and market labor between women and men. But the egalitarian family is, even in principle, a troubling ideal. Strictly equal sharing seems unduly constraining, not merely because families today deviate from the ideal, but because free people might *want* to organize their lives differently.[15] What about couples who prefer traditional gender roles, or the reversed traditional pattern in which the mother works and the father stays home? What about single parents by choice? Divorcing couples who prefer to give one spouse sole custody and the other a fresh start? Communal living arrangements or extended families?

In contrast, the No Exit theory makes continuity of care rather than parental role sharing its defining ideal, and in doing so, makes fewer demands on the parental relationship. Two parents in a cooperative relationship may function adequately as psychological parents while still playing different roles in a child's life and providing unequal amounts of care. Some parents may share child rearing equally, but others may choose to specialize in either child rearing or market work. Although gender plays too great a role in individuals' choices about child rearing, even in an ideal world people might choose a variety of roles with respect to child rearing. Some will adopt the egalitarian, equal-sharing ideal of partnership, but others will not; for religious, ethical, and personal reasons, these people will value the chance to devote themselves primarily to child rearing. Some of these may form partnerships with a "breadwinner"; others may not have a partner at all.

Put another way, the No Exit theory emphasizes parents' obligations to children, and not to each other; it is the state and not the marital (or parenting) partner who bears responsibility for protecting caretakers' life-planning possibilities. For children's sake, the law should discourage parental exit from the child's life, even if the adults' relationship founders. But nothing in the theory requires a strictly equal division of labor in intact families, or any attempt to recreate a partnership that one or both parties have rejected.

The egalitarian family prescription rests on the premise that gender subordination always follows from the unequal sharing of child care duties. But although child-rearing work is, today, a source of gender inequality, must it necessarily be so? It may be possible to challenge gender inequality while preserving for individuals the freedom to define and pursue a variety of roles within the family. Today, the injustice is that many men and women expect mothers to shoulder the autonomy burden of caretaking unassisted. It has come to seem natural that women take on more and achieve less, that mothers interrupt their working life or work a "second shift" of care and housework, while fathers concentrate on their jobs and exit their parental role at divorce rather frequently.

But it is not clear that gender injustice can be remedied only if every mother and every father take an equal role in child rearing.[16] We can imagine a society that is gender-free, in the sense that men and women are free to choose life roles without gender constraint, and that also permits women and men to choose to devote some portion of their lives to child rearing without having a partner of the opposite sex who is prepared to do the same. The motivating ideal should be a society in which individuals, male or female, can choose the parental role as one option among many. The state can help by ensuring that those who choose the caretaker role retain the capacity to remain fully involved in the enterprise of life planning. The key is that the decision process, and the structure of opportunity, should be as free as possible from the constraints of gender. More vigorous state action should attack gender injustice in its many forms—for example, by countering discrimination in the workplace and in the educational system.

This chapter has begun to demonstrate what caretaker resource accounts might mean for parents' lives. Still, there are a host of practical details to be worked out. Why should the yearly grant be $5,000 rather than $1,000 or $10,000? How would the program work for divorced parents? And could the government enforce the rules requiring the money to be spent only on child care, education, or retirement?

In Chapter 10, I consider these questions (and more) in some detail. I intend caretaker resource accounts to be a workable, real-world program, and so it is important to engage these administrative questions.

But first, I want to finish outlining my basic program. Caretaker resource accounts would provide important assistance to parents, but the program cannot adequately address the special needs of parents whose children have serious illnesses or disabilities. For these parents, the economic burden of child rearing will be especially large, and they will require greater and more individually tailored assistance than caretaker resource accounts can provide. How might we craft a program to address their needs?

7

Life-Planning Insurance: Extra Help for Parents of Ill or Disabled Children

A child in my extended family (I'll call her Sarah) has an autistic spectrum disorder. (What we often call "autism" comprises a range of related conditions.) Like many children with autism, Sarah seemed typical in her development until she became a toddler. Her parents became a bit concerned as Sarah lagged in language acquisition and missed other developmental milestones, but they did not suspect any serious problem. When Sarah was 3, the doctors diagnosed her as autistic, and the news turned her parents' lives upside down. They felt crushed, but they did not have time to indulge their own emotions, because early intervention is crucial for children on the autistic spectrum. All of a sudden, Sarah's parents had to navigate the special education system to get the best possible therapy for her. And they had to educate themselves, *fast*, about autism, so that they could act as Sarah's advocate with the special-education authorities.

With boundless energy and love, Sarah's parents embarked on an intensive program of education, therapy, and dietary modification. Several years later, Sarah is a happy, cooperative child, who is making good progress in a special school. What the future holds for her remains uncertain. Her parents cope with that uncertainty by doing the best they can for her, each day and each year.

Sarah's parents have been closely involved in her therapy and treatment, but managing her care has not been easy, and they have made some significant changes in their own lives. Sarah's mother initially took a leave from her job but concluded after a few months that it was impossible to care for Sarah and keep her job. For Sarah's sake, the family eats a special diet, which is time-consuming and expensive to shop for and prepare. Someone must drive Sarah an hour or more to school in the morning and again at night. And both parents work with her continually to reinforce the language and social skills that she is working so hard to learn.

The experience of Sarah's parents and other families like them raises some pointed questions about U.S. social policy. Should the law permit parents to take time away from work if their child needs special care? What happens to parents who must leave their jobs but who cannot afford to lose one income? How can parents manage to care for their other children when one child's needs consume the family's reserves of time, energy, and money?

The policy literature provides some sobering answers. The families of children with serious disabilities and chronic illnesses are under severe stress, and yet existing programs do relatively little for them. Studies confirm what everyday experience tells us: these parents often find it difficult or impossible to continue with paid work and other outside activities. They suffer fatigue and high levels of stress. Most parents cope, but some do not; there is evidence that children with severe illnesses and disabilities are at greater risk of parental exit than ordinary children.[1] Sometimes parents leave because the child's care can no longer be accomplished outside an institution; in other cases, they simply cannot handle the economic and personal burden without assistance.[2]

Low-income families face special hardships. Studies suggest that they are more likely than affluent families to have seriously ill or disabled children. They have less financial capacity to absorb extra expenses, including skilled child care for children with special needs. And they may suffer most from missed work and lost jobs.[3]

For these parents, the No Exit obligation weighs heavily, and society should respond with extra help. Caretaker resource accounts address the economic situation of the typical parent. But parents whose children suffer severe illness or disabilities have a different experience of child rearing.[4]

Their children require more protection, more attention, more advocacy, and more care. Support targeted to these parents could help reduce parental stress and improve families' economic options.

In this chapter, I propose a program of life-planning insurance, which would provide income support and social services to parents whose children require intensive, personal care due to a serious illness or disability. The goal should be to mitigate the impact of the child's condition on the parent's independence: to preserve for the parent, if possible, some capacity to pursue life projects in addition to child rearing. A child's illness or disability will still alter her parents' lives, but the extra help may enable parents to carve out some room for their own plans while still attending to their child's special needs. (Just as in the case of caretaker resource accounts, life-planning insurance would target assistance to *caretakers*, meaning parents who persist in caring for their child for the long term. As I discuss in Chapter 11, this can be fairly readily accomplished, because the program would provide benefits that would be valuable primarily to parents who take day-to-day responsibility for the child's care.)

Today, public and private medical and disability insurance focus on the child suffering the illness or disability, not on the parents' situation. Although the state provides education and medical care to children with disabilities, there is no comprehensive, national program that guarantees parents access to supportive social services such as skilled child care, respite care, and housekeeping assistance. Services vary greatly depending on the nature of the child's condition, the family's income, and the state in which the family lives. The only national program of income support is Supplemental Security Income (SSI), which pays small benefits only to quite poor families. Apart from the Family and Medical Leave Act (FMLA), which provides unpaid leave to parents for children's medical care, there is no national program that mitigates the impact of children's crises on their parents' life-planning capacity. Consider a hypothetical but realistic example:

> Larry and Lori have three children, ages 6, 4, and 2. Their oldest son, Linc, has been diagnosed with a developmental disorder, as well as some physical disabilities. At age 6, he cannot speak more than a few, single words. He is not toilet trained, and he is some-

times physically clumsy. Although Linc is a good-natured child, he sometimes has tantrums that can be hard to handle.

Larry and Lori have been active in negotiating with the local school board to provide appropriate therapies for Linc. The school board is legally obligated to provide a free and appropriate education, and it has done so. Linc attends a special education class in his local school and goes to speech and occupational therapy several times a week. But the school and therapy schedule is set according to the child's needs and the therapists' convenience; there is no provision in the law for accommodating parents' needs. Some days, Linc is out of school at 2 P.M. Other days, he may have therapy sessions all afternoon.

Larry and Lori are getting worried about how they can care for Linc and their other children while keeping their jobs. They feel pushed to the limit. Lori's mother used to watch Linc after school and drive him to medical appointments, but now that he is bigger and Grandma is older, she can no longer look after all three children. They have searched for alternative afterschool arrangements for Linc, but without luck, so far. The school district provides a bus from school to the speech and occupational therapists, but Linc has been terribly distressed (and aggressive) for days after the experience of riding the bus alone. They have searched for a babysitter willing to help out, but they cannot afford a nanny to work just for them. Day care providers have told them, over and over, that Linc needs more care than they can handle.

The family is facing a tough financial choice. Larry works in an auto body shop, and Lori works as a receptionist. To make ends meet, they need both paychecks, and if one parent quits work, they would have to go into debt or sell their house and move in with their in-laws. Lori is about ready to cut her hours to part time, and Larry thinks that they might get by if he takes a second job. But that solution isn't ideal. The family would hardly ever see Larry, and Lori would be left to handle Linc and the two other children mostly on her own. In the meantime, everyone feels stressed. Larry and Lori fight over money more than usual, and Linc has been aggressive. The other two kids need attention too, but their exhausted parents don't have much left to give.

This family's situation is not unique. The law ensures that children with disabilities have access to appropriate therapies and special programs, but parents complain that the programs are not designed with an eye to their needs.[5] Studies confirm that parents of children with serious disabilities, especially married mothers, tend to cut back their paid work.[6] One study of parents of children with multiple disabilities showed that mothers reduce their work hours, and fathers follow one of two patterns, either reducing their work hours or working very long hours.[7]

What if Lori were a low-income single mother? Statistically, low-income families are more likely to have a chronically disabled or ill child. Low-income children are especially vulnerable because poverty brings with it risky environmental conditions and, too often, poor health care. In addition, caring for children with serious illnesses and disabilities can push working-class families into poverty.[8] Faced with a child like Linc, what could Lori do? SSI may provide a cash benefit of a few hundred dollars a month and ensure access to Medicaid for Linc. This is useful, but it won't make up for the loss of Lori's income if she must quit her job. Lori might apply for welfare benefits, but in most states such benefits are time-limited and require recipients to hold jobs as well.

It is both possible and desirable for the United States to make greater efforts to support these parents. Life-planning insurance should be understood as analogous to catastrophic insurance. The goal is not to provide routine assistance to parents whose children suffer minor illnesses or small accidents. Rather, the program is intended to mitigate the impact of the No Exit obligation on parents' lives when it becomes especially heavy.

More concretely, life-planning insurance would provide a menu of income support and social services to all parents whose children suffer a severe illness, accident, or disability. The program also presumes the continuation (and perhaps the modification) of FMLA, which now permits parents to take a temporary, unpaid job leave to care for a child. Job leave responds to the special needs of paid workers, but the new program would also meet the needs of nonworkers as well. A child's illness may interfere with activities outside paid work, including cooking, cleaning, and caring for other children, so that even parents not formally employed may find their normal lives compromised by their child's extraordinary need for care. For these reasons, I propose that life-planning insurance should extend income support and social services to all eligible parents, regardless of their employment status.

Some of these reforms might be adopted as part of a broader effort to overhaul the U.S. health care and disability system, which is badly broken. The United States continues to spend huge amounts on an inefficient system that excludes millions of people, including children.[9] But health care reform, as important as it is, is not my agenda here, and I will not attempt to explore how health care and disability programs for children should be coordinated. Instead, I want to highlight a defect in the current system that is sometimes overlooked: our failure to provide reliable assistance to parents who care for children with serious illnesses and disabilities.

Two Kinds of Luck and Two Kinds of Insurance

The No Exit obligation forges a link between children's luck and their parents' luck. Whether children are healthy or ill, disabled or fully abled has an enormous impact on parents' lives. Children's brute luck—the raw, unmanageable misfortune of life that is no one's fault—becomes their parents' brute luck as well.

The link between children's luck and parents' luck has not been fully recognized in either political theory or real-world social programs. Liberal egalitarians have asked whether society should make special provision for individuals who suffer illness or disability or other misfortunes, but their rich and detailed theories concentrate on variations in individuals' *own* luck.[10] Feminist theorists have seen more readily the close linkage between parents' and children's fates. Eva Kittay,[11] for instance, has written a vivid account of caring for a child with disabilities, and she explores the self-transformation that such care requires. This chapter attempts to harmonize the insights of liberal and feminist theory and to suggest concrete policies that would be workable in the U.S. context. I begin with a brief introduction to liberal theories of luck.

Life is a risky enterprise. Individuals' plans may fail because of bad planning or bad luck; they may run afoul of foreseeable risks or unanticipated acts of God. Recognizing these risks, most liberal theorists suppose that society should make it possible for individuals to insure against potential hazards at an actuarially fair price.

Liberal theories commonly distinguish between *option luck* and *brute luck*.[12] Option luck occurs when adults take on a calculated gamble. If I choose to ride a horse and break my arm, that is option luck. Brute luck is bad luck that cannot be characterized as option luck, because one did not have the opportunity to foresee the risk and to choose whether or not to take the gamble. Children's luck is brute luck, because they do not have the moral capacity to take a deliberate gamble and to be held responsible for their decision. Thus, most accidents, illnesses, and disabilities suffered by children should be understood as instances of brute luck.[13]

In contrast, adults usually have the capacity to anticipate the risks of disability, illness, and old age and may bear greater responsibility for arranging their own care. Because individuals will adopt different priorities, they may make provision in different ways, or not at all. Some adults may persuade a partner (or adult child) to provide care. Others may save (or buy insurance) to buy paid help in the marketplace. Some will take their chances without insurance and trust to the social safety net should bad fortune strike. Of course, real-world conditions such as poverty and market failure may unfairly deprive individuals of the opportunity to make such arrangements. For that reason, remedial measures and social provision may be important. But in ideal theory, social provision for adults should be less extensive than for children.

Insurance plays a key role in liberal egalitarian theory: a bedrock principle is that individuals should be responsible for their option luck but not their brute luck. In principle, adults should have the opportunity, but not the duty, to insure against bad option luck. In contrast, the state should provide (and pay for) insurance against brute luck: because individuals did not, by hypothesis, take a deliberate gamble, they should not be held responsible for what is a morally arbitrary outcome.

The theory implies that two types of insurance should exist in a fair society. First, the state should ensure that individuals have the opportunity to buy *optional insurance* against a range of life hazards. The convenient feature of insurance is that it transforms some types of brute luck into option luck. Although it may be brute luck whether I develop heart disease, declining to buy health insurance when I have the chance to do so is option luck. Ideally, each person should weigh his or her insurance options and decide whether the reduction in future risks is worth the premium demanded. Those participating in the insurance plan should pay an actuarially fair premium out of their share of social resources. Those who decline to participate should bear the consequences of their actions. Thus, when I go horseback riding, I should have a chance to buy accident insurance ex ante at a premium that reflects my skill level and the inherent risks of the activity. But if I choose not to buy the insurance, preferring to take my chances and save my money for something else, then I should not (generally) be able to require others to compensate me ex post if I suffer an accident. A decent society may wish to provide a safety net to ensure minimally decent care. But a liberal society should otherwise permit—and require—individuals to determine for themselves how much and what kind of calamity insurance they wish to buy.

Normally, optional insurance should be provided by private firms. But in some cases, market failures may require government action to shore up or create functioning insurance markets. Insurance markets, for instance, may fail when contracts cannot control moral hazard or when asymmetric information leads to adverse selection, which prevents buyers and sellers from agreeing on an actuarially fair price. When the government acts to correct insurance market failures, it should do so in a manner that replicates, as closely as possible, the bargains that individuals would have made.[14] Participation should be optional, and every person should pay an actuarially fair premium.

In contrast, the state should provide *mandatory insurance* against brute luck at no cost to the recipient. For instance, the state should guarantee every child medical, educational, and social support to preserve, to the greatest possible degree, their normal development. The proper scope of brute luck insurance is a debated issue, because it raises the question of how "disability" should be understood:[15] Should society guarantee a variety of abilities to its citizens, or should it define "disability" narrowly? Here, I want to acknowledge the general debate but not enter into it. My purpose is not to debate which conditions represent disabilities but, instead, to consider the impact of children's disabilities on parents' lives. Once we understand parenthood as a No Exit relationship, we must revisit the distiction between option luck and brute luck.

No Exit, Revisited

The No Exit obligation requires parents to give appropriate priority to their child's need for care as long as the child's development depends on that care. But what is "appropriate" priority? If a child is severely injured, ill, or disabled, should his parents be required to persist, no matter what the hardship for their own lives? Or should the No Exit obligation be relaxed in such cases? This is a difficult, and sad, question, because it highlights the conflict between children's needs and parental autonomy. I begin with an abstract standard, and then suggest a more compassionate way to apply it.

In principle, the parents of children who are ill or have disabilities should abide by the No Exit obligation to the same extent as parents of other children: they should care for their child until their exit no longer shortchanges the child's needs or damages her development. The ideal of continuity of care, expressed in the No Exit obligation, represents society's commitment to the development of each child's capabilities. Acting as faithful representatives for children, we should guarantee each child a parent (or parent figure) who is bound by the No Exit obligation, even if that child turns out to be severely ill or disabled. Each child should have a parent, and each adult, having benefited from parental care herself, should share the obligation to provide the same resources to the next generation of children.

In practice, society cannot compel parents to remain. The law should encourage them to do so, and it should take measures to support their efforts. But there is no point in punishing the parents of ill or disabled children who exit (provided, of course, that they exit in a careful and respectful way that does not violate their obligation to care for the child until they secure substitute care). At the same time, however, society should do more than it now does to support parents who are willing to persist but who need help in doing so. The best-intentioned parents may be exhausted or overwhelmed by the demands of caring for children who are ill or who have disabilities, and here the state *can* do something constructive by providing the material, emotional, and social support they need. It is not enough for society to enunciate the No Exit ideal; it should also take an active role in helping willing parents provide continuity of care.

The No Exit obligation transforms children's brute luck into parents' brute luck as well. Good luck—a healthy child, a happy child, an "easy" child—lightens the parent's days. But a child's bad luck may carry severe penalties for his parents. Some children may have chronic illnesses or developmental disabilities that require extensive programs of medical care and therapy. Their parents may find it difficult, or even impossible, to maintain independent activities; they may find that holding a job, caring for other children, and even running the household will all suffer. Of course, the degree of personal presence required and the permissibility of delegating care will vary depending on each child's situation and according to the parent's own choices and beliefs. But the No Exit obligation defines a core of nondelegable parental responsibility.

The link between a child's brute luck and his parent's opportunities suggests a role for social insurance. Parents should be eligible for ordinary types of optional and mandatory insurance that protect against their own disability or misfortune.[16] But, beyond the standard protections, parents deserve special consideration. Society should not burden parents' autonomy with the No Exit obligation and then treat with indifference the consequences of that rule for parents' lives. Caretaker resource accounts respond to the ordinary burden of the No Exit obligation for the average parent. But caretaker accounts will be insufficient to respond to extraordinary misfortune.

These ideas raise immediate questions. How should we distinguish between routine child rearing, which poses ordinary risks to parents' opportunities, and extraordinary events, which pose severe risks to parents' ability to pursue outside projects? What kind of benefits should such insurance provide? And how should the program be funded? I explore some of these issues later in this chapter, and in Chapter 11 I devote more attention to issues of implementation. But first, I want to address an objection: Why shouldn't we treat children's misfortune as their parents' *option luck?*

The unfortunate events I describe are clearly brute luck as to children. But from a would-be parent's perspective, these events are to some degree foreseeable. Children are notably risky creatures. Some percentage of them will fall from trees, get struck by lightning, develop cystic fibrosis or autism or cancer; and when they do, they will be incapable of caring for themselves and will require extra parental time. Accordingly, the objection runs, anyone who steps into the parental role is taking a deliberate gamble. On liberal principles, it should be up to each parent to protect herself against bad outcomes. Even if society should insure *children* against brute luck, it should be up to each *parent* to protect her own opportunities.

This criticism simply repeats the private project view; it restates the idea that parents should bear the entire autonomy burden of the No Exit obligation. The reply, then, is parallel to the answer I developed in Chapter 4. An egalitarian society should remain mindful of the autonomy burden that the No Exit obligation creates. Caretaker resource accounts help preserve the opportunity for parents to pursue a variety of life projects over time, independent of their child-rearing work. Life-planning insurance adds an extra measure of assistance when very disabled children require special care that sharply limits their caretakers' life options.

Extraordinary Needs and Neutral Remedies

Life-planning insurance should help mitigate the risk of severe damage to parents' opportunities in cases of children's severe illness or disability, including mental and developmental disabilities. But when is a child's need for care sufficiently serious to warrant assistance?

In existing programs, the standards for children's disability have been extensively debated, and the controversies continue today. In 1996, the SSI program (which aids disabled adults and children) narrowed the definition of disability for children, in part because policymakers feared that normally abled children were being classified as disabled.[17] The standards for learning disabilities for purposes of the Individuals with Disabilities

Education Act (IDEA) have also been debated with some heat. Some advocates for people with disabilities applaud the growing recognition of learning disabilities, but critics worry that the diagnosis is too malleable and can become a tool for middle-class parents to claim resources that could be better used for disadvantaged children.[18]

Here, I will not attempt to revisit existing disability standards in detail. In Chapter 11, I consider how life-planning insurance might be coordinated with existing programs, but for now I want to begin with two general principles.

First, parents should be eligible for life-planning insurance only if their child's care places extraordinary demands on their life. "Extraordinary" should be understood in contrast to "ordinary"; the program should identify those parents whose children have needs that go well beyond routine childhood illnesses and injuries. The governing standard should be objective: Would the child's condition require *any* parent to devote time to his care that significantly exceeds the time a parent would commit to the care of a healthy and normally abled child?[19]

Second, life-planning insurance should provide assistance that is as neutral as possible across life plans. Benefits should not, to the extent feasible, be made conditional on or otherwise linked to a parent's paid work participation. Instead of giving the greatest weight to disruptions in paid work, we should frame the problem more generally as disruptions in life planning. At-home parents, no less than working parents, have projects they are pursuing wholeheartedly; they may be rearing other children, volunteering at their church, or attending school, for example. When crisis hits, there is no good reason to protect workers' life plans while ignoring other parents'. The analogy to disaster relief is telling. It would be odd for the government to aid, say, only those flood victims who hold paid jobs. It would be similarly inappropriate to limit life-planning insurance to employed parents.

To this end, life-planning insurance should aim to provide financial assistance and social services that would help any parent reclaim some time for projects other than the child's care. For example, a program might provide skilled child care, respite care, or domestic help to help caretakers return to outside activities or better manage their home life.[20] Families under severe stress might also benefit from social work assistance as they coordinate a child's medical care and seek out available public services.

To illustrate, consider several situations that would meet the extraordinariness and neutrality standards. Some children who are ill or have a disability require expensive, skilled care. A child with medical needs—one who is tube-fed, for instance—may need trained medical supervision.[21] But here, there is a gap in existing programs. Home care may be available for some medical needs, but often families are expected to provide quite sophisticated care that many ordinary child care workers cannot or will not perform.[22] In addition, medical care may not be a good substitute for child care; depending on the child's condition, insurance may provide nursing help only a few hours per day. In the age of managed care, the health care system has increasingly sent children home with significant medical needs and no assistance at all.[23]

If medical insurance will not pay, it will be beyond the average parent's financial capacity to pay the $20,000 (or more) that even semiskilled nursing care would cost each year.[24] The $5,000 annual caretaker grant would help, but would defray only a fraction of the cost. In this situation, poor and working-class families will be pushed beyond their means, and even middle-class families will find it a strain on their finances.[25]

More generally, ordinary child care providers often cannot (or will not) accommodate children with significant developmental or physical needs.[26] The Americans with Disabilities Act (ADA) requires child care centers, in theory, to admit children with disabilities without extra charge, but many centers do not comply. And the law permits centers to reject disabled children whose care would require a "fundamental alteration" in the nature of the program. Although the boundaries of the ADA remain contested, that law is not well designed to create inexpensive care for children with extremely high needs.[27]

Some children need parental care that is time-intensive and cannot be delegated. For example, children with autism may require intensive speech and behavioral therapy, which requires parental participation. Although experts may design and demonstrate the techniques, the program may require a parent to participate in the therapy and to apply its lessons nearly continuously during the child's home life.[28] Children with other disabilities may also require intensive therapy. For instance, Helen Featherstone quotes a physical therapist who later had a disabled son:

> Before I had Peter, I [assigned physical therapy] programs that would have taken all day. I don't know when I expected mothers to change diapers, sort laundry, or buy groceries. . . . Tasks like dressing, bathing, and toileting, which most children manage unaided after the first few years, may challenge a disabled child for a long time. Each specialist will suggest a few (perhaps small) things the mother can do at home. By gradual increments, the program grows beyond what is doable.[29]

A parent in this position cannot responsibly delegate his duties, yet the time commitment, as well as the emotional and physical demands of the therapy, may foreclose (or sharply limit) paid work and other outside projects. These parents may need extensive help, including not only social services but income transfers as well.

Other countries provide aid to parents in this situation. For example, in Denmark, local authorities help parents pay extra expenses related to caring for a disabled child and also compensate parents for lost wages when they care for a disabled child at home. Sweden has provided an array of accommodations for care for children with disabilities, including financial allowances for parents, priority in public day care placement, and a menu of social services including respite care, summer camps, home help, and transportation.[30] Even Great Britain, which typically resembles the United States more strongly in its social welfare system than the Scandinavian countries, provides special financial assistance to parents of children with disabilities.[31]

It will not be a simple matter to demarcate "severe" illnesses and disabilities from less serious ones. A child with cystic fibrosis (a lung disease that requires intensive treatment and often results in early death) obviously requires greater parental care and attention than one with, say, mild asthma, which is usually treatable and controllable. But in a range of close cases, the lines will be difficult to draw. For instance, what if the child has quite severe asthma, not well-controlled by the standard medications, and requires intensive home monitoring and hospitalization once or twice a month? Does that family need skilled child care, or is it reasonable to entrust the child's care to a day care situation? Can an average babysitter monitor the child's condition and administer breathing treatments correctly? What if illnesses caught from other children in day care would worsen the child's condition?

These line-drawing problems, although difficult, are not qualitatively different from the standard setting that is required in many social welfare programs. The effort to help those in need always requires a determination about individual situations, and that can be complicated. Disability programs offer the obvious parallel. Am I disabled if I have arthritis that is excruciating on some days but bearable on others? Am I disabled if I could work, but only at jobs that are quite different from my usual one? Analogous distinctions between serious and minor (or transient) disability and illness pervade FMLA workers' compensation, tort law, and the health care system.

Should life-planning insurance be income-tested? The case for income testing is somewhat stronger here than in the case of caretaker resource accounts. Life-planning insurance takes the form of ex post relief (rather than ex ante prevention) and by necessity will require bureaucratic administration that should be capable of relatively fine judgments about parents' circumstances. The aim should be to tailor assistance appropriately to the situation, to preserve the caretaker's time and basic financial resources in light of the child's extreme need for care.

Still, traditional income testing is a crude instrument for situational judgments, and we might do better. The difficulty with income testing (just as in the case of caretaker resource accounts) is that family income is a rough proxy for caretakers' opportunities. Unless the caretaker herself controls the income, she may have a limited capacity to use resources to preserve her own independence. One approach would be to income-test financial assistance but to make in-kind services available without regard to income. It would be absurd to provide, say, $1,000 per month in income support to a rich family; income support by its nature supplements general family finances. But it may still be appropriate to permit the caretaker in a well-off family to take an unpaid job leave (FMLA does not contain an income test) and to utilize services such as respite care and social work assistance. Providing this sort of assistance in kind (rather than in the form of a reimbursement right) would give every caretaker access to basic assistance.

These broad principles leave unresolved a number of prudential concerns. For example, like any social program, life planning insurance may create "moral hazard." The task will be to screen out parents who exaggerate (or lie about) their child's condition in order to gain extra assistance. Administrative coordination is also a critical piece of the puzzle: Are there existing bureaucracies that have expertise well-suited to the new program?

I return to these issues in Chapter 11. For the present, I want to round out the preliminary sketch of life-planning insurance with a comparison to existing programs and a series of preliminary examples showing how the program might work.

The Inadequacy of Present Programs

Current social insurance programs provide some cushion against illness and disability. But the major programs respond primarily to events in *one's own life*—disability, injury, unemployment—rather than events in a child's life that affect his parents. For example, Social Security Disability Insurance (SSDI) provides income support (and Medicare) for workers who suffer a long-term disability. That program provides aid to a disabled worker's dependents, but a child's disability does not trigger coverage.[32] Programs for short-term disability and unemployment also do not extend benefits to parents whose children suffer short-term but dire emergencies. Workers may be eligible for unemployment compensation or short-term disability coverage if they leave work for their own illness or other "good cause," but a child's need for temporary care due to an accident, illness, or trauma is not considered good cause.[33]

Present programs provide fragmented assistance to parents of children with severe disabilities and illnesses.[34] FMLA gives some workers the right to return to their job following an unpaid leave of up to 12 weeks, if necessary to attend to a child's illness.[35] But FMLA permits parents to take only relatively short, unpaid leaves, and only when children require continuing medical treatment. A developmentally disabled child, for instance, may require a caretaker's participation in and constant reinforcement of therapeutic techniques. For that caretaker, 12 weeks of leave will pass terribly quickly, and FMLA provides neither income support nor social services.[36]

As Michael Graetz and Jerry Mashaw have emphasized, the current system of public disability insurance is inadequate and badly organized. The system for disabled children is, if anything, even more tangled and uneven.[37] Disabled and ill children may have access to SSI, to Medicaid, to special education, and to other services provided by states, localities, and charities. But there is no standard, national menu of services, nor is there an integrated system for identifying needs and delivering services. The services to which children and their families are entitled vary significantly depending on three factors.

The first is family income. A disabled child from a poor family may receive income support under the federal SSI program, often with state supplementation. But the eligibility rules are stringent, and the program pays benefits, which are modest, only to quite poor families. SSI benefits typically do not raise a family to the national poverty threshold.[38] In 2000, for example, maximum federal benefits per month ranged from $340 to $512, depending on the child's living situation.[39] Although the SSI program is a useful barrier against dire poverty, it is officially presented as a "program of last resort"[40] and not a front-line effort to make decent provision for families of disabled children.

The second factor is the nature of the child's condition and needs. Two types of needs are relatively well provided for: children's medical care and special education. Some children have private health insurance to cover the cost of medical care. Those who have no health insurance, or whose health insurance benefits have been exhausted, are often eligible for medical insurance under Medicaid.[41] A child with disabilities is also entitled to individualized therapy and public education under IDEA at the expense of the local school district.[42]

Although these are laudable programs, they do not systematically address parents' need for assistance. Medicaid focuses on medical treatment for the child and does not typically fund custodial care outside a residential institution (e.g., a hospital or group home). Some children qualify for home medical care under private insurance or Medicaid. But although it is valuable, and crucial, to have a nurse or aide present to help care for a gravely ill child, that person may not (depending on the child's condition) be in the home for periods long enough to permit the parent to work. In effect, the public and private health care systems presume that parents have unlimited time to devote to children's care.

A third variable is the state and locality in which families live. Depending on local rules, a family with an ill or disabled child may or may not have access to respite care, child care assistance, home help, or other services. Some of these services are funded by federal grants, but they are not funded as universal entitlement programs.[43] Depending on where the child lives, and how aggressive his parents are in seeking out assistance, there may be state, local, or charitable social service programs. For instance, child welfare laws may authorize housekeeping and other home services for children with disabilities, but these services are discretionary, not an entitlement, and seem most likely to be used when a family has already been called to the attention of child welfare authorities.[44] Nor is respite care readily available to all parents. Although the federal government provides some funding, the provision of care is delegated to an "intricate web" of agencies and charities, and parents complain that available services are inflexible, limited in arbitrary ways, and unresponsive.[45]

This state of affairs reflects two related problems: the disorganization of the U.S. disability system (for children and adults) and the absence of attention to parents' needs. Existing programs may or may not provide adequate services. The services that do exist will often require considerable efforts to locate, given the fragmented nature of the system. *Nowhere in the system is the demand on parental time the deciding factor for aid,* with the exception of FMLA.

From Principles to Programs

What would life-planning insurance look like "on the ground"? In this section, I offer two examples to illustrate the program's operation and highlight some legal and administrative questions for further attention in Chapter 11.

When children's emergencies arise, one central concern of employed parents may simply be keeping their job while they spend time away from work. Job retention may have significant value in protecting parents' long-term opportunities. Parents may have developed job-specific human capital, which means that their opportunities are better in their current job than in a new one.[46] In addition, keeping one's job may help prevent the child's crisis from snowballing into a more general family crisis.

For prudential reasons, which will become clearer in the discussion of workplace regulation in Chapter 9, feasible job leave rights should be of relatively short duration and should be unpaid. FMLA today provides 12 weeks of unpaid leave.[47] Although many feminists have advocated adding pay to the FMLA leave entitlement, we shall see that unpaid leave helps minimize the possibility that leave rights will damage women's labor market opportunities.

Critics worry that unpaid job leave amounts to no job leave at all for parents who cannot live without their wage income. This is an important issue, but the best way to resolve it is to provide income support as well. Instead of requiring employers to pay all workers on leave, the government should provide income assistance to those workers whose leave creates financial hardship. The critical point is that government-funded income support takes pressure off the employment relationship. The employer still must replace the absent worker but does not need to pay double wages. Income support also extends assistance to parents on a more equal footing: working parents whose paycheck no longer funds the mortgage and utility bills quite obviously need financial assistance, but so too might an at-home parent whose family must now pay someone else to help care for the other children, cook the family's meals, and so on.

The program should also offer social services, including respite care and assistance in navigating the medical, educational, and disability programs that provide care to ill and disabled children. For reasons I explore in Chapter 11, the implementation of this principle will be a challenge, because there is currently no national program in place that has the infrastructure to provide uniform services across jurisdictions.

Recall the case of Larry and Lori and their son, Linc, who suffers from developmental and physical disabilities. He attends special education classes and requires an array of different therapies, and his parents have difficulty finding appropriate afterschool care for him. Life-planning insurance might provide Larry and Lori with income support, which could ease the pressure on Larry to work a second job and on an exhausted Lori to take a part-time job. Alternatively, or in addition, the program could help fund skilled, paid care for Linc to enable Lori to return to work full time. The program could also furnish respite care and other social services.

Now consider Maria, who has two children, Maribel and Mikey. One day, Maribel is hit by a car as she exits the school bus. She fractures her skull and sustains internal injuries, and she undergoes several surgeries, spread over a week. She remains in the hospital for three weeks and requires intensive physical therapy and home care for another two months. Maria is a single mother who is not sure how she can manage to continue at her full-time job while paying for home care for Maribel and providing the personal attention that she needs.

Maria may initially seem an unusual candidate for life-planning insurance. Maribel's condition is severe, but it is also short term; there is every reason to suppose that in a few months, life will be back to normal for this family. It is not obvious that life-planning insurance should respond to transient events such as these. In past chapters, I have emphasized the importance of *long-term* life planning. Why, then, should short-term emergencies be covered?

The answer is that short-term crises should be covered *if* they are likely to have a severe impact on a parent's long-term opportunities. The standard should be whether Maribel will need such intensive, personal care that Maria will have to neglect her other projects—a job, running the home, caring for Mikey—for some significant period, with severe consequences. Short-term job leave, income support, and social services may help prevent a transient event from snowballing into a longer-term disaster if Maria loses her job, her house, or goes deeply into debt.

By this point, some readers may wonder whether my analysis has overlooked a crucial problem: the inflexible structure of most paid jobs. Many of my hypotheticals illustrate the situations of parents who find the demands of paid employment at odds with their children's needs. Couldn't we attack that problem more directly by requiring employers to adopt family-friendly programs for parents? Wouldn't workplace programs serve just as well the goal of improving parents' long-run options? And wouldn't it be easier (and cheaper) to require employers to accommodate parents than to create new government programs?

These questions occupy the next two chapters.

Part 4

Why Workplace Programs

Aren't Enough

8

Parents and Paid Work

How should we think about parenthood and paid work? Most of us spend years of our lives working, and for many people paid work brings status, income, and long-term financial security. But not everyone experiences paid work in this way. Many parents feel ambivalence toward their paid jobs, which make demands incompatible with child rearing. Some workers, especially low-paid ones, find that their jobs provide little in the way of dignity or economic security.

The programs I have proposed would help parents choose a balance between paid work and child rearing and enable them to change their plans over time. Caretaker resource accounts and life-planning insurance would assist parents who wish to remain in the workforce, while also improving options for those who wish to de-emphasize paid employment for a time.

But I have not yet considered proposals to make paid employment the primary form of assistance to parents. Instead of offering equal grants to working and at-home parents, should we structure programs that would encourage all parents to take jobs? Could we (and should we) use the law to restructure jobs to mitigate the conflict between parenthood and paid work? Would promoting employment for mothers help in the battle against workplace discrimination?

These are the questions that motivate this chapter and the next. This chapter examines the normative case for work-centered assistance to parents: *Should* we make paid employment the central aim of programs to assist parents? Chapter 9 considers some practical issues of policy design: *Could* we restructure paid jobs if we wanted to do so?

Programs for Parents—or for Parents Who Work?

Some policymakers and scholars conclude that the best way to help parents is to integrate them more seamlessly into the paid workforce. The pragmatists argue that parents, especially mothers, could earn more if they participated continuously in the paid workforce. Higher earnings would mean greater economic security for mothers and their children, and perhaps even greater gender equality at home.[1]

The theorists take a more idealistic view. They posit that paid work permits (or could be restructured to permit) every individual to participate in a collective endeavor that takes him or her out of the familial sphere into the wider world. Paid work, these theorists say, provides a unique venue for the development of individuals' capabilities and for human engagement and interaction. Too many mothers, they conclude, are missing out on one of life's most important experiences.[2]

One policy response would be to subsidize the costs that working parents incur: child care and transportation, for instance.[3] The 1996 welfare reforms represent one example; the idea is that if low-earning mothers work, they can become financially self-sufficient with limited assistance from the state. More moderate versions of this strategy recognize that low-wage workers need considerable assistance, and even middle-class mothers often need some help, with working expenses if they are to hold traditional jobs.[4]

Another approach would attempt to alter the jobs themselves to accommodate parents' need for flexible schedules. Family-friendly workplace proposals would require (or, in some cases, just encourage) employers to offer part-time work, flextime work, job leave, and other measures tailored to parents' needs. Some advocates acknowledge that parents taking such jobs might not earn as much or be promoted as quickly as if they held traditional jobs, but they reason that it is better for parents to remain in the game. More ambitious proposals aim to improve the earnings and promotion opportunities associated with part-time and flexible-schedule work.[5]

All these policies could help many parents live the life they wish to lead, and that is all to the good. Indeed, my own proposals share elements of both approaches. Caretaker resource accounts include a child care voucher, which would help parents remain in the workforce. Life-planning insurance endorses the continuation of FMLA, which permits all parents a 12-week, unpaid job leave to care for a sick child.

But I hesitate to make workplace reform the sole method of assisting parents. Instead of portraying parents as people, who might or might not choose to hold paid jobs at different points in their life, such proposals portray parents as workers who just need better jobs. Today, it is true, most parents work. But it does not follow that most parents ought to work.

Some parents, especially mothers, would like to work more but are unfairly constrained by gender attitudes or finances, including the high cost of child care. Women in this situation could benefit from child care subsidies or perhaps flexible- or part-time job options. But we also know that some mothers (and fathers) prefer to take time away from paid work to care for their children. If parents had better economic options, some might work more, but others might work less.

Poll data and interview studies confirm that many parents place considerable value on personal involvement in child rearing.[6] And a significant percentage of mothers in every income class, including many highly educated women, interrupt their working careers. We should not be too quick to ascribe those attitudes to gender bias. Some mothers who opt out of paid work may have mixed feelings, but not all experience their choice as disempowering. It is significant that there is a tiny but growing percentage of married couples in which the father works part time or not at all to care for young children at home. These fathers are challenging gender roles to spend more time with their children.

The problem with policies that seek only to send parents to work is that they exclude parents who wish to structure their life differently. Child care is useful only to those who currently hold paid jobs; similarly, flexible- and part-time jobs are only valuable to those who want them. Caretaker resource accounts take a more expansive approach: they offer a menu of choices with value to a wider range of parents. The working parent can use $5,000 each year for a child care subsidy, and the sequencer can save his funds for future child care, education, or retirement needs.

Paid work should not be the exclusive route to self-realization in a society that respects the way of life chosen by each citizen. Parents plan their lives according to their values and particular situation. Every care-taker bears the burden of the No Exit obligation, but each responds differ-ently. Some parents work full time for financial security and for the dignity they find in that endeavor. Others willingly forgo income and job prospects to take time away from paid work to rear their children. These parents may be motivated by religion, or tradition, or a personal convic-tion that parental care is best. Some have children with special needs, who require more intensive care than even a flexible paid job will permit. Some parents find that their skills are not highly valued in the marketplace and qualify them only for routine jobs they dislike, whereas child rearing may give them a chance to make a difference in their children's lives. I do not intend to romanticize the life of an at-home parent; many find it isolating and stressful. Still, a pluralist approach should grant each caretaker equal resources and permit her to decide for herself which life to lead.

Child rearing is not a mechanical task. It is value-laden work, and how we accomplish it is as central to our identity as our religion, our politics, or our ethnic affiliation. A fair society should respect the different ways par-ents choose to meet their No Exit obligation.

Some proponents of workplace reforms recognize that many parents deliberately opt out of paid work. Joan Williams, for instance, is sensitive to parents' desire to care for their children themselves; she proposes paid work reforms as well as family law reforms intended to enhance mothers' economic security regardless of their paid work involvement.[7]

But other advocates quite deliberately make paid work normative for parents. They talk in utilitarian terms about the benefits of paid work for workers or the virtues of high-quality day care. They argue, in effect, that caretakers who reject or delay employment are mistaken or uninformed. But the psychological evidence is too often overstated. For example, some claim that at-home mothers are more depressed than working mothers. But that conclusion requires a strained reading of the psychological studies, which find that autonomy—choosing one's role—matters more than which role one chooses.[8]

Some feminists defend paid work programs for mothers on the ground that women's choices have been so distorted that the best route to equality is to reorient them firmly toward the workforce. There is certainly some truth here. We live in a society that still considers child rearing to be women's work. Gendered attitudes push and pull women toward care work and may lead women to be unduly self-sacrificing in their choice of life plans.

But the recognition that gender shapes women's preferences should not necessarily lead us to make paid work the focus of programs for parents. Caretaker resource accounts adopt a subtler approach; they would encourage mothers to make future-oriented investments in themselves, while leaving greater room for the expression of individual values and aspirations. The program could improve economic options for mothers without excluding sequencers and at-home mothers. Caretaker resource accounts could also complement other efforts to promote women's autonomy in many spheres of life: in paid employment, in education and early socialization, in medical care, in the administration of justice.

Should We Regulate Jobs to Improve Parents' Options?

To this point, I have argued that efforts to support paid employment should not be the primary means of assisting parents. But why couldn't the programs I propose be combined with additional measures to expand parents' job options?

Caretaker resource accounts and life-planning insurance would improve caretakers' capacity to compete in the marketplace, but they do not directly enhance the terms of the jobs that employers offer. (The one exception is the job leave program I endorse as part of life-planning insurance.) We know that some parents would value the chance to work part time or otherwise to work at jobs with more flexible terms. So why not add family-friendly workplace measures to my agenda?

The case for workplace accommodations for parents is not as straightforward as it seems. At this point, I want to question the normative case for workplace accommodations. Later, in Chapter 9, I consider the practical difficulties of regulating labor markets.

Both here and in Chapter 9, my aim is to raise questions, not utter the final word. I am open to the conclusion that workplace accommodations may be both fair and practical, but it seems to me that some serious questions about the merits of family-friendly workplace regulation have not yet been adequately addressed.

To begin with, we should be clear that workplace accommodations for parents would not simply redistribute opportunities *to* caretakers; instead, they would redistribute opportunities *among* caretakers as well. Consider three hypotheticals:

> Florence works full time as a police officer. She works overtime when she has the chance, and she sometimes volunteers for special assignments to impress her superiors with her commitment to her work. Florence values her earning power and her financial independence. She expects her long hours to pay off in opportunities for promotions in the long run. Florence's children attend a day care program, and she arranges alternative care when she works late.

> Patricia currently works 40 hours per week as a sales clerk at a clothing store but would prefer to work part time, 30 hours per week, in order to spend more time with her children. She usually refuses overtime, even during the busy Christmas season. Patricia might be able to reduce her hours to 30 per week, but she knows that her employer does not always grant such requests. Nor is Patricia eager to take the cut in hourly pay and the loss of promotion opportunities that the change to part-time status would entail.

> Beatrice owns the small business that employs Patricia. Beatrice believes that the working conditions and promotion criteria she has established are well-tailored to the needs of the business and will reward workers according to their economic contribution to the firm. Beatrice became an entrepreneur so that she could have

greater flexibility to pursue her own ideas and set her own schedule to meet her children's needs.

Patricia is the person that workplace accommodation proposals intend to help. She could benefit from rules requiring employers to offer part-time hours, and to grant such workers equal (hourly) pay and seniority rights. But we might expect Florence and Beatrice to object to such changes, because they would sacrifice some of the relative gains they enjoy from their willingness to work longer hours (Florence) or to take the risks of entrepreneurship (Beatrice). Florence might have to contend with a larger pool of (part-time) competitors for promotions, and she would be more vulnerable to layoff if part-timers also earn seniority. Beatrice might find her business less profitable if costs of employment increase in ways that cannot be shifted to workers, and if she has less flexibility to reward workers for working harder by giving them greater promotion opportunities.

These hypotheticals do not, of course, prove that a policy that redistributes toward Patricia at the expense of the other two mothers is unfair. There is no reason to treat the status quo as a normative baseline for fair working conditions. For instance, not everyone has the entrepreneurship option that Beatrice found so valuable; perhaps it would be fair to try to extend similar flexibility to a larger group. And yet, the uneven pattern of redistribution does raise questions. If the rationale for workplace accommodations is to improve the opportunities of parents *as a group*, why should we take steps that benefit some caretakers at the expense of others? The autonomy burden of the No Exit obligation falls on all three mothers, but only Patricia would benefit from adding workplace accommodations to the menu for reform. These questions intensify if the full-time-working Florences are more likely to be low-paid or single mothers and the part-time Patricias are more likely to be better off or married.

Here is the problem: Should parents who choose to work part time (or who work shorter hours or flexible schedules) bear the costs of doing so? Today, Patricia suffers if she cuts back to part-time work. At a minimum, she loses wages and promotion opportunities. As a part-time worker, she may also lose benefits and will find that she has a smaller array of (worse) jobs to choose from, compared to her full-time peers. If this situation is unfair, we need to be more precise about what a fairer arrangement would look like. Caretaker resource accounts take one approach: they give Patricia extra options over the long term but without alleviating the immediate costs to her of choosing part-time work. Florence and Beatrice would receive the same funds. In contrast, workplace accommodations would offer special protections for Patricia's wages, benefits, and promotion opportunities. But by increasing the rewards for part-time work, those policies would reduce the relative gains to parents who work full time.

My argument is not that current working conditions are ideal or that the government should never intervene in the labor market. On the contrary, there is good evidence that gender discrimination persists in the workplace and that labor markets fail in other ways as well. It is important for the government to take vigorous measures to combat discrimination and to ensure equal access to the marketplace for all. But when the agenda is to improve parents' opportunities, workplace regulation may not be the best place to begin.

Would Initiatives for Parents Worsen Workplace Discrimination?

The existence of employment discrimination raises still more questions about the interplay of initiatives for parents and working conditions. How would new programs affect the fight against gender discrimination in the workplace? Would caretaker resource accounts help or hurt? How about workplace accommodations of the family-friendly kind? If it turned out that caretaker resources would undermine such efforts, then perhaps workplace accommodations would be a useful corrective measure.

A preliminary analysis suggests that this is not the case. It is difficult to make any firm prediction, because the impact of different policies will be empirically contingent and context-sensitive. But, at the level of theory, it is not clear that caretaker resources would worsen discrimination, or that workplace accommodations would combat it.

To begin, it is important to define "discrimination" and "accommodation" more precisely. Legal scholars conventionally distinguish antidiscrimination rules and workplace accommodations in the following way. "Simple" discrimination occurs when employers treat female workers worse (in terms of hiring, pay, or promotions) than they treat male workers whose net marginal product is no higher. Discrimination unjustly limits women's opportunities to participate in the market, to bid for resources and opportunities that they desire to implement their life plans. The goal of *antidiscrimination rules* should be to guarantee women and men equal access to the marketplace. *Accommodations,* by contrast, would require an employer to hire, promote, or tailor working conditions to the needs of parents *even if* their net marginal product is lower than that of other workers.[9] Thus, accommodations would impose a net cost (in terms of forgone marginal product) on someone; any proposal for accommodations should be explicit about the proper allocation of that cost.

The dynamics of discrimination are not well understood. In the empirical economics literature, discrimination is literally a residual, the portion of occupational sex segregation or the wage gap that is not correlated with observable human capital factors such as age, education, and job experience. Sociological studies have captured more nuance in observing workplace behavior and in identifying pathways through which discrimination can operate. But there are a number of different theories of discrimination, with evidence to support each.

Two theories—statistical discrimination and differential visibility—suggest that workplace accommodations for parents could do both harm and good. Statistical discrimination occurs when employers assume that an average woman will quit (or otherwise be less persistent) than a man.[10] Employers engage in statistical discrimination when they assume that the average woman will behave in a stereotypical way: quitting more often, especially to meet family responsibilities, and perhaps being less committed while on the job. Statistical discrimination may reflect incorrect information, unconscious gender biases, or social stereotypes. But it may also reflect correct (aggregate) information, because women do, on average, have more interrupted careers than men do. Statistical discrimination of this latter type is rational, in the narrow sense that employers engage in it when it is not cost-effective to evaluate each worker as an individual. As a consequence, statistical discrimination will not (even in theory) be driven out by market competition. Instead, individuals will take measures to signal to employers that they do not fit the stereotype. Some women take off their wedding ring before job interviews, a fairly trivial signal; other women remain childless or unmarried for life, in part as the price of career success.

Workplace accommodations for parents could reduce *or* worsen statistical discrimination. To the extent that mothers (on average) responded by working with greater continuity, the change would help undermine the perception, and the reality, that women quit more often than men or cut back their effort when children arrive. Accommodations could lure some mothers back into the paid workplace, reducing turnover for women as a group. At the same time, however, accommodations could lead some mothers to cut back to part-time or flextime work. The net effect on the profile of the "average" female worker is uncertain. More troublingly, to the extent accommodations require employers to bear the productivity cost, they could raise the cost of employing mothers, an issue I return to in Chapter 9.

Perhaps surprisingly, workplace accommodations have no clear advantage over caretaker resource accounts in combating statistical discrimination. Caretaker accounts would also have an ambiguous effect on statistical discrimination. Like accommodations, they would have positive and negative effects on mothers' paid work profile. Some mothers would not change their paid work behavior at all. Others would respond to the program by increasing their hours of work, reentering the workforce immediately, or returning to work sooner or at a higher level because of the program. But a third group would work less, changing from committed workers to sequencers.

One great advantage is that caretaker resource accounts would not increase the cost to firms of employing female workers. Caretaker accounts also should promote more diverse patterns of sequencing, and this diversity should make it more costly for employers to engage in statistical discrimination. The greater the dispersion of work behavior, the less cost-effective it becomes for employers to use average behavior as a proxy for individual behavior.

Differential visibility theory offers an account of workplace discrimination that initially seems to offer stronger support to workplace accommodations for parents. According to this theory, a scarcity of female workers in a particular setting may predestine them to failure. If there are few women in the workplace (or in supervisory positions), then female workers (supervisors) will be the target of greater attention, often negative.[11] Women's failures are highlighted because they cannot "blend in" and because peers may not empathize. In addition, women may be excluded from social and professional networks that transmit valuable information, so that failure becomes a self-fulfilling prophecy. On this theory, discrimination may range from the subtle and unconscious (e.g., exclusion from gossip networks) to the extreme and deliberate (e.g., sabotage of working equipment).

These theories tend to imply that increasing the percentage of female workers could undermine the conditions that foster discrimination. Women may affirmatively help one another (e.g., by creating their own informational networks). Alternatively, a critical mass of women may by itself limit harassment and exclusion opportunities.

But it is not clear that accommodations can deliver this happy scenario. Workplace accommodations would indeed make it easier for mothers to participate in paid work. But the productivity differential associated with accommodations could undercut the positive effect on workplace discrimination. By hypothesis, caretaker *accommodations* would require employers to change workplace rules in ways that ignore the productivity differential. The catch is that employers and coworkers will understand the productivity gap and may resent the accommodated employees. Childless workers sometimes express this kind of resentment today.[12] These attitudes may reflect accurate assessments or biased ones, but for purposes of the differential visibility/networks theory, perception is reality. Further, the greater the actual productivity difference, the longer these resentments are likely to persist.

By contrast, caretaker resource accounts would foster different dynamics. Caretaker accounts would enhance mothers' opportunities to play by the (standard) rules of the workplace. The program could increase the number of caretakers who persist as continuous workers, with positive effects on differential visibility, critical mass, and networks. At the same time, caretaker accounts might lead some caretakers to withdraw from the labor force and become sequencers. The net effect, compared to workplace accommodations, is uncertain. Workplace accommodations could create a larger concentration of female workers but leave them concentrated in part-time jobs and branded with a productivity differential. Caretaker accounts might produce a smaller net gain in critical mass but would not brand caretaker-workers with a productivity differential.

Although I am committed to improving parents' economic opportunities, I worry that workplace reform has come to be too uncritically accepted as the best (or only) way to help parents.

I want to turn now to some practical problems with the family-friendly workplace. Whether or not one agrees with my initial reservations about work-centered programs, it is important to understand that reforms intended to promote parents', especially mothers', job opportunities could have the opposite effect.

Practical Limitations of the Family-Friendly Workplace

Family-friendly workplace policies seek to improve job options for parents, but they could produce unintended—and distinctly unfriendly—side effects: they could cut women's wages, increase women's unemployment, and reinforce sex segregation in the workforce. These problems arise because, in a free market, employers can shift the costs of workplace regulation to workers, and to female workers in particular. In this chapter, I present economic theory and empirical evidence that suggest caution in adopting family-friendly regulations.

Although the social science evidence is not as conclusive as one could wish, existing studies raise troubling questions. The risks of harmful side effects are particularly acute in programs that adopt numerous workplace regulations at once; the greater the cost burden on employers, the more likely it is that they will react by shifting costs to female workers.

To begin, it is important to be clear about the type of program that can generate these effects. The "family-friendly workplace" is, of course, an imprecise term. Some use it to describe *voluntary* changes in workplace practices intended to attract or retain workers with child care responsibilities. For example, employers may offer part-time or flextime work, on-site child care, or paid family leave. These voluntary arrangements are not my focus here. Instead, I want to concentrate on proposals for *government-mandated* benefits for parents, that is, legal regulation that requires employers to alter the terms of jobs in ways valuable to caretakers.

To simplify the analysis, I focus on just one kind of workplace mandate: job leave for parents. The example of job leave is useful for several reasons. First, job leave is a core component of most family-friendly workplace plans, and job leave programs have been the subject of numerous empirical studies. Second, I have endorsed limited job leave rights as part of life-planning insurance.[1] It will be useful to see why I support some job leave and yet reject more ambitious efforts to reshape working conditions. My conclusion is rooted in an empirical judgment: the existing studies suggest that the kind of job leave I endorse is not particularly problematic, but that more extensive (and expensive) workplace regulation could produce unintended harm to women's employment opportunities.

How Employers Can Shift the Cost of Workplace Regulations to Workers

To understand why workplace regulation for parents may disadvantage female workers, begin with some simple economics. A job leave mandate (i.e., a regulation requiring employers, under penalty of law, to offer job leave to caretakers) may impose one or both of two costs on firms. First is *job protection,* the worker's right to return to the same or a similar job at the same pay. FMLA, for example, requires a large employer to grant 12 weeks of unpaid leave to workers with at least a year's experience with the company.[2] The second possible cost, not mandated by federal law today, is *leave pay,* the requirement that workers be paid their normal salary and benefits during their absence. For simplicity, I focus on the costs of job protection, and thus on unpaid leave. The analysis could readily be extended to paid leave; any requirement that companies pay absent workers would tend to intensify the effects I describe.

Job protection requires firms either to hire a temporary worker to hold the absent worker's place, or to hire a permanent replacement and guarantee an equivalent position when the absent worker returns. Thus, from the employer's perspective, any particular worker's leave will be expensive (or cheap) depending on how costly it is to hire a substitute or to create (or hold open) a similar job for the returning worker. The cost of job protection is likely to be highly variable across jobs, employers, and industries; it will depend on the employer's cost structure and organizational flexibility and the nature of the job at issue, as well as the timing of the leave relative to the demands in the company's business. For example, job leave may be less costly when the absent worker is part of a large cohort of similar workers or when there is a high rate of turnover among workers in equivalent jobs.

The costs of job leave may be mitigated, or even outweighed, by the benefits to employers, including reduced worker turnover and improved morale.[3] But economic theory suggests that firms that anticipate net benefits should adopt job leave voluntarily, unless there is a market failure (a possibility to which I return later). In the absence of market failure, we would expect that companies responding to a new mandate would be those experiencing net costs.

At first glance, job protection costs appear to fall on employers, which must literally pay the costs of hiring substitute workers and of guaranteeing equivalent positions. But economic theory suggests that, to the extent legal and market conditions permit, employers will attempt to recoup their costs by reducing workers' wages or by reducing employment.[4]

In effect, the costs of job protection act like a tax on the employment of workers likely to take family leave. Conventional employment taxes (such as the Social Security payroll tax) are shifted to workers, as are the costs of mandated employment benefits such as workers' compensation.[5] Minimum-wage laws too tend to shift the costs of regulatory mandates to workers, this time in the form of reduced employment.[6] In a similar fashion, economic theory predicts that the costs of the job protection rule will be shifted to workers.

When job leave mandates benefit an identifiable group of workers, the "tax" will tend to shift to those workers (rather than to workers as a group). A job leave program for parents, for example, makes caretakers more expensive to employ than other workers, on average. Although it is difficult to distinguish caretakers with great precision, gender is (unfortunately) a reasonably good proxy. The great majority of women have children, and mothers are more likely than fathers to take job leaves related to children.[7] Thus, wage and job cuts are likely to be targeted to younger women (i.e., women of childbearing age). Employers will respond by reducing the wage payable to such workers and/or by substituting other, "cheaper" workers when possible. Importantly, these effects operate even when employers bear no animus toward women; the incentive arises because, by operation of law, younger women become (on average) more expensive (i.e., less productive) workers than men and older women.

Because employers can observe age and gender but cannot make finer predictions about which workers will likely take leave, it is likely that all young female workers will pay the same wage or employment penalty. More precisely, the wage or employment penalty is likely to be uniform for all young women who hold jobs with equivalent leave costs. Women who hold high-leave-cost jobs would likely pay higher wage or employment penalties than women in low-leave-cost jobs.

The shifting of costs can be illustrated with a simple economic model, depicted in Figures 9.1 and 9.2.[8] In both graphs, a new regulation requires employers to provide job leave to caretakers. The net cost of the mandate to employers is $C, and the net value of the benefit to workers is $V. In response to the mandate, the labor demand curve shifts downward by $C. That is, employers will pay $C less in wages for each quantity of labor, because they must pay $C in nonwage costs. This effect occurs in both graphs.

The two graphs differ in their depiction of workers' reaction. In Figure 9.1, $V is less than $C; that is, workers value the benefit (on average) at less than its cost. The result is that wages and/or employment will fall. The labor supply curve does shift outward, because workers are willing to work for reduced (cash) wages to the extent of $V, but the demand curve drops by the larger amount, $C. Of course, the magnitude of the wage and employment effects depends on the shape and slope of the supply and demand curves. The graph merely illustrates the *tendency* of wages and/or employment to fall to some degree in response to a low-value mandate (i.e., a mandate with a value less than its cost). Workers are (on average) worse off than before enactment of the mandate, because their wage falls by more than $V.

Figure 9.2 anticipates a happier result, produced when the value of the benefit to workers exceeds the company's cost. The same shifts in supply

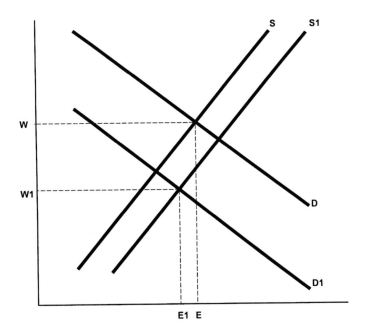

Figure 9.1

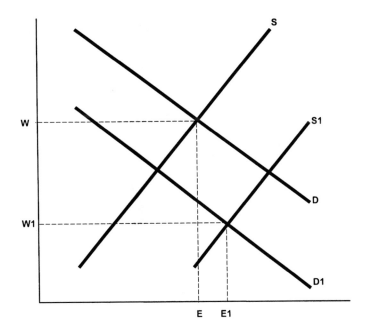

Figure 9.2

and demand occur, but because $V exceeds $C, workers feel as if they have gotten a raise, despite the fall in cash wages, and so employment increases. The puzzle about Figure 9.2, however, is that, in theory, a *mandated* benefit should not be necessary in this case; if markets work properly, no state action should be needed to create a value-enhancing bargain between employers and their workers.

This much is standard economics. Christine Jolls's recent work adds an important nuance regarding the impact of antidiscrimination law.[9] Simplifying a bit, there are two possible outcomes. If antidiscrimination laws prevent employers from differentially adjusting *women's* wages or employment levels, then employers will respond to a job leave mandate by cutting wages or employment for all workers, both male and female. In this case, a job leave mandate looks, from the market's perspective, like a general employment tax. Put another way, the Figure 9.1 or 9.2 results will apply to all workers, regardless of their gender.

If, however, antidiscrimination laws cannot prevent differential treatment of female workers, then employers will respond to a job leave mandate by cutting (young) women's wages or employment but not men's wages or employment. In the second scenario, the job leave mandate acts as a tax on women's employment, and the Figure 9.1 or 9.2 wage and employment effects apply (basically) to women alone.

Which of these scenarios will prevail? Studies from both the United States and abroad confirm that workplace mandates can reduce women's wages. Jonathan Gruber, for example, found that state and federal regulations requiring employers to provide health insurance coverage for childbirth reduced young women's wages but not their employment levels.[10]

Although Jane Waldfogel's study of FMLA failed to detect any impact on women's wages or employment, critics have questioned her methodology.[11] One confounding fact is that FMLA represented only an incremental change in prior practice. Some states had mandated job leave before the federal statute took effect, and FMLA's many exemptions weaken the force of the mandate. Softer evidence of FMLA's impact comes from Labor Department surveys, which asked employers about the costs and disruption of mandated job leave. The majority of employers reported no costs or small costs in complying with the FMLA mandate.[12]

Despite their limitations, the FMLA studies support three conclusions. First, the current program of modest, unpaid leave seems not to have produced large changes in wages or employment, either for all workers or for women in particular. Second, FMLA's many exemptions may help produce this result. For example, FMLA applies only to large employers and to workers with a significant work history.[13] FMLA also permits employers to deny leave to the highest-paid 10 percent of workers in each worksite under certain circumstances; these are likely to be managers for whom even unpaid leave might be costly to the company.[14] Third, it is difficult to predict whether expanding FMLA to cover more workers would produce large changes in women's wages or employment. Here, the European experience is relevant: most EU countries offer job leave to nearly all workers, often including wage replacement payments and longer leaves than FMLA requires. Christopher Ruhm found that European parental leave mandates increased women's employment but reduced their wages.[15]

For these reasons, the program of life-planning insurance that I propose incorporates a job leave right, but a modest one, basically, a continuation of FMLA. The evidence, such as it is, suggests that FMLA has produced minimal effects on women's employment. (Whether FMLA's unpaid leave could be extended to smaller companies without producing greater effects is an open question.) But life-planning insurance would not amend FMLA to require employers to pay workers on leave; instead, it would use government funds to provide income support to some parents while on leave.[16]

It is worth pausing a moment on the question of leave pay. Leave pay seems inherently attractive, because it helps make real the promise that parents can take time away from work if they need to. But the structure of leave pay matters: there is a critical distinction between requiring *employers* to pay absent workers and creating a program under which the *government* pays income support or leave pay. The preceding analysis shows why: if employers must pay absent workers, the cost of leave will be higher, and so will the incentive to shift costs to female workers. Thus, mandated leave pay is a risky proposal; it could produce serious unintended effects. In contrast, when leave pay comes from the government, there is a much smaller impact on employers' costs. This is what policy wonks call a social insurance structure: the leave pay comes from a government-sponsored fund rather than from one's employer.[17]

Creating a social insurance program to pay workers on leave does raise serious issues. For instance, employers' costs for job protection may rise a bit, because more workers are likely to take leave if it is paid. The taxes imposed to fund the social insurance program also require some deliberation; an employment tax, for example, could cut wages or employment for workers, although the impact would not fall disproportionately on women. Recently, California enacted a parental leave program with pay funded by the state government;[18] it will be instructive to watch how that experiment turns out.

My proposal for life-planning insurance sidesteps these complexities, for now, in the interests of offering a plan that would be immediately helpful and with minimal risks to women's employment. Life-planning insurance would not extend full leave pay to all FMLA-eligible workers, but instead would offer income support to the hardest-pressed families, those caring for children with severe illnesses and disabilities who meet some kind of income test.

Finally, a cautionary note. Not all family-friendly workplace policies can be redrawn as social insurance. Job leave pay is a relatively good candidate for such a structure: the government can create a fund to pay cash to absent workers. But it will often be difficult, if not impossible, for the government to compensate employers for the costs of restructuring to comply with family-friendly mandates. Proposals to require employers to offer parents part-time and flextime work, to pay part-timers a proportional full-time wage, or to ban mandatory overtime might raise employers' costs sufficiently to set in motion the shifting mechanisms described here. And there is no straightforward way for the government to ascertain these costs, or take steps to defray them.[19]

How Job Leave Mandates Can Worsen Sex Discrimination

In the basic model (Figures 9.1 and 9.2), a job leave mandate reduces young women's wages or employment or both. This simple story, however, fails to take full account of antidiscrimination laws. Employers faced with a job leave mandate (or other workplace mandate) may experience a double bind: the mandate creates an incentive to cut young women's wages, but the employment discrimination laws prohibit employers from doing this. Employers may react to the double bind in one of two ways. The optimistic story is that employers will obey the law. In this case, as we have seen, the job leave mandate will be paid for by a reduction in wages for all workers. In effect, the mandate serves as a general employment tax.

But some studies, notably, those by Gruber and Ruhm, suggest that employment discrimination laws do not prevent adjustments in women's relative wages. This possibility will not be entirely surprising to lawyers. Although it is in theory a violation of federal law to discriminate against mothers in wages or hiring,[20] it is costly for plaintiffs to detect and prove sex discrimination. Some employers may play the "litigation lottery," relying on collective action problems and the high cost of investigation and litigation to deter enforcement of the law. The pattern of discrimination produced by a family-friendly mandate may not be easily detectable, particularly in a sex-segregated environment, where pay cuts for women can be disguised as pay cuts for workers in a particular job category.

Employers can also create internal structures that facilitate wage discrimination. They need not engage in obvious, large-scale firing or wage cutting for young women. More subtly, they can cut wages by denying promotions and raises to young women; more insidiously, they can take advantage of or create patterns of job segregation that shunt young women into job categories that "coincidentally" will pay less over time. Employers can also segregate young women into low-skill or low-compensation job categories in which granting job leave (or other mandated benefits) is cheaper. By reinforcing the glass ceiling, employers can exclude women from high-responsibility, high-visibility positions for which mandated job leave is costly.

The stakes here are high. Job leave mandates (and other workplace regulations) will create market pressures for employers to discriminate. Unless antidiscrimination laws can prevent *both* wage and employment adjustments, job leave mandates may reinforce workplace structures that facilitate discrimination. Jolls shows, for example, that if employment discrimination rules prevent wage cuts but *not* hiring cuts, then mandates will reduce the employment of young women. [21] The logic is that young women become "more expensive" than other workers; because, by hypothesis, their wages cannot be cut, fewer are hired (or more are fired). The mandate also increases the incentive for employers to segregate workers by sex and to engage in other practices that minimize the cost of an absent female worker (e.g., discrimination in promotions).

I have found no studies on whether mandates reinforce sex segregation. The cautionary example sometimes offered is Sweden.[22] Sweden offers up to 12 months of paid childbirth leave at 80 percent of full pay, followed by the right to work 3/4 time until one's youngest child is 8 years old.[23] The leave pay is funded by a combination of employer mandates, payroll taxes, and general revenues. Sweden's policies apparently succeed in promoting women's attachment to paid work. In 1999, a larger percentage of Swedish mothers than U.S. mothers were in the paid labor force.[24] Still, some feminists worry that Sweden is not a model of gender equality in the workplace.[25] A large percentage of mothers work part time (although part time tends to mean 3/4 time rather than half time). In addition, there remains a significant gender gap in wages and a high degree of sex segregation in the workforce. Women tend to cluster in lower-paying, public sector jobs, with flexible or reduced hours, and men dominate higher-paying, private sector employment, which demands long hours.[26]

The Swedish evidence is limited, and in any event, one country's experience may not be reliable as a general model. Still, the Swedish experience suggests the possibility that a cumulation of workplace mandates could create a trade-off: greater employment for mothers but greater sex segregation as well.

Would Family-Friendly Mandates Correct Market Failures?

To this point, I have presented family-friendly mandates as an effort to benefit parents. But some advocates have a different goal in mind: market correction. They argue that current labor markets misallocate resources and that efficiency might be improved by corrective workplace regulation.

The market failure argument for workplace mandates runs like this: many workers would probably like to be able to insure against conflicts between child rearing and paid work. Workplace mandates such as job leave, part-time work, and flextime would be attractive to many parents. But the market, the argument runs, has failed to respond to demand for such arrangements. The standard argument concludes that because the market has failed, the government should step in to require employers to provide workers with the right to job leave, part-time work, and perhaps other workplace benefits as well.

To be persuasive, however, the market failure justification for workplace regulation requires more thorough theoretical and empirical groundwork. To begin with, not every working condition that disadvantages parents is a market failure. From an efficiency perspective, markets fail when some structural problem prevents the market from allocating resources at a price that willing buyers and sellers would otherwise agree on. For example, suppose that supply and demand for widgets would clear at $1 per widget, but for some reason the going price is $10 per widget. That is a market failure, because willing buyers and sellers are denied the opportunity to strike a bargain.

By contrast, markets that clear, but at a price that leaves parents with fewer opportunities than they would like, are not malfunctioning. For example, suppose that an employer offers Sarah a job for $40,000 per year, with two weeks' vacation and a standard 9–5 workday. Sarah would prefer to work 7–1, and she would even be willing to take a pay cut of $2,000 in return. The employer balks, however; she will offer only $35,000 for a non-standard workday, which is inconvenient for others in the office who work 9–5. In this case, *the market has not failed*; instead, the market price for Sarah's preferred accommodation was simply too high.

Insurance markets sometimes fail (in this stricter sense) because of moral hazard or adverse selection. Suppose that a hypothetical market would offer insurance for paid work disability at a premium of $100 per worker in risky jobs and $50 per worker in safe jobs. But suppose that insurance companies cannot distinguish riskier jobs from safer ones, and so set the price of insurance at $75. In that case, the market may fail, because the price is both too high and too low. As adverse selection occurs, only risky workers will remain in the pool, driving the premium up toward

$100. Thus, adverse selection is a pathology of information and of pricing: because insurers cannot charge high prices to the bad risks and low prices to the good risks, the market price for all buyers will be set too high, and good risks will be denied the chance to insure at a fair price.

Adverse selection might operate in the market for workplace accommodations. It may be difficult for companies to price such benefits accurately, because the productivity costs of accommodations may depend on so many variables. A right to take job leave, for example, might be a trivial cost to an employer, or a significant one, depending on how many workers take leave at once, whether the company is entering a seasonally busy period, and whether individual workers are cooperative or flexible in how they structure their leave. It might be that employers' effort to price such benefits would degenerate, as good risks left the pool, leaving the rest to pay higher prices for their leave rights. In the end, only those workers highly likely to take leave (or to abuse it) might remain in the pool, paying high prices for their leave rights.

In addition to adverse selection, there may be other market failures. For example, if workers or employers have mistaken or incomplete information, they might be unable to strike mutually beneficial bargains for workplace accommodations. For example, managers acting out of ignorance, fondness for tradition, or animus toward women may overlook or undervalue the benefits of job leave for employers in terms of reduced turnover and higher employee morale.

This theory has some appeal because information is never perfect and people are often uninformed or biased. It also seems plausible that workplace traditions have not adapted to the rapid entry of married women into the workforce in the past 30 years. But it is not entirely clear why such ignorance would persist today, when many firms have adopted parental leave programs, and FMLA and state statutes have performed some educative function. Twenty-five years ago, parental leave policies were relatively rare (as were long-term female employees with young children), but today the business sector seems fairly well versed in the possibilities.[27]

Empirical studies have proved of limited value in detecting such market failures. Return, for a moment, to the example of job leave from the previous section. In principle, we should be able to determine whether the market for job leave failed by examining how the labor markets reacted to past mandates. If FMLA or other job leave mandates caused employment to *rise*, that would be good evidence (according to Figure 9.2) that workers value the benefit at more than its cost (i.e., that the market failed to effect a value-enhancing exchange).

Unfortunately, the available studies fail to produce clear results. FMLA, as discussed above, had little or no effect on wages or employment. But FMLA is a questionable test case, because its coverage is limited and because many states (and federal law on pregnancy) required similar job leaves before FMLA was enacted. Ruhm's study of European parental leave policies did detect a positive effect on young women's employment (relative to men and older women). But because Ruhm was considering paid leave programs funded by social insurance, the increase in employment is ambiguous. On the one hand, higher employment would be consistent with a market failure story: young women's observed (gross) wage falls, but their perceived (net) wage rises, leading to higher levels of employment. On the other hand, the increase in employment could instead reflect young women's positive reaction to the government-funded leave pay, which implicitly increases young women's wage.[28] The latter story is consistent with the mandate's having a negative employment effect, which is then swamped by the larger positive effect of the government-funded benefit.

Advocates of family-friendly workplace programs sometimes present positive testimonials from companies that have adopted such programs, to the effect that the programs produced large benefits at small cost.[29] But this evidence is of questionable value; companies that have *voluntarily* adopted such benefits would be expected to predict large benefits and small(er) costs. It would be odd (and probably grounds for a shareholder lawsuit) for a firm to announce proudly that it had awarded benefits to workers that were not value-producing for the firm. There is no reason to infer that companies *not* offering job leave could duplicate the same ratio of benefits to costs.

Equally soft is evidence from public opinion polls showing that workers (male and female) favor family-friendly policies in order to spend more time with their families.[30] One major problem with such polls is that they typically do not show whether workers would be willing to accept the necessary wage cut to obtain the policies. Asking someone if he would like a new, free program of job leave is rather like asking whether he would like a free ice-cream cone. Although a few oddballs will reject the goodie, most will accept it. But that does not imply that the ice cream market has failed. A few polls address the problem by asking workers whether they would accept some cut in pay.[31] That is helpful, but still not sufficient, because we do not have information about what the market price for job leave would be, and whether the workers would accept a pay cut large enough to compensate employers for its cost. If you would buy ice cream at $.50, but I will only sell it at $3.00, the market has not failed if ice cream is unavailable.

Without better evidence, it is extremely difficult to know whether market failures exist and, if so, whether workplace accommodations represent an effective response. Adding confusion to the mix, a 2001 study of FMLA produced some modest evidence suggesting that benefits markets may be functioning relatively well in matching supply and demand for family-friendly benefits. According to the study, commissioned by the Department of Labor, 45 percent of employees report having access to flextime, 16 percent report access to telecommuting arrangements, and 9 percent report on-site child care. The survey also asked employees which two benefits they would most like to have. Surprisingly, the responses correlated rather well with the actual availability of such arrangements: 60 percent put flextime in their top two, 16 percent listed telecommuting, and 7 percent listed on-site child care.[32] This evidence provides only a rough measure of worker demand, but the correspondence between availability and employees' priorities is striking. Another survey, conducted in 1992, also found that a large percentage of employees had access to family-friendly policies. In that study, 38 percent of parents indicated that they would change jobs to gain access to flextime, but virtually none would do so to gain access to part-time work or telecommuting.[33]

Even if the evidence of market failure were quite clear, it is tricky to design an appropriate remedy. The ideal should be to duplicate a well-functioning market, which permits but does not require workers to "buy" flexible workplace benefits. But voluntary opt-in can be problematic if the market failure is due to adverse selection. For that reason, the standard solution to adverse selection is mandatory coverage. In the case of job leave, for instance, the government might solve an adverse selection problem by requiring all employers to provide paid parental leave.

But we should be cautious about the use of mandates. Mandated benefits will tend to redistribute among female workers in an unintended way. Suppose that workers *as a group* value paid job leave at an aggregate amount $V greater than its cost $C. In this setting, mandated leave would be efficient, in the sense of enhancing aggregate welfare. But some individuals would be treated unfairly, relative to an ideal market. Instead of being given the option to buy insurance, they would be forced to do so. Individuals are likely to value leave differently depending on the amount of leave they intend to take and perhaps on their family circumstances. For example, young women who intend to remain childless or to take minimal leaves will value the benefit less than those who plan to have multiple children or take longer leaves per child. Even some who intend to take time off from work may not value job-protected leave highly if they plan to change jobs or if their job already offers leave. The result is that a mandated benefit that is efficient in the aggregate could leave some individuals worse off.

From a utilitarian perspective, there is no problem; the objections of the losers are irrelevant, because $V > $C, and aggregate social welfare rises. But from an individualist perspective, the issue is less clear-cut. On the one hand, a market failure has (by hypothesis) denied some individuals the opportunity to purchase a job leave benefit. On the other hand, mandatory insurance will tend to overcharge young, childless women and mothers who do not take leave, while undercharging fathers who take leave. Here, the problem is not that women's wages will fall by $C; when the goal is market correction, it is appropriate for workers to bear the cost of their own "insurance." Rather, the problem is that an average premium of $C will overcharge some workers and undercharge others, relative to a pure insurance system with voluntary participation.

One practical response is to use alternatives to mandates when possible. Although this inquiry is beyond the scope of this project, it would be worth asking whether a failed market for job leave could be replicated by some system other than universal mandated coverage. For example, Stephen Sugarman has proposed that workers be permitted to accrue time off and to use it for a variety of reasons, including vacation and sick days.[34] Perhaps some variant of this system would give parents who desire to do so greater flexibility to reserve days off for child care, while not mandating standard coverage for workers who would place little value on it. To simi-

Part 5

Implementation

10

Implementing Caretaker Resource Accounts

In contrast to the uncertainty of workplace regulation, caretaker resource accounts would be relatively straightforward to implement. There is no need to nail down every detail at this stage, but it is useful to anticipate a few of the biggest issues that arise in turning ideas into workable rules.

In this chapter, I consider four issues:

- First, how much money should caretakers receive? I suggest that the annual grant should be about $5,000. That amount would make a significant difference in parents' economic options but at a budgetary cost that is politically reasonable.

- A second question is how to identify which parents bear the autonomy burden of the No Exit obligation. When parents live together or share physical custody of their child, they may—or may not—share the economic costs of child rearing. Although there is no perfect solution, there are several reasonable approaches that the program might adopt.

- Third, I consider whether caretaker resource accounts might be undermined by psychological "myopia," which leads people to make short-term decisions at odds with their long-range interests. Caretaker resource accounts encourage a long-term perspective by restricting funds to future-oriented uses. Although the program might adopt additional restrictions, it is probably better to preserve flexibility for individuals to change their decisions over time.

- Finally, how would the vouchers for child care, education, and retirement operate? Could caretakers use child care vouchers for informal care in a neighbor's home as well as for state-licensed day care? Which institutions should be eligible to receive tuition vouchers or retirement funds? In most cases the program could build on existing regulations that govern child care subsidies, education loans, and retirement investing.

Why $5,000?

In principle, the annual caretaker grant should be large enough to support meaningful efforts at life planning. A small sum, say $500 per year, would be a token payment and not a good-faith attempt to alleviate the No Exit obligation. Although there is no simple way to translate society's obligation into a dollar figure, several benchmarks suggest that an annual grant of $3,500 to $5,000 could make a substantial difference in parents' long-term opportunities. Throughout the book, I have endorsed the higher figure because it would provide greater assistance, still at a reasonable cost. But even a grant at the lower end of the range would represent a significant initiative.

The first benchmark is the motherhood wage gap. As Chapter 2 notes, the consensus figure is that mothers earn about 70 percent of what the average man earns, and childless women earn 80 to 90 percent. Using these percentages, in 2001, the annual motherhood wage gap was between $3,600 and $7,250.[1] As I have emphasized, the wage gap represents a rough measure of the autonomy cost of caretaking; still, it helps quantify the economic disadvantage of the caretaker role.

A second set of benchmarks asks how much it would cost to give caretakers the opportunity to go to college or to save a substantial amount for retirement. The average annual tuition at a public, four-year college in 2000 was $3,744; tuition at public two-year colleges was much lower, at

$1,336 per year.[2] A caretaker grant of roughly $1,500 to $4,000 would thus pay full tuition at an average public college.[3] To be sure, tuition varies by state and by region and even year to year. Still, the price of public college tuition provides a reference point for judging what might be meaningful assistance for higher education.

Another benchmark, retirement savings, is harder to document because data on individuals' contributions to private pension accounts are sparse. In 1996, individuals and employers together contributed an average of $3,400 per worker to 401(k) savings plans for retirement.[4] The tax law permits workers to save between $3,000 and $160,000 per year tax-free.[5] These sums may represent some past legislative judgment about desirable levels of individual retirement savings (but they also, of course, represent purely political judgments about the feasible level of tax subsidies).

A final benchmark is the cost of child care (Table 10.1). Parents spend varying amounts, depending on the age of their child, the type of care they use, and the local cost of living. Costs are highest for infants and toddlers and for nanny care and day care centers in big cities. Costs are lowest for relative care and family day care (meaning small operations in private homes) and outside metropolitan areas.[6] An average family spends $2,600 to $4,500 on paid child care.[7] These averages may seem low relative to the cost of day care centers in large cities, which may charge $12,000 per year (or more). But many families live in less expensive areas and use a mix of paid and unpaid arrangements. Not every family requires full-time child care, and older children often require only afterschool care. And, as we have seen, many families prefer relative care for emotional and security reasons.

Table 10.1
Average Annual Expenditures on Child Care,
by Family Income, for Families That Purchase Care

Family Income (annual)	Cost of Child Care (annual per family)
Less than $18,000	$2,585
$18,000 to $35,999	$3,275
$36,000 to $53,999	$3,500
$54,000 and over	$4,430

Table 10.1 annualizes the weekly figures in U.S. Bureau of the Census (2002, p. 17, Table 8).

Table 10.2
Benchmarks for Annual Caretaker Grant

Benchmark	Implied caretaker grant per year
Motherhood wage gap	$3,600–$7,250
Public college tuition	$1,500–$4,000
Retirement contribution allowance	$3,000–$160,000
Child care costs	$2,600–$4,500

These benchmarks suggest a reasonable range for caretaker resource grants of $3,500 to $5,000 per year (see Table 10.2). In 1999, the median family income was $48,950. For the typical family, these amounts would represent substantial support for future-oriented endeavors. For poorer parents, the boost in resources would be even more significant; for instance, single-mother median income was just $24,000.[8]

I have not addressed in detail how the program might be financed—how taxes ought to be raised, or spending cut, to finance the net cost of the program. In principle, the program ought to redistribute to parents who bear the burden of the No Exit rule. I have suggested a few existing programs for parents that might be cut, because the new initiative would render them duplicative (see Figure 10.2). But the remaining net cost of the program ought to be paid by people who remain childless and by parents who do not fulfill their No Exit obligation.

Translating these principles into real world tax programs would be complex. Ordinary income, wealth, and consumption taxes make (at most) rough adjustments for parental status. We do not have any ready tax rule for determining whether one bears the burden of the No Exit obligation. There are also serious life-cycle issues that present tax systems do not deal with adequately. Ideally, caretaker resource accounts should be funded by taxing the lifetime childless (and other noncaretakers) and not those who are currently childless. Otherwise, the program would only accomplish a temporal redistributin, giving parents funds during their child-rearing years but taking the money back in old age. Another complexity arises when we think about the difficulties inherent in taxing families; when a caretaker and noncaretaker live together, is it really possible to tax one but not the other?[9]

I have not attempted to design an ideal tax to fund caretaker resource accounts. In the real world of politics, it is most likely that caretaker resource accounts would be funded by incremental increases in existing taxes and cuts in existing programs. Although existing taxes may not produce an ideal pattern of redistribution, it should be possible to accomplish, albeit in a rough-and-ready way, the goal of increasing the net resources available to most caretakers.

There are two additional issues that should affect how much each parent receives. First, how long should caretakers continue to receive a grant? Conventionally, we think of childhood as ending at age 18, and so there is something to be said for concluding the caretaker's entitlement when her child reaches that age. But the economic cost of the No Exit obligation is likely to be highest for younger children. One break point might be age 13, by which age most children no longer need constant supervision, although they still require parental guidance and care. Existing tax rules for child care subsidies follow this approach.[10]

Second, should the caretaker grant be tailored to reflect variations in the autonomy burdens that caretakers bear depending on family size and structure? More children require more work and more attention and leave even less time for parents' independent projects. Studies suggest, for example, that the motherhood wage penalty is larger for mothers of two children than for mothers of one child. Paid child care also is more expensive for more than one child. Still, there is no principled way to ascertain *how much more* burdensome each child is. The economic literature on poverty and taxation has developed methods for adjusting welfare benefits and income taxes for family size and composition. But these methods aim to measure differences in family consumption needs, not differences in parents' opportunity sets. For purposes of caretaker resource accounts, it is not helpful to learn the amount of food or square footage in the house that extra children require. Even paid child care costs do not necessarily increase in proportion to the number of children; the incremental cost depends on the type of care used and the ages of the children. In addition, the variability among children in behavior and needs seems to be at least as

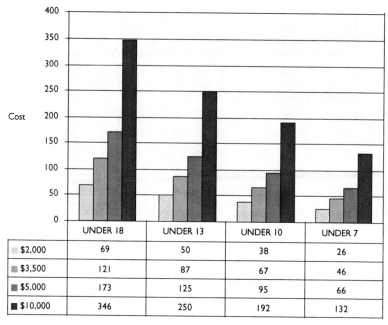

Program	UNDER 18	UNDER 13	UNDER 10	UNDER 7
$2,000	69	50	38	26
$3,500	121	87	67	46
$5,000	173	125	95	66
$10,000	346	250	192	132

Program

Figure 10.1
Annual Revenue Cost (billions of dollars) for Caretaker Resource Accounts
The table reflects author's calculations, based on data from U.S. Bureau of the Census
(2000c, Tables 1, 66).

important as the number of children; one very difficult (or ill) child may impose a greater burden than two quiet, compliant, healthy ones.

For similar reasons, it would be difficult to adjust for family structure, even though a caretaker's opportunities may vary depending on whether he is a single parent or shares child-rearing work with another parent. It is not even clear which way an adjustment would run: Should a single parent receive more or less than a caretaker who shares child-rearing work with a partner? On the one hand, the average single parent probably works harder, feels more stress, and has less flexibility for the obvious reason that there is no one else to help out. On the other hand, we know that some mothers in traditional marriages are more economically vulnerable than some single mothers: they spend less time in the labor force and, in some couples, do most of the child-rearing work while also caring for the hus-

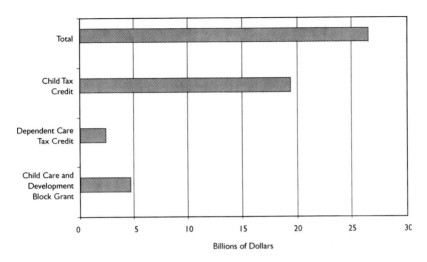

Figure 10.2
Annual Revenue Cost of Selected Federal Programs
The table reflects statistics for 1999 spending for all programs except the child care and development block grant, which is a 1998 figure. See Bureau of the Census (2000c, Tables 539, 605).

band. There are a host of additional complicating factors: Does the single caretaker (or the couple) have an extended family to help out? And so on.

For these reasons, any attempt to adjust the caretaker account for family size and structure will represent a rough cut. I recommend the simplest approach, although I recognize that there may be equally defensible alternatives. My approach takes the child as the focal point. The first child in any household should have one caretaker account allocated to her parent(s). (I discuss how to divide the funds between parents in the next section.) The second child in each household would not increase the amount of the annual grant but would extend the duration of the caretaker's eligibility: each caretaker should remain eligible until the youngest child is 13. For example, suppose that Nancy is the single mother of two children, born three years apart. Each year her caretaker resource account receives a deposit of $5,000. Assuming that Nancy retains custody, she will participate in the caretaker resource program for a total of 16 years.

Based on these preliminary specifications, I estimate that the gross annual revenue cost of caretaker resource accounts would range from $87 billion to $125 billion. Figure 10.1 demonstrates the connection between program cost and the terms of the program. The revenue range reflects annual grants ranging from $3,500 to $5,000. The chart also presents additional variations: grants ranging from as low as $2,000 to as high as $10,000, with age cutoffs as low as age 7 and as high as age 18. Figure 10.2 suggests some existing child care subsidies that could be repealed or reduced in size to offset the cost of the new initiative. After these offsets, the *net* cost of a $5,000 annual caretaker grant to caretakers of children under age 13 would be about $100 billion per year.

Who Are a Child's Caretakers?

In principle, caretaker resource accounts should assist all parents who abide by the No Exit obligation and who suffer some significant loss of opportunity because of it. In some cases, there will be one identifiable caretaker, and only one. A mother whose husband has long ago abandoned the children would, under the No Exit obligation, be the children's sole caretaker. That father may technically remain a parent, in legal terms, but he is no longer sharing day-to-day responsibility for the child's care. Similarly, a divorced or separated parent who has sole physical custody of his children would ordinarily be the only parent eligible for a caretaker account. This is not to say that the noncustodial parent suffers no constraint at all. For example, if she wishes to continue to see the children often, she cannot move far away to take a new job. Still, the sole custodial parent in such situations generally does most of the hands-on work of child rearing.[11]

The difficult cases involve children who live with more than one parent. Married couples usually live together with their children, and so do many unmarried, cohabiting couples. Even caretakers who do not live with each other may live with their children if they share joint physical custody. The administrative difficulty is that the state cannot readily observe the division of labor between the parents: the law cannot determine whether they share the No Exit obligation equally.[12]

In many couples the division is far from 50-50. Sociological studies suggest that two-parent families fall along a spectrum. Some couples share child-rearing work equally; others follow a traditional division of labor, allocating most child care to the mother; and still others engage in some middle course, with fathers taking on something more than the traditional paternal role but something less than the mother's commitment of time and energy.[13] The data suggest that the strict traditional model is waning a bit, but that truly equal sharing has not become the dominant pattern.

Put another way, many parents aspire to equal roles but do not live them. Mothers still, on average, bear the lion's share of child-rearing responsibilities and pay the greatest economic cost in terms of forgone job opportunities, earnings, and old-age security.[14] But the difficulty is that these aggregate statistics do not help identify the pattern that prevails in any individual household.

It would be costly and probably unwise to attempt to determine the facts of each family's situation. In theory, the government could authorize an administrator to inquire into each family; a social worker might quiz parents about the children's daily activities, checking to see who knows the baby's shoe size or who has declined a better job in favor of one closer to home. But that system would be prohibitively intrusive, costly, and slow (there are tens of millions of families with children). It would be impossible to ensure that bureaucrats could implement the law fairly, in light of their own, very human biases about how to rear children. Administrative and judicial appeals of fact-specific judgments would create litigation costs and additional avenues for variable outcomes. There is no point in introducing annual social work visits and adversarial adjudication into the lives of ordinary families. Moreover, for caretaker resource accounts to be effective, parents should be certain about their claim to resources and not anxious about legal nuances that could, on adjudication, force them to repay amounts already spent.

If individualized evaluations are impossible, we must use what lawyers call a "bright line" rule: a hard-and-fast rule that is easy to apply but that may be inaccurate in any given case. There are three possibilities. When two parents appear to be providing continuity of care to a child, the program could award the caretaker resource account to one caretaker, split it equally between them, or permit the two to negotiate on a division.

None of the three rules is entirely satisfactory, because there is such a gap between our aspirations for child rearing and the reality. Ideally, every child should have two parents bound by the No Exit obligation. But today, it is more often mothers who act in accordance with it, both during marriage and after divorce. Ideally, child-rearing work should be freely chosen and ungendered, but in fact, the household division of labor remains heavily gendered. Ideally, mothers and fathers should make rational decisions about how to share child-rearing work, negotiating from positions of equality, but in many cases, mothers are at an economic disadvantage because women's (typically) lower earning power and shorter reproductive life leave them with worse options outside marriage.

Compounding the difficulty of choosing a rule is the diversity of families. In some families, both parents make significant sacrifices for their children. Even if they do not put in strictly equal time day to day, both have rearranged their lives to play an active role in their child's life for the long term. Some couples cooperate better than others. And in some couples the women have better (or far worse) bargaining power than in the average case. The range of real-world situations will render any simple rule inaccurate.

The administrative dilemma is neither novel to caretaker resource accounts nor so intractable that it renders the program unworkable. Any public program capable of large-scale redistribution must rely on rules that produce approximate rather than finely tuned results. Many programs adopt simple proxies for complex real-world situations. The law permits children to drive at age 16, ignoring the variability of temperament and maturation among individual teens. The welfare system conditions benefits on low income, even though poverty is complex in its causes and effects. The Social Security system awards retirement benefits at age 65, regardless of individuals' ability to work and their need for resources. These rule-of-thumb standards are quite acceptable, and indeed inevitable, in large-scale public programs.

It is also crucial to bear in mind that caretaker resource accounts allocate *money* between parents: they do not govern child custody or divide child-rearing rights and duties. Money is, of course, important; the premise of the program is that money can promote opportunity. But we should not conflate money rules with substantive rules for child custody or the ideal division of labor.

In the end, I conclude that it would be best to award the caretaker resource account to one "primary" caretaker. But in doing so, I am responding to the fact of the gendered division of labor. In the following discussion, it is crucial to bear in mind that the primary caretaker rule is an administrative accommodation, not an ideal of child rearing. In an ideal world, we might do more to encourage and support both parents to remain by their children's side for the long term. But in the real world, the No Exit obligation weighs most heavily on mothers.

The Primary Caretaker Rule

I propose two rules, loosely modeled on the existing rules for the EITC. First is the residence rule: only a parent[15] who resides with his child for the majority of the year may claim a caretaker resource account. The marital status of parents should be irrelevant; the test deliberately focuses on the caretaker's physical presence in the child's life, which is relevant to continuity of care. If only one of a child's parents meets the residence test, then that caretaker receives the grant. For example, in the case of divorced parents, the child's primary custodial parent ordinarily will qualify under the residence rule, with no need for further determinations. However, if both parents live together with their children, both caretakers will ordinarily meet this test, and they will need to proceed to the second rule to determine which is primary.

Second is the earnings rule: if both parents meet the coresidence test, then the parent with the lower labor market earnings should receive the caretaker grant.[16] The logic is that the relative earnings of the mother and father provide some indication of how they have divided the work of child rearing and the autonomy burden of the No Exit obligation. Of course, relative earnings are far from a perfect indicator. Market earnings reflect not only each parent's efforts at child rearing, but also individual preferences, education and work experience, labor market discrimination, and sheer good or bad luck. Nor is income always a good proxy for autonomy. Indeed, in Chapter 5, I argued *against* using family income as a proxy for the economic burden of caretaking. But there is a key difference here: the primary caretaker test does not use a parent's market earnings to gauge her autonomy relative to every other citizen. It is that claim I rejected earlier, in pointing out that even caretakers in middle-class and well-off families may bear a significant economic burden traceable to their parental obligations.

Instead, the logic of the earnings test is that, *as between parents in the same household,* relative earnings are a reasonable, if imperfect, proxy for the incidence of the economic cost of child rearing. The earnings test works because it makes use of two facts. First, most husbands earn more than their wife. In 25 percent of couples, the wife is not employed; among the remaining, dual-earner couples, only 20 to 25 percent of wives earn more than their husband.[17] Second, when households have children, wives, on average, assume greater day-to-day responsibility for child rearing and make more significant changes in their working life after having children. Even when fathers participate actively in children's lives, it is mothers who tend to do more child care, to sacrifice leisure, and to cut back hours worked or job status. We know less about families in which *husbands* earn less. Perhaps they are doing more child care. Some may be at-home dads by choice; others may take care of the children during a spell of unemployment (which explains their temporarily lower earnings).

Why not simply award caretaker resource accounts directly to *mothers?* Instead of using earnings as a proxy for gender, the program could use gender directly. But there are serious problems with that approach. A caretaker benefit awarded to mothers and not to fathers would likely be ruled unconstitutional.[18] There is also a small but increasing percentage of fathers who leave the workforce or take part-time jobs to rear children. They should, in fairness, receive a caretaker resource grant. And a gender-based presumption would be useless when coresident parents are a same-sex couple.

The primary caretaker rule has two advantages. First, it would allocate resources appropriately in the average case, in which the mother earns less and carries the greater share of the economic burden of child rearing. In contrast, the alternative rules (we shall see) would dilute the effectiveness of the program by allocating significant resources to parents who do not bear much of an economic burden.

Second, the earnings test permits two parents to share access to care-taker resources *across several years*. The primary caretaker test should not be a once-and-for-all determination. Over time, mothers and fathers may shift roles, and as their relative economic status changes, so will the alloca-tion of the caretaker grant. Of course, not all changes in relative earnings reflect a shift in child-rearing responsibilities. And not all changes in the division of labor within the household will produce a relative income shift. Still, the rule rewards gender role change in a way that neither of the alter-natives can; we shall see that both of those rules would be invariant to the actual division of labor within the family.

At the same time, the primary caretaker rule has drawbacks. Like any simple rule, it would be inaccurate in important cases. In some situations, relative earnings fail to indicate relative sacrifice due to child rearing. The primary caretaker rule awards 100 percent of the caretaker grant to one parent, even if both share child rearing and limit their outside obligations. The rule is not irrational: fathers *on average* spend less time on child care and housework and are far less likely to interrupt their working life for child rearing. Still, this rule will seem both unfair and outdated to couples who share child rearing.

The earnings test will also be inaccurate when one parent earns more *and* bears primary responsibility for child rearing; in this case, the earnings test will award the grant to the wrong person. If Olga earns $40,000 per year and Oscar earns $30,000 per year, but they pursue strictly traditional gender roles in the home, Olga will lose out and Oscar will receive an undeserved bonus. Changes in relative earnings may also be inaccurate signals of changes in child-rearing responsibilities. If Oscar earns a pro-motion to $50,000 per year, the caretaker grant will shift (in this case, properly) to Olga, even if they do not change the allocation of child care duties.

A simple rule can also invite parties to engage in strategic behavior. When caretakers are hostile to each other, they may seek to use the pro-gram's rules to gain an advantage. For example, suppose that, in a divorce situation, the mother wants custody of the children and the father is con-tent with a visiting role. Under current law, the father already has some incentive to contest custody in order to gain a bargaining advantage in the financial settlement. Caretaker resource accounts could increase the rewards to such behavior, because the rules award the grant based on physical custody.[19]

Finally, the earnings test incorporates some predictable technical problems, which arise in any program that uses income as a metric. Any earnings test inaccurately measures the economic situation of students and other nonworkers who have temporarily low incomes but are enhancing their future earning capacity. Although special rules can anticipate these cases, the cost is greater rule complexity. Parents could also attempt to understate their annual earnings, either illegally (through fraud) or legally (through deferred compensation arrangements). More troubling, the earnings test represents, in effect, an extra "tax" on primary caretakers who begin to earn more than their spouse. In an extreme case, the program would create a "cliff": just one dollar of extra earnings could mean the reallocation of $5,000 in resources. To mitigate these problems, the program could make more gradual transitions between primary caretakers, but at the cost of delaying the program's responsiveness to true changes in caretaking roles.[20] These familiar problems arise in any program that attempts to use a simple financial concept to measure a complex social phenomenon.[21]

The shortcomings of the primary caretaker rule arise because it presumes that there is a single primary caretaker, whose lower earnings reflect (at least in part) her interrupted working life. As a consequence, the earnings test is likely to award the greatest resources to caretakers whose opportunities are most compromised. But as gender roles continue to change over time, the earnings test may come to seem more and more dated. At some point, the balance of equities may support a different rule. In the end, the best defense of the primary caretaker rule is that it is, at least today, better than the two alternatives, to which I now turn.

Splitting the Grant between Two Parents

When two parents live with their children (or share joint physical custody), the program could split the caretaker grant equally between them. The advantage of this approach is that every parent who makes an economic sacrifice on account of child rearing would receive something, simply because every resident parent would receive half a grant ($2,500). Thus, the equal split would avoid some of the inequities of the primary caretaker rule: higher-earning caretakers would get a full $2,500, and the program would accurately award grants when parents share child rearing equally.

Initially, the equal split has great appeal. It seems to recognize the contributions of fathers as well as mothers, and to encourage *both* parents to honor their No Exit obligation. Although I feel the symbolic pull of the equal split, I worry that the price of symbolism could be quite high. Splitting the grant equally would dilute the impact of the initiative by awarding large sums to parents who are not significantly burdened by the No Exit obligation.

Today it is mothers, and not parents as a class, who sacrifice economic opportunity due to child rearing. In effect, the equal split would award a $2,500 windfall as a prize for managing to live with one's children. Although everyone gets something, some parents would receive far too much and others far too little. The program would still direct greater resources than today to (true) caretakers, but the equal-splitting rule would dilute the effectiveness of the program for such caretakers by as much as half, depending on the division of labor in each household.

The equal split would respond to the administrative difficulty of observing child-rearing practices in an outsized fashion: to get half of the caretaker grant to the right person in the average case, the program would give the other half to the wrong person. The recurring problem, of course, is the inaccuracy of any bright-line rule. The primary caretaker rule presumes traditional gender roles and a gap in relative earning power, whereas the equal split presumes egalitarian gender roles and equal earning power. Neither assumption accurately captures the reality of family life.

An equal split would create new opportunities for strategic behavior in hostile situations. The splitting rule would put additional pressure on the residence test: any caretaker who could claim residence with a child could gain $2,500. (Under the primary caretaker rule, in contrast, this possibility arises only in the rarer case in which the noncustodial parent is also the lower earner.) For the same reasons, the equal-splitting rule would also alter dynamics at divorce; parents might be more likely to seek shared physical custody, or to threaten to do so, because with shared custody comes the annual $2,500 grant (regardless of relative earnings).

Perhaps the most troubling feature of the equal split is its lack of responsiveness to changes in family roles. The equal split expresses an aspiration of equal sharing, but ironically, that expression of equality would dampen the program's responsiveness to real change in household roles. Under the equal split, every father who lives with his children would claim $2,500, whether or not he shares child care and whether or not he makes any compromise in his working life relative to the mother. The father would receive the same symbolic sum regardless of his actions, unless he formally exits the scene.

In the end, the program might adopt *either* the primary caretaker rule or the equal split. Neither is perfect, and both represent an administrative accommodation to the messiness of real life. Still, the choice is important, because each rule deploys the power of public policy in a different way. The primary caretaker rule would use the financial power of the state to redistribute resources within the household; by vesting title to the money in mothers' names, the program would take an affirmative step toward empowering women engaged in women's traditional role. The equal split, in contrast, would use the financial power of the state to make a moral point; the state would distribute resources aspirationally, hoping to prod parents into dividing child-rearing work more equitably.

A middle ground is also visible. For example, the program could divide the caretaker grant in some way so that both parents receive a minimum amount, but the lower earner gets somewhat more. Perhaps the higher-earning caretaker receives $1,250, while the lower-earner receives $3,750. These intermediate solutions mingle the appeal and drawbacks of the two basic approaches.

The Negotiation Alternative

Instead of adopting an automatic rule, the caretaker resource program could permit a child's parents to decide how to split the grant. They might agree to designate one parent as primary or might split the grant in any way they chose. The rules would require them jointly to sign an election and should establish some default rule when the parties cannot reach an agreement. For example, in the absence of an express election, the funds might be divided 50-50, or they might revert to the lower earner.

In theory, negotiated outcomes would permit caretakers to tailor the annual grant to the specifics of their situation. Equal-sharing couples could share the money equally, and traditional couples could award the grant to the primary caretaker spouse. But that rosy picture dissolves when we confront the realities of gender inequality in household bargaining and the prospects for abusive behavior in a divorce (or other conflictual) setting.

Although caretaker resource accounts emphasize individual agency, they do not require a naïve belief that all women's choices, in all circumstances, are equally likely to be free. I have argued that we should generally respect parents' choices about how to live their lives, out of respect for their individual values, because of the unfairness of projecting "better" choices for them and the impossibility of constructing gender-free choices on their behalf. But these are reasons for permitting individuals to choose how to deploy their resources among the three options. They do not imply that eligibility for caretaker resource accounts should be determined by bilateral bargaining between men and women in a family setting. We have far better information about who caretakers *are* than about what they should do with their lives or would do in the absence of gender.

Today, mothers tend to have less bargaining power in a marital setting.[22] Permitting parents to negotiate over the division of the annual grant would tend to undermine the purpose of the program, which is to challenge, rather than to replicate, the autonomy burden created by the caretaker role.

Even in cooperative marriages, wives and mothers tend to have less status and less power, manifested, for example, in errors of perception. For example, studies reveal that husbands and wives often *perceive* that they share the burden of housework and child care more evenly than time studies show that they do.[23] We should anticipate that some of the same power dynamics will come into play as caretakers choose how to use their funds; spouses (and other family members) will exert their opinions and influence. But the identification of the primary caretaker is the critical step; once the resources are in her hands, the terms of the program require them to be spent in ways that will benefit her.

In cases of divorce or open hostility, an election would be even less desirable; it would create another opportunity for hostile parties to threaten, to bargain, and to hold one another hostage for other purposes. An election option would permit the greatest degree of destructive, strategic behavior, permitting either spouse to harm the other (depending on the default rule) by withholding consent.

Even though I argue for a primary caretaker rule, I acknowledge that the equal split has considerable appeal. Stepping back for a moment, we ought to keep in mind that the program could do good in the world with either rule. Either would offer much needed help to parents who are struggling to care for their children and to preserve their own options.

The next question is whether caretaker resource accounts adequately deal with some predictable psychological barriers to long-term planning.

Will Caretakers Take Self-Defeating Actions?

The purpose of caretaker resource accounts is to enhance parents' ability to make future-oriented plans and to revise those plans over time. But psychology suggests that it is not a straightforward matter to promote long-term planning while permitting revisability. Individuals tend to suffer from time inconsistency in their preferences. They simultaneously want to wait and pursue Project X, while spending their money now on Project Y. Sorting out which of these desires should be acted on raises serious normative questions. In this section, I argue that caretaker resource accounts should direct caretakers to future-oriented plans but preserve substantial opportunities for revision.

To see the problem, recall that caretaker resource accounts permit deferral. Each caretaker can spend $5,000 each year on child care, education, or retirement planning or she may defer her money to a future year and decide then. This deferral option reflects the program's orientation to individual choice and long-term planning; ideally, parents should choose for themselves how best to plan for their future. Some will choose current investments with a long-term payoff (e.g., staying on the job while paying for child care). Others will choose to direct their investments to some later time (e.g., education once the children are in school or retirement savings for old age).

This deferral option creates an opportunity for caretakers to save toward some future goal. But this savings opportunity squarely poses the time inconsistency problem. In slightly stylized form, the problem is this. Suppose that Pam has $10,000 in a conventional bank account. (Later, I consider how a caretaker resource account would differ.) She has taken a break from her job as an elementary school teacher to spend time with her young children. Some time in the next few years, she plans to use her money to return to school to obtain a master's degree in special education. But the presence of the money in the bank is a constant temptation; it "burns a hole in her pocket." In Year 1, when Pam leaves her job, she fully intends to return to school in Year 5. But in Years 2, 3, and 4, as Pam sits at the kitchen table paying the monthly bills, she will be tempted to raid her savings to live a little more comfortably. On any given day, she may keenly feel the need for a new car or house repairs to the point that she will invade her savings, perhaps "just a little at a time," until there is nothing left by Year 5.

From one perspective, Pam is a rational maximizer, making ordinary trade-offs. If she raids the bank account to fund day-to-day consumption, then she must "prefer" to do so. But that is a tautology. It is worth taking seriously the idea that Pam has preferences that conflict, in one of two senses. In the first interpretation, Pam's Year 1 self intends to save for graduate school, but her Year 2 self decides that a new car is more important. If Pam is satisfied with both choices *at the time she makes them*, we have the familiar problem of intrapersonal conflict: Should Year 1 Pam be permitted to bind her later self to the education plan, even if Year 2 Pam really would be happier with the new car? This is a deep question, and the answer is not obvious. Theorists of autonomy who emphasize the unity of the self over time might permit Pam to precommit herself in Year 1, but those who prefer to protect the revisability of one's life plan over time might reject precommitments.

There is a second and somewhat simpler interpretation. Perhaps Pam's impulsive Year 2 behavior consistently frustrates her ability to carry out a long-term life plan. If Year 2 Pam *experiences her own actions as self-defeating*, then her situation reflects a cognitive failure, or perhaps a failure of self-discipline. In that case, there seems to be a stronger justification for precommitment: for permitting Pam to anticipate and to guard against her own weakness.

Although the psychology literature on "hyperbolic discounting" is not clear on this normative distinction, a variety of experiments find a clear discontinuity between Time 1 decisions and Time 2 actions. Typically, someone decides at Time 1 to take some action (e.g., to begin a savings plan) at Time 2. But when Time 2 rolls around, the person fails to do so (e.g., he spends the money instead of saving).[24] Because people anticipate this kind of behavior, they adopt (at Time 1) a variety of precommitment devices to constrain their own impulses at Time 2. This literature explains, among other things, why people use Christmas clubs (non-interest-bearing savings accounts that prohibit withdrawals until December) and individual retirement accounts (which bear a heavy tax penalty for spending before retirement). Workers may be adopting a similar strategy when they authorize tax overwithholding during the year to produce a large tax refund check in April.

But none of this answers either the normative question, *Should* the Time 1 self be permitted to constrain her future choices?, or the psychological one, Does the constrained Time 2 self bitterly protest these constraints or feel (at some level) that they help keep her "on track"?

The problem of time inconsistency is relevant to caretaker resource accounts, but less so than may first appear. Caretaker accounts are less vulnerable to impulsive behavior than ordinary cash, because they channel spending toward activities with future benefits. Pam may not withdraw cash in Year 2 to buy a car or fix the roof. Instead, she has to spend on some item that is relatively likely to have a future payoff. As I have discussed, not every caretaker will make wise or successful choices. But the structure of the program prevents caretakers from making choices with no forward-looking component at all.

Thus, the *temporal paternalism* of caretaker resource accounts mitigates the time inconsistency problem to some degree. Caretakers do not choose between present and future (unlimited) consumption, but between present and future child care, education, or retirement savings. Each of these uses is, in effect, a production good: it will produce future income if used wisely. Continuous paid work enhances long-term earning power; education is of course a classic investment in human capital; and retirement savings directly promote long-term financial security.

Still, Pam in Year 2 can take actions that will frustrate her plan to return to school. She might, for example, take a part-time job and spend her $5,000 on child care. Or she might, in a fit of excessively future-oriented behavior, commit her $5,000 to retirement savings. If it were desirable to prevent such behavior, we might modify the caretaker resource account to permit Pam a precommitment option, that is, the opportunity to elect, in Year 1, to make funds unavailable until Year 5, and then only for education.

But the appeal of a precommitment option is limited because it reveals the normative problem hidden by the labels of time inconsistency and hyperbolic discounting. On the one hand, there is no reason to prevent individuals from recognizing, and guarding against, predictable myopias that undermine their capacity for long-range life planning. On the other hand, there *is* good reason to prevent younger selves from tyrannizing older ones, and to preserve revisability in life plans over time. For each impulsive Pam who might benefit from precommitment, we must imagine a Pam whose plans legitimately change over time. Perhaps Year 2 Pam chafes at the life of an at-home mother and wants to go back to work but cannot draw on her funds for child care. Perhaps Year 3 Pam gets divorced and needs the funds for child care or to supplement her retirement savings.

In the ordinary case, it is impossible to distinguish between self-defeating spending and deliberate revisions in life plans, because people constantly make and change their good-faith guesses about the right timing for childbearing, for education, and for retirement savings. Given the impossibility of making these distinctions, and the already future-oriented character of the caretaker resource accounts, precommitment devices seem an unwise addition to the basic structure.

How Will the Vouchers Work?

The final issue for caretaker resource accounts concerns the design of vouchers for child care, education, and retirement savings. The policy challenge is a familiar one: how to provide well-targeted assistance to large numbers of people at reasonable cost and with simple rules. These final issues are important, but for the most part, there is a range of solutions with ample precedent in existing programs.

The three vouchers in caretaker resource accounts would operate in a straightforward way. Caretakers would obtain a voucher or authorization from a government agency, with the voucher stating its amount and its intended use. (This might be done with paper vouchers or electronically.) The caretaker would use the voucher to pay for a service: child care, school tuition for herself, or a deposit in a retirement account. The service provider would file a claim for reimbursement with the government, documenting the service provided and the identity of the recipient. The voucher arrangement is familiar in the private sector for health care and in the public sector for benefits programs such as child care subsidies, Food Stamps, and Section 8 housing.

The term "voucher" can encompass a variety of arrangements, so it is useful to be more specific.[25] Caretaker resource accounts would offer first-dollar reimbursement for covered expenditures; that is, if a caretaker paid $1 or $100 for child care, she could claim payment of the entire amount from the government, up to the balance in her caretaker account. The vouchers would not vary in amount based on the income or wealth of the caretaker and should be available for the widest variety of services. For example, child care vouchers should be made available not only for day care centers, but for family day care homes and individual babysitters. Both full-time and part-time workers should be eligible to withdraw child care funds.[26] Education vouchers should be available not only for four-year colleges but for GED programs, vocational schools, and job skills courses (e.g., typing or WordPerfect).

The design of the three vouchers poses several challenges. For example, the program will require appropriate measures to prevent fraud. The danger is that diploma mills, fake child care centers, and fictitious financial institutions will either take caretakers' money and run, or else collude with caretakers and split the cash payout with them. This is a problem for any social program that attempts to impose use restrictions, and there are several strategies for preventing and detecting abuse. The education voucher can most readily take advantage of existing regulation and enforcement: the federal government monitors educational institutions for purposes of student loan assistance and other kinds of grant making to ensure that loans are not made to fictitious or shady "schools." (These procedures also help filter out purely recreational education, such as aerobics classes.) Caretaker resource accounts could tap into these rules, making tuition vouchers available only to schools that may receive student loans and on the condition that schools provide appropriate verification of services.

By contrast, there is less governmental oversight in day care, and informal arrangements are common. If I list "Rosie Smith" as my nanny, how is the government to know whether Rosie is really my sister-in-law, who does not babysit my kids but will kick back to me the cash she receives minus a small fee? The tax law faces a similar problem and has arrived at an ingenious, and largely successful, solution. The dependent care tax credit permits parents to reduce their tax liability by a portion of their child care costs. The rules now require taxpayers to list the social security number of their child care provider to ensure that he or she is reporting the income. That sort of rule could help by ensuring an audit trail should questions arise and by identifying some co-conspirators in a scam. In the case of caretaker accounts, however, the solution of taxing the income reduces, but cannot eliminate, the fraud incentive. Even if Rosie must pay tax on every dollar of child care income, she and I will have money to divide once the taxes are paid, although I will have reduced the balance in my caretaker account to use for myself. Still, the disclosure rules could create an *in terrorem* effect for people who are opportunistic but not criminal.

Alternatively, the program could adopt a rule restricting voucher redemptions to licensed child care centers, but the gain in fraud prevention would be bought at the cost of limiting child care options. Center care is currently used by only a minority of preschool children, for two reasons.[27] One is that center care is relatively expensive. Although the $5,000 caretaker grant would enhance families' ability to pay, mandating more expensive care would limit some caretakers' capacity to reserve part of their grant for education or retirement. This concern might be less serious if center care were clearly the highest-quality option, but studies suggest that the quality of day care centers is uneven (as are all forms of care) and that parents have difficulty judging the quality of care that centers provide. Many parents also prefer the greater convenience and home-like setting provided by smaller, family day care homes or the true home setting of relative care.

An additional challenge for the child care voucher will be to deny claims for child care for leisure activities. Most parents of modest means are unlikely to waste their voucher in this way, but a few better-off caretakers could create a damaging, public scandal if they used their subsidized child care to go out to lunch or the golf course. In principle, caretakers should use their child care funds only for projects that in some way expand their long-term opportunities; caretakers should not be permitted to draw on a caretaker resource account to fund babysitting for a Friday night at the movies. In practice, however, it may be quite difficult to distinguish between "serious" charitable work and "mere" fun. Running the American Cancer Society 5K race falls in the latter category, but how about serving as a volunteer docent 30 hours per week at the art museum? There are two ways to draw the line. One would be to reimburse only child care costs required for paid employment. This is the rule for the present child care tax credit. A second alternative, fairer but more open to abuse, would permit child care funds to be withdrawn to pay for child care related to volunteer work, provided that the caretaker works for a tax-exempt charity for a substantial period (perhaps 20 hours per week or more) in a job that directly and substantially furthers the charity's core mission.

The retirement voucher can also take advantage of current federal regulations but may need additional rules. The main administrative task is to ensure that funds transferred from caretaker resource accounts to retirement accounts cannot be withdrawn in cash before retirement. Otherwise, the retirement option would be a back door for parents to convert their grants into cash. Today, there are two types of tax-favored pension accounts. Although neither of them follows this model, it should not be prohibitively difficult to graft on the new restriction.[28] Another challenge is to reflect on whether the program should restrict individuals' control over investment decisions. Paternalism and administrative considerations (e.g., the high transaction cost of individual trading in small accounts) suggest caution in giving individuals unfettered investment discretion. I will not pursue these issues further here, because there is a lively and informed debate regarding the structure of proposed private retirement accounts within the Social Security system.[29]

One objection to any voucher system is that government subsidies for tuition, retirement, and child care will raise the price of these items, in effect transferring caretaker dollars to the education sector, to financial institutions, and to child care providers. In technical terms, the question is whether the government's infusion of cash will be capitalized into prices for goods and services. Capitalization may occur whenever the government introduces a subsidy for the purchase of a good. Buyers initially benefit, because they can pay more than they otherwise could. But the increase in demand for the good also enables sellers to charge a higher price, capturing some, or, in extreme cases, all of the value of the subsidy. To take an outer-bound example, if the enactment of caretaker resource accounts caused the price of tuition and the price of child care each to *rise* by $5,000 per year and the annual interest rate on retirement savings to *fall* by $5,000 per year, caretakers would receive no net economic benefit from the program.

But two related features of caretaker accounts should constrain capitalization.[30] The program endows individuals with a fixed dollar amount (rather than an unlimited voucher), creating an incentive for caretakers to shop carefully. A worker who pays more for education will have less for retirement. Most important, the accounts are not single-purpose subsidies; because there are four uses (three options plus deferral), the worker is not restricted to the purchase of just one good. Thus, unlike subsidies that can be used *only* for child care, for example, caretaker accounts do not simply introduce "free (government) money" into a market transaction and invite the actors to split it. Instead, it functions (more) like an increase in caretakers' wealth. Their greater wealth may permit some increase in prices, but less so than in dedicated subsidies, because if the price of one good rises by too much, caretakers will shift their resources to another.

11

Implementing Life-Planning Insurance for Parents

When we turn from caretaker resource accounts to life-planning insurance, we leave the realm of large, universal programs with standardized benefits and enter the world of smaller programs paying more tailored benefits. Caretaker resource accounts are a mass program, which should deliver a uniform package of resources to a large number of individuals. In contrast, life-planning insurance would provide individualized assistance to a small group of parents and will come into play only in catastrophic situations. The corollary is that life-planning insurance will inevitably require more bureaucracy to ascertain the facts about families' particular situations and to craft appropriate remedies. There are ample precedents for this sort of program. Disability insurance for adults and children, workers' compensation, special education—all require individualized determinations. None of these is a model of perfection, and indeed, the disability system requires major reform. Still, life-planning insurance represents an extension of familiar principles and not an entirely new enterprise.

In this chapter, I consider two major issues of implementation. The first is moral hazard: parents have an obvious incentive to exaggerate (or invent) children's illness or disability in order to claim benefits. How might a program limit parents' ability to game the system? The second is how to structure the bureaucracy that will be necessary to administer the program. To what extent can life-planning insurance build on existing programs?

I do not attempt to elaborate all of the rules and administrative structures that would be necessary to enact the program. I offer some preliminary suggestions, but further study is necessary, both to craft workable rules for eligibility and to choose appropriate agencies for administration.

The Problem of Moral Hazard

Moral hazard plagues most kinds of insurance. In the textbook example, moral hazard reduces people's incentive to take care; an insured homeowner may build too close to the river, or an insured driver may drive more recklessly. Moral hazard may arise in life-planning insurance in a somewhat different way. The problem is not, usually, that people will knowingly take greater risks with their children's safety or health, but instead that people whose children have *not* suffered an extraordinary calamity may misrepresent their circumstances in order to claim benefits.

This kind of moral hazard is most familiar in disability programs.[1] The law sets a disability standard—usually, for adults, the inability to pursue gainful employment. But the existence of the program creates an incentive for people to exaggerate or feign health problems in order to claim benefits. Because it is difficult for bureaucrats to evaluate individuals' ability to work, there is significant room for slippage in the system. Moral hazard also plagues other kinds of social insurance. For example, unemployment insurance rules require that individuals be available and looking for work. Individuals have an obvious incentive to exaggerate their efforts (or to hide jobs they hold), and the system is not set up to monitor claimants' activities.

The entry point for moral hazard in life-planning insurance is likely to be the threshold criterion that caretakers' children have suffered severe ("extraordinary") injuries, illnesses, disabilities, or developmental crises. The difficulty is to create a legal standard and a monitoring apparatus that can administer this standard with some degree of accuracy. In concept, there are two ways to counter moral hazard, each based on existing programs.

The first and more conventional model is *bureaucratic*. The law would set a medical standard, informed by psychological and educational expertise regarding children's need for intensive, personal care. Parents would apply for benefits, offering medical evidence to document their claim. Cases would be reviewed and approved or denied; some kind of internal, due process rights to appeal would be provided.

Once approved, parentss could claim benefits based on the duration and nature of the personal care that the child needs. Paid workers would be eligible for unpaid job leave, and families would be eligible for income support and social services designed to mitigate the disruption in their normal projects. For example, a child with a skull fracture might require a month of parental presence at the hospital and another few months of careful home care. For the first month, the family might receive income support and perhaps home help or other services to keep the household running if there are other children at home. For the next few months, the family might receive assistance for purchasing skilled child care to enable parents to return to work. Different underlying problems would trigger different benefits options.

Within the bureaucratic model, administrators may have greater or lesser opportunities for discretion and individual determination. On one end of the spectrum, school districts implementing IDEA, which governs special education, tend to use individual assessments, with each child undergoing testing with a variety of specialists. At the other end of the spectrum, SSI, the federal program that provides cash disability payments to children in low-income families, relies on a relatively rough, binary determination (Is the child "disabled" or not?) as the basis for authorizing a standard, monthly cash payment.[2] For adults with disabilities, Social Security disability and state temporary disability insurance (TDI) programs provide additional precedents.

The bureaucratic model obviously raises government expenditures per dollar of benefits paid. For example, the cost of administering the Social Security disability program, which makes individualized determinations, is much higher per dollar of benefits paid than the cost of the Social Security retirement program, which provides benefits based simply on a worker's wage history. The determination of eligibility and benefits may be slow, depending on the staffing of the program and the nature of the processes involved.[3] In a badly designed or underfunded program, "street-level" decisions may not accurately implement the program's objectives.[4]

A second model would make use of a wealth-endowment structure to combat moral hazard. For example, each caretaker might be awarded a sum of money that could be used only in the event of a child's extraordinary illness, injury, or disability. The idea is that individuals will, to some degree, monitor themselves if three conditions are met. First, individuals should be entitled to the residual balance in the account at some future date; otherwise, they will adopt a use-it-or-lose-it attitude. Second, the account balance should grow at a market rate of interest, to avoid any time-value incentive to withdraw. Third, individuals must not be able to claim additional benefits for life planning from some other source.

The precedents for this structure include medical savings accounts and two proposals, made separately by Graetz and Mashaw and Sugarman, to convert unemployment insurance to an account structure.[5] Very generally, both of these plans would endow workers with an unemployment insurance account and would require them to pay all or a portion of unemployment benefits if they became unemployed. These proposals use the account structure in combination with worker contributions to create a kind of copay mechanism that, the authors argue, would cut down on moral hazard.

Although the account model is promising in some regards, it is unsuitable as the primary vehicle for life-planning insurance. Caretaker resource accounts deliberately award a standard grant in anticipation of routine child-rearing burdens. In contrast, life-planning insurance should be rarely invoked but should provide generous benefits when needed. Disability, rather than medical care or even unemployment, is the better analogy here. Most parents should never need the protections of life-planning insurance, just as most workers never suffer a long-term disability. But when parents do experience a severe disruption in their life-planning capacity, the program should be in a position to award them significant resources. For this purpose, a few thousand dollars per caretaker would give most families too much and some too little.

Even a bureaucratic model can adopt some standard methods to minimize moral hazard. Waiting periods, copayments, and deductibles tend to discourage small claims and to make fraud more difficult and less lucrative. Here, the existence of the caretaker resource account may be helpful; the program could require that the first $X of income support, or the first Y percent of benefits, be offset by a deduction in the caretaker resource account. Although such rules would have to be administered carefully to prevent parents from casually withdrawing cash, the deductible or copayment structure could make limited use of the wealth-endowment method of discouraging moral hazard.

One issue of moral hazard can be relatively easily solved. Whereas caretaker resource accounts require somewhat mechanical rules to distinguish "parents" from "caretakers," life-planning insurance focuses quite naturally on the household in which the child lives. The problem arises because the options that caretaker resource accounts provide would be valuable to most people, whether or not they care for a child; virtually anyone would value a grant that might be used for education or retirement savings. In contrast, life-planning insurance can target benefits more accurately because the program's benefits will be valuable primarily to the person who would otherwise provide the child's care. To take an oversimplified example, if one parent does all the child care and housework, a program that provides skilled child care, respite care, and housekeeping assistance will primarily benefit that parent. The other parent cannot grab the extra resources for himself or herself.[6]

Making the Most of Existing Programs

To this point, I have described life-planning insurance as if it were a freestanding program. But, as a practical matter, the better route to implementation is probably to graft the elements of life-planning insurance onto existing programs. The following two examples illustrate how a program might work and how it might be coordinated with existing programs. (The examples expand on the Larry/Lori and Maria cases first presented in Chapter 7.)

Recall that Maria has two children, Maribel and Mikey. Maribel suffers a skull fracture in a car accident, remains in the hospital for three weeks, and then requires intensive physical therapy and home care for months.

Maria should be entitled to up to three months of unpaid leave under the FMLA, which should be retained and possibly extended. An expanded program of Temporary Disability Insurance (TDI), which now exists in five states (but currently applies only to workers), could provide a vehicle for authorizing income support and social services for Maria. Existing TDI programs should be amended to cover parents' needs arising from children's short-term disabilities, including income support and vouchers for social services.

This example suggests several reforms in existing TDI programs. First, they should be adopted by every state, a reform that policy analysts concerned with disability have recommended. Second, the scope of TDI should be expanded to make determinations about *children's* as well as *workers'* short-term disabilities, with the term understood, in the case of children, to encompass any serious but short-term injury or illness that requires intensive and personal parental care. Third, TDI's benefit structure and menu would have to be amended. Today, TDI typically provides only cash benefits, which are linked to workers' past wages. Life-planning insurance, in contrast, should pay income support (possibly with income testing) and should provide social services (skilled child care, home help) or at least vouchers for their purchase.

These changes would require major reforms in TDI. Today, TDI exists in only five states, has no uniform rules or funding structure, and is often administered through the unemployment insurance or workers' compensation bureaucracies, which have some experience in dealing with wage replacement for workers but not disability benefits for severely ill or injured children. It may be feasible to retain a relatively standardized approach to short-term life-planning insurance for caretakers; perhaps the program might offer a standard income-support benefit for three to six months and a shortish menu of social services likely to be useful to most families. Even these changes would require significant expansion and adaptation by the TDI bureaucracy. But other scholars have spotted TDI as a potentially promising vehicle for disability reform,[7] and life-planning insurance might be added to the menu.

Recall that Larry and Lori's son Linc has developmental and physical disabilities and requires intensive therapy as well as special education. The parents find it difficult to meet Linc's needs while working. The couple would face severe financial pressure if Lori quit work or cut her hours, but they see no alternative.

Initially, Lori should be able to take a three-month leave from her job and receive temporary income support from the (modified) TDI program. At the end of that time, Linc's therapy will continue in the same intensive mode for the foreseeable future. Suppose that Lori decides to resign permanently because she cannot manage Linc's care and hold a full-time job. She should be able to apply for long-term caretaker benefits under an expanded version of the Social Security disability program. The benefits should include income support, as well as an automatic entitlement to respite care and other family services as appropriate. If Lori later returns to work, the family should be eligible for skilled child care assistance if needed.

Institutional coordination will be a significant challenge in implementing life-planning insurance. As Michael Graetz and Jerry Mashaw point out, the existing system of disability benefits is full of gaps and oddities and is not well-integrated with medical care.[8] To their critique we might add that programs for *children* with long-term disabilities are especially fragmented, so that there is no ready foundation for life-planning insurance. Educational accommodations for children with disabilities are made by local school systems; thus, it is the local school district that provides not only pre-school but also a therapist for Linc. The federal SSI program provides income support for some children in very poor families. Children with high medical needs may also receive assistance from Medicaid, depending on state-by-state rules. There is also an array of specialized state programs, which may be coordinated by child welfare agencies or by health and human services departments.

There is no simple way to transform this hodgepodge of programs into a unitary program of life-planning insurance. We can imagine many possibilities. For example, one approach would be to have disabled children evaluated by the local school system or by doctors but to have a standard menu of benefits administered by the federal Social Security program as part of Social Security disability (SSDI, which is distinct from SSI). This would be a considerable expansion of SSDI, which does not now cover children's disabilities, and which covers only work-related disabilities. But of all the eligible bureaucracies, SSDI has particular appeal because it is a national agency of a familiar kind and is equipped already to perform an analogous set of tasks. Although the Social Security infrastructure would not be well suited to providing social services, at a minimum, the agency might coordinate income support, medical benefits, and caretaker support services, providing a "one-stop shopping" experience to families.

But it may be that some other coordinating mechanism would work better. My goal here is not to offer a final decision on that issue, but simply to highlight the question for further inquiry: Given existing institutions, and directions for reform, how can we best coordinate the input of different bureaucracies to ensure that parents receive timely and appropriate support?

Conclusion

What Kind of Society?

America's public policies have not come to terms with our evolving attitudes toward child rearing. To our credit, we have begun to recognize the dignity and equality of every child. We understand that every child deserves a fair chance at a good life and that parents have an obligation to provide it. Thanks to technological and social change, parenthood has become a costly pursuit. We expect parents to protect their children's developmental chances, even at the expense of their own opportunities.

But our commitment to higher and higher standards for children's care comes at a price, measured in lost autonomy for parents. We love our children dearly, and yet their care constrains the kind of lives we might lead. Today, parenthood, to a greater extent than any other social role, requires a significant, and decades-long, restructuring of one's economic and personal life. We care for our children out of love and a deeply felt sense of duty, but we should also recognize that society regulates parenthood with a heavy hand.

The autonomy costs of parenthood are most apparent in women's lives. Social science research is often maddeningly equivocal, but not on this point; a truckload of research documents the ways motherhood limits the economic options of mothers in every income class. Low-income

mothers struggle to make ends meet while fulfilling their parental obligations, and sometimes they cannot. Middle-class and even upper-class
mothers struggle with inflexible jobs, and a substantial minority of them
simply exit the workforce, with severe consequences for their long-term
financial independence.

But the costs of parenthood are not just a by-product of gender
inequality. Children deserve good care, and that care will inevitably burden some adults' lives. Even if fathers shouldered half the burden, the No
Exit obligation would still shrink parents' economic options compared to
nonparents'.

The Curious Appeal of the Libertarian Response

The libertarian reply is, essentially, "So what?" Parents know, or ought
to know, what they are getting into, and they should plan for the economic burden of parenthood by saving, marrying, or remaining childless
if need be. On this view, every family ought to be financially self-sufficient,
and parents have no right to complain: they chose their own path, and it is
unfair to ask their childless peers to help out at this late date.

This perspective has dominated U.S. social welfare policy, especially
during the past two decades. Meager, time-limited welfare benefits express
the view that poor single mothers should not have children they cannot
afford. Child benefits in the tax code provide small sums rather than real
assistance to parents. Federal subsidies for child care are also small in
amount and require most parents to pay large sums out of pocket.
Although social welfare policy does provide major subsidies for middle-
class life, they take the form of benefits for the childless and parents alike.
Deductions for home mortgage interest and retirement savings confer no
special assistance to parents as *parents*.

The libertarian view of parenthood is integral to the conservative
movement that has dominated electoral politics and public policy dis-
course for much of the past 20 years. Most obviously, the Reagan and Bush
Sr. presidencies initiated efforts to reduce the size of the welfare state and
to insist that families be economically self-sufficient, a trend that contin-

ued, in some notable ways, even during the Clinton administration, which approved the 1996 welfare reforms.

But even people who reject conservative political views may find attractive the vision of equality that is implicit in the libertarian claim. Why should a parent be able to claim a greater share of social resources than her childless neighbor? As we become more aware of our multicultural society, and as greater numbers of women remain childless, it may seem, well, retrograde, to insist that parenthood merits special, and rather extensive, state support. Aren't we all equal now?

This book has tried to show that the assertion of equality between parents and nonparents is superficial because it overlooks the child in the picture. Once we recognize parents' special duty to their children, we can begin a conversation about society's obligations to parents. Whether society owes parents a lot or a little is an open question, and one I've tried to address here. My vision is one in which we mitigate the costs of parenthood without attempting to erase them: the goal is to pull parents back from the economic margins without trying to eradicate the impact of parenthood on parents' life chances.

But whether readers embrace my programs or reject them, I hope to help shift the terms of the debate. Society stands in an exceptional relationship to parents and children; for children's sake, we must regulate parents' lives far more extensively than we regulate other ways of life. A good society can and should recognize that reality.

Our current neglect of parents' situation is far from benign. Although most parents provide continuity of care to their children, they do so under unduly stressful conditions. This situation is unfair to parents, and it has serious consequences for children's lives. When social welfare policy deems parental obligation a private matter, we pit children's interests against their parents'; we tell parents, in effect, "Do the right thing for society, but don't ask for help."

Confronted with this command, many parents will still put their children's interests first, but some will not. When the No Exit obligation weighs so heavily, some parents will protect their own prospects at their children's expense. Sadly, some of the neediest children, including those with serious disabilities, may be most at risk for abandonment or breaks in continuity of care, simply because their care is so very costly for their parents' lives. There is no way to make it cost-free for parents to care for severely ill and disabled children; those parents' lives are forever changed. But we should not, and need not, require those parents to bear their load alone.

Treating the parental obligation as purely private also reinforces gender roles. Today, a good parent, a parent who provides continuity of care, must pay a dramatic price in terms of economic success and life-long opportunities. Given that situation, it is not especially surprising that fathers have been slow to embrace the caretaker role. The crude way to interpret the situation is as a raw exercise of gender power: fathers continue to expect mothers to take the harder, less rewarding, and more precarious role in the family. More sympathetically, we might spot a more nuanced dynamic: today, public policy pits a father's desire to be a good provider against his desire to be a good parent. A man may feel that the sacrifice of economic opportunity and lifetime autonomy is too great, not merely for selfish reasons but in the interests of his family as well.

What Public Policy Can Do—Now

Both of the programs I propose could be adopted right now. Caretaker resource accounts would be straightforward to administer and could be enacted for a reasonable budgetary cost. One hundred billion dollars annually is not a small commitment, but neither is it outsized for a social initiative of such importance in a federal budget of more than $2 trillion per year. The proper comparison is to other major programs that express our collective commitment to vulnerable groups. Compare the more than $400 billion we spend each year on Social Security retirement benefits and on public education. Consider, too, the current president's successful effort to enact tax cuts worth more than $1 trillion over 10 years.

In predicting the impact of caretaker resource accounts, I have invoked both anecdote and social science research. Parents, mothers especially, need child care, education, and retirement savings to expand their economic options and improve their long-term prospects. These are key ingredients in staying in the labor market, reentering it after a period of absence, and securing a degree of financial independence in old age.

But you can take a further step. Think about the parents you know, and consider how caretaker resource accounts might change their lives. Would your daughter, your wife, your mother make different choices if she could count on $5,000 every year to invest in herself? How about your son or your husband? How might the caretaker resource account open up new options and new conversations in your family when the topic turns to how to care for the kids?

Life-planning insurance is a smaller initiative, in a budgetary sense, and even more manageable, despite its administrative challenges. It may at first seem difficult to identify children who are seriously ill or disabled and to gauge the extra effort they require from parents, until we recognize that there are already regimes in place that assess illness and disability and might be adapted to the new task of securing appropriate assistance for parents. The SSI program already evaluates childhood disability, and every school district in the country must assess and assist children with special needs. Ideally, life-planning insurance for parents should be part of more sweeping reform of the disability system, but even in the short run we might do far more than we now do to recognize and address the unmet needs of parents who care for children with extraordinary medical needs and disabilities.

A number of trends make life-planning insurance especially important. Technological and medical advances provide greater treatment options for childhood illness and disabilities, but they also impose greater demands on parents. A second, troubling trend is the rise in certain kinds of serious and chronic diseases. Asthma has increased more than twofold among U.S. children since 1980, and autism too appears to be on the rise. Frustratingly, these new ailments seem to be an increasing part of modern life. And in this era of managed care, parents often must take responsibility for administering sophisticated medical care at home.

Just the Beginning?

Caretaker resource accounts and life-planning insurance are, quite deliberately, incremental in spirit. I have chosen to focus on policies that might be adopted *today,* but we can and should think about longer-term reforms.

The Social Security retirement system requires major reform to ensure its financial soundness during the next generation. As part of that effort, policymakers ought to give serious consideration to changing the rules that make retirement security contingent on one's own (or a spouse's) long-term, paid employment. Those rules were adopted in the 1930s on the assumption that every mother would have a working husband to rely on. Today, those rules leave too many mothers financially insecure in old age. Rising rates of divorce (and motherhood outside marriage) mean that the husband assumption no longer holds true. And although far more mothers now hold jobs of their own, mothers' interrupted labor force participation limits the benefits they can earn independently.

Scholars and policymakers have suggested different options for improving old-age security for parents. An incremental approach would retain the basic structure of Social Security but give parents extra credit for years spent out of the workforce or in part-time work while their children are young. A more sweeping plan, which I favor, would convert Social Security into a system of "citizens' pensions," which would pay a flat bene-fit to every person over age 65.[1] The universal benefit would provide a decent floor of retirement income for everyone and leave individuals free to supplement with private savings.

I am leery of some forms of labor market regulation, for the reasons of fairness and practicality that I outlined in Chapters 8 and 9. Our under-standing of the labor markets is too limited, in my judgment, to risk the potential ill effects of well-intentioned regulation. Still, it may be that we could encourage the markets to provide a greater array of more flexible job options to parents; there is no reason to assume that current markets func-tion perfectly. Over the longer term, research may yield better information about what works and what doesn't. California's recent adoption of paid job leave will provide administrative experience and data on the conse-quences for women's wages and employment.[2]

The special challenges confronting poor children and their parents deserve further attention as well. The libertarian ideal of family self-suffi-ciency is especially hollow for parents whose limited education and lim-ited skills earn meager rewards in the labor market. Poverty also tends to cause (or be caused by) a host of other stresses. Poor children are more likely to suffer disabilities and serious, chronic health problems.

None of these problems can be easily solved, but they require attention if we are to make it possible for parents to provide continuity of care to their children. Caretaker resource accounts and life-planning insurance take initial and deliberately incremental steps. We might do more, but we should not do less.

Notes

Introduction

1. The phrase "author of [her] own life" comes from Raz (1986, p. 204), in the context of a general discussion of individual autonomy.
2. See, e.g., Blustein (1982); Scott (2001).
3. See Bumpass and Lu (2000; marriage patterns of unmarried parents); Federal Interagency Forum on Child and Family Statistics (2001, p. 9; births to unmarried parents); U.S. House of Representatives (2000, p. 1236, Table G-1, marriage and divorce rates; p. 1236, Table G-2, never-married adults; p. 1241, Table G-6, marital status of single parents).
4. See U.S. Bureau of the Census (2001d, p. 355, Table 547).
5. See Blank (1997, pp. 52–71, wage trends); Langbein (1988, wealth trends); Schneider and Brinig (2000, pp. 341–353, noting the limited success of efforts to divide human capital at divorce); U.S. Bureau of the Census (2001b, pp. 4–5, stepfamilies).
6. See Chapter 5.
7. See, e.g., Crittenden (2001); Fineman (1995); Kittay (1999); Williams (2000).

Chapter 1. What Is Continuity of Care?

1. This story is based on *In Re Marriage of Allen*, 626 P. 2d 16 (1981).
2. For a compelling account of how parents come to identify with and even feel the needs and wants of their children, see Kittay (1999).

3. Under the law, it is not easy for a stepparent to challenge a parent for custody of a child. (There are notable exceptions to this rule, which I discuss later in Chapter 3.) Because Jeannie did not formally adopt Joshua, in the eyes of the law, she had a lesser legal claim to Joshua's custody than did Joe, his biological father. But a wise court awarded her custody anyway. 626 P. 2d 16 (1981).

4. Goldstein, Freud, and Solnit (1973, 1979a, 1985). A second edition of the 1973 book was published (1979b) with a helpful epilogue, and so I usually cite to that version.

5. Goldstein, Freud, and Solnit (1979b, pp. 5–6). I make extensive use of Goldstein, Freud, and Solnit in the text because their work highlights beautifully the continuity that is essential to healthy child development. But one need not subscribe to their particular brand of psychoanalysis to value continuity; attachment theory, too, endorses a similar ideal. See Fonagy (2001).

6. Goldstein, Freud, and Solnit (1979b, pp. 14, 31–32).

7. Ibid., p. 32.

8. Ibid., p. 12.

9. For instance, their 1973 book is extensively cited, with approval, by leading family law scholars today. See, e.g., Bartholet (1999, p. 39); Mason (1999, p. 89); Sanger (1996, p. 443); Scott (1992, p. 630); Scott and Scott (1995, p. 2412).

10. See, e.g., Bartlett (1984). Although Goldstein, Freud, and Solnit were psychoanalysts, continuity of care has also been advanced by attachment theorists. Psychoanalysis and attachment theory differ in important respects, but both agree that continuity of care (at least in the general formulation I have presented) should be an important value in determining arrangements for children's care. For an account of continuity of care that draws on a variety of psychological sources, see Bartlett (1984, pp. 902–911); for an account of continuity based on attachment theory (and rejecting psychoanalysis), see Waters and Noyes (1983–1984).

11. For a critical perspective on mother-infant bonding theories, see Eyer (1992). The mainstream view is that children may develop attachments with multiple caretakers, and studies have generally rejected the simple prediction that maternal employment compromises children's development. For research on attachments to multiple caretakers, see R. Kelly and Ward (2002); for a review of studies of maternal employment, see Sanger (1996, pp. 434–438, 478–483).

12. Some older examples of attachment theory and psychoanalysis contain stereotypes that are jarring to a modern reader, but we should understand these as artifacts of an older culture and not as fundamental flaws in the underlying theory of child development. The dramatic change in gender roles and social arrangements since some of the major sources were written

renders their attitudes anachronistic at times. See, e.g., Goldstein, Freud, and Solnit (1979b, p. 32): change in infants' routines due to the use of a babysitter may produce distress; the authors do not seem to anticipate that a babysitter might become part of the daily routine rather than a disruption of it.

13. See, e.g., the advice, guidelines, and model correspondence offered by the Autism-PDD Resources Network website, at www.1autism-pdd.nt/ (parents' guide), accessed 8 July 2002.

14. Buss (2002); Scott and Scott (1995).

Chapter 2. The Cost of Continuity for Parents' Lives

1. *In Re Guardianship of Verona Jonice N,* 177 A.D. 2d 115 (1992). Carol Sanger mentions this case in her excellent article, "Separating from Children" (1996).

2. 177 A.D. 2d 115, 119 (1992).

3. See Edin and Lein (1997).

4. See Demo and Acock (1993); Shelton and John (1996).

5. A further difficulty is that ideal data would give us a rich picture of parents' opportunities over a lifetime. What might caretakers do at different life stages? How do their options ebb and flow as their child-rearing obligations vary? But there is no easy way to measure autonomy, or even individuals' opportunity sets: what they *might* do. Instead, most real-world studies provide statistics on economic *outcomes*, what people *actually* do, measured in "snapshot" fashion at just one point in time. I make use of the standard measures, supplementing them with better data where I can.

6. For employment statistics on mothers and fathers, see U.S. Bureau of Labor Statistics (2000); for statistics on at-home mothers by income class, see U.S. Bureau of the Census (2001a, p. 8, Table 4); for women's and men's reasons for being out of the workforce, see U.S. Bureau of the Census (2001c, p. 6); for data on mothers' job interruptions, see Klerman and Leibowitz (1999).

7. See Waldfogel (1998a, 1998b). Researchers find no family penalty for men; indeed, married men earn more than single men (1998b, p. 147).

8. For the motherhood wage gap, see Waldfogel (1998a); for similar results, see Budig and England (2001) and Waldfogel (1997). For long-term effects, see Anderson, Binder, and Krause (2001).

9. See Anderson et al. (2001, finding that after controlling for human capital, family income, and unobserved heterogeneity, mothers still face a wage penalty of 3 percent for one child and 6 percent for two); Waldfogel (1997, 1998a, finding wage penalties of 4 percent for one child and 12 percent for two, even after correcting for unobserved heterogeneity); Budig and England

(2001, finding a wage penalty of 5 percent per child after using fixed-effects models to help correct for unobserved heterogeneity). Discrimination against mothers may explain part of this gap, but it is not clear that a discrimination story could explain the wage differential that increases with the number of children and with marriage. See Budig and England (2001, pp. 218–220).

10. Anderson et al. (2001).

11. For efforts to use twin births to eliminate selection effects, see Bronars and Grogger (1994, focusing on unmarried mothers); Gangadharan and Rosenbloom (1996, focusing on married mothers); see also Angrist and Evans (1996, making use of twin data and finding that children reduce mothers' but not fathers' labor supply).

12. For data on business and the professions, see Fagenson and Jackson (1994); see also Hewlett (2002). For data on politics, see Burrell (1994).

13. For studies of working mothers, see Hochschild (1989, 1997); for studies of doctors and lawyers, see Chambers (1989) and Grant, Simpson, Rory, and Peters-Golden (1990).

14. See Hundley (2000).

15. See Goldin (1997, pp. 44–48).

16. For a study of midlife work patterns, see Moen, Downey, and Bolger (1990, pp. 237–238); for Social Security and pension coverage, see Ackerman and Alstott (1999, pp. 145–146); Burggraf (1997, pp. 58–63); Choudhury and Leonesio (1997); Social Security Administration (2000, pp. 11–12, Tables 5A1, 5A7).

17. See Blau (1998).

18. The phrase is from Hochschild (1989).

19. See U.S. Bureau of the Census (2001a, Table 4). These data are for mothers, age 15–44, whether married or unmarried, *excluding* mothers of infants under age 1, who work much less.

20. Author's calculations based on U.S. Bureau of Labor Statistics (2000).

21. See Blau, Ferber, and Winkler (1998, p. 52, Table 3.3); Bianchi, Milkie, and Sayer (2000); Demo and Acock (1993); Shelton and John (1996).

22. Yeung et al. (2001, p. 143, Table 1, p. 146, Table 3). According to the Yeung study, fathers spend 46 percent of the time that mothers spend with infants and toddlers. Thus, for every 10 hours an average mother spends, an average father spends 4.6 hours, meaning that the mother provides 10 of 14.6 hours, or 70 percent of total hours.

23. See, e.g., Orrange (1999).

24. Yeung et al. (2001, p. 148).

25. Among two-parent families, 85 percent were headed by two biological parents, and another 10 percent included one stepparent (U.S. House of Representatives, 2000, p. 1245, Table G-10). For data on single parents, see p. 1239,

Table G-4; p. 1240, Table G-5. The 82 percent figure in the text is a calculation based on data in Table G-4. For patterns of custody after divorce, see Maccoby and Mnookin (1992); Melli, Brown, and Cancian (1997). For the decline in fathers' (but not mothers') visitation over time, see Maccoby and Mnookin (1992, p. 171, Figure 8.4).

26. See Catalyst (1997); Hochschild (1989, 1997); Malin (1994, pp. 1049–1050).

27. See Schultz (2000, p. 126). The U.S. Bureau of Labor Statistics (2000) reports that, in 2000, 4.1 percent of married fathers were not employed, while their wives were employed. Note that this figure *excludes* the unemployed, that is, those who are out of work but looking for work.

28. A majority of Americans from every income class prefer to have one parent take time out of the paid workforce to care for young children. See Sylvester (2001); see also Public Agenda Online (2000a).

29. See Capizzano et al. (2000, p. 3, Table 1). I infer that couples who use parental care are (primarily) using split shifts or other staggered working hours, because of the small percentage of fathers who are out of the labor force. Other studies confirm that as many as 25 to 33 percent of dual-earner couples work split shifts (Presser, 1994).

30. Conlin, Merritt, and Himelstein (2002); Morris (2002).

Chapter 3. Should Society Expect Parents to Provide Continuity of Care?

1. This story is based on *Painter v. Bannister*, 140 N.W. 2d 152 (1966).

2. *Painter v. Bannister* is a classic case, taught widely to students of family law. The case is sometimes cited as an example of judges' cultural biases; some suspect that the Iowa courts in the mid-1960s were too quick to conclude that Mark's "Bohemian" father could not provide him with continuity. While it is indeed possible to read the case in that way, it seems to me that there are deeper issues at stake, too, and a close reading of the case suggests that the Iowa Supreme Court was doing its best, within its admittedly fixed cultural context, to resolve the core emotional issues.

3. Goldstein et al. (1979b, pp. 5–6).

4. I talk at greater length about some of these institutions later in this chapter and in Chapter 4.

5. The importance of families as the first school for citizens is a central theme in Okin (1989). See also Ackerman (1980, pp. 139–167); Rawls (1971, pp. 462–472).

6. Studies document the suffering of children who lose psychological parents to death or voluntary exit, and they emphasize that one of the key prescrip-

tions for recovery is to maintain a continuing relationship with the remaining caretaker. See Daniel, Wassell, and Gilligan (1999, pp. 93–94); Davies (1999, pp. 67–68); Dixon and Stein (2000, pp. 505–509, divorce; 561–562, parental death). For studies of children deprived of parental (or substitute) care for extended periods, see Cole and Cole (1993, pp. 251–257).

7. Some critics contend that representatives in the original position would *not* reach that result, but I will not engage that larger debate here; instead, I begin with Rawlsian principles that have held wide appeal, despite the debate over their derivation. For readers who are methodological sticklers, I point out that there are other ways of reaching the result I describe in the text. For instance, we might follow Dworkin's (2000) method of asking what kind of "insurance" each person would buy. Would each person (hypothetically) agree to purchase "continuity of care" insurance? (Although Dworkin does not address this question, he uses a similar method to address other questions of social organization. We can reasonably suppose that the answer is yes, because continuity of care is a basic building block for human development. Alternatively, consider Ackerman's (1980) assembly, governed by the principle that no individual can assert she is better than another. Only someone who had already had continuity of care could meaningfully stand up in the assembly and assert that she rejected continuity; and if such an adult asserted that her values were more important than continuity for the next generation, a member of the next generation (recall that Ackerman's assembly abstracts from temporal constraints) could stand up and object, decisively in Ackerman's scheme, "I am just as good as you."

8. Rawls (1971, pp. 463–464).

9. Ackerman (1980, p. 141).

10. For principles along these lines, see Blustein (1982, pp. 103–114, 113): "Parents have a right to satisfy their own individual interests, parental and non-parental, *as long as this is consistent with the satisfactory performance of their parental duties.* These interests include the need for a certain degree of privacy within the family, the desire to engaged in activities unrelated to child-rearing, and the desire to care for a child."

11. The phrase is from Goldstein, Freud, and Solnit (1979b, p. 3).

12. For an account of the difficulties in striking the right balance between family preservation and adoption for foster children, see, e.g., Bartholet (1999).

13. Not every disability will necessitate continuing *parental* care; a child who cannot walk, for example, but who has no other disabilities will generally make the psychological transition to adult life. Although she may need physical assistance in some aspects of daily life as an adult, she will ordinarily be able to take responsibility for arranging her care, and it will not be critical to

her psychological well-being that those tasks be performed by a parent. In contrast, some children with developmental disabilities may require a parent's care for far longer than 18 years.

14. See Chapter 7.
15. See Fishkin (1983).
16. See Bergmann (1996).
17. The themes in this section draw on Buss (2000, 2002); Scott and Scott (1995); Woodhouse (1993, 1995).
18. Buss (2000, 2002), Goldstein et al. (1979b), and Woodhouse (1995) emphasize state incompetence as a rationale for parental authority. For criticism of foster care, see, e.g., Bernstein (2001); Chaifetz (1999); Toth (1997).
19. The Supreme Court has also expressed this functional understanding of the parental authority doctrine. For example: "The law's concept of the family rests on a presumption that parents possess what a child lacks in maturity, experience, and capacity for judgment required for making life's difficult decisions. More importantly, historically it has recognized that natural bonds of affection lead parents to act in the best interests of their children" (*Parham v. J.R.*, 442 U.S. 584 (1979), upholding state procedures for committing minors to state mental hospitals).

      See also *Troxel v. Granville*, 530 U.S. 57, 69–70 (2000), noting the "traditional presumption that a fit parent will act in the bests interest of his or her child."
20. Buss (2000b, 2002); Scott and Scott (1995).
21. For First Amendment reasons, the state grants somewhat greater latitude to parents who advance religious reasons for their decisions. Most famously, in *Wisconsin v. Yoder*, 406 U.S. 205 (1972) Amish parents were permitted to keep their children out of high school, even though the state insisted that the children had an independent interest in an education that could widen their horizons. For criticism, see, e.g., Arneson and Shapiro (1996); Feinberg (1980); Gutmann (1987). Still, even the religious exceptions have a limited scope; parents may not generally deny life-saving medical treatment to children for religious reasons, and parents may not violate the child labor laws even if the children's work is religious in nature. See *Prince v. Massachusetts*, 321 U.S. 158 (1944), upholding the application of child labor laws to a Jehovah's Witness who took her niece and ward out to sell the *Watchtower*); *Jehovah's Witnesses v. King's County Hospital*, 278 F. Supp. 488 (W.D. Wash. 1967), upholding statute authorizing declaration of children as wards of the state for purposes of permitting blood transfusion over parental religious objection).
22. *Painter v. Bannister*, 140 N.W. 2d 152 (1966).

23. For example, a line of famous Supreme Court cases involved disputes between biological fathers and stepfathers. These cases involved mothers who had remarried and whose husbands wished to adopt the children from the prior marriage, over the objections of the biological father. In these cases, the stepfathers prevailed because they had established long-term relationships with the children and the biological fathers had not. In *Lehr v. Robertson*, 463 U.S. 248 (1983) the father had not been given notice of the child's adoption, but the Court emphasized the father's prior failure to take steps to see or to claim the child. In *Quilloin v. Walcott*, 434 U.S. 246 (1978) the Court also approved adoption by a stepfather when the biological father has little involvement with his child.

24. U.S. House of Representatives (2000, p. 1239, Table G-4, and p. 1240, Table G-5).

25. U.S. Bureau of the Census (2001d, p. 3, Table 1).

26. For data on visitation by noncustodial parents, see Maccoby and Mnookin (1992); for accounts of fathers' reasons for not maintaining postdivorce relationships with their children, see Arendell (1995).

27. Goldstein, Freud, and Solnit recognize this point, as do attachment theorists. See Goldstein (1984); J. Kelly and Lamb (2000); Waters and Noyes (1983–1984).

28. Goldstein, Freud, and Solnit (1979b, p. 38, 117–118).

29. Ibid., pp. 116–121. For critics of Goldstein, Freud, and Solnit, see, e.g., Bartlett (1984); Waters and Noyes (1983–1984).

30. Bartlett and Stack (1986); Chambers (1984, pp. 527–538); Roman and Haddad (1978).

31. ALI (1998, sec. 2.09); Bartlett (1984, 1999).

32. Maccoby and Mnookin (1992, p. 103).

33. See Scott (2001).

34. A parent who (in technical terms) seeks to "relinquish" or "surrender" her parental rights must typically execute a formal document before a judge or legally approved witnesses. See Haralambie (1993, sec. 13.19). In New York State, for example, a parent must obtain court approval of the surrender of her parental rights; she must sign a surrender either before a judge or before two witnesses with court approval within 15 days (Carrieri, 1991, pp. 141–146).

35. See Goldstein, Freud, and Solnit (1996), pointing out that a parent who wishes to abandon her child probably is no longer a good "psychological parent," and that in such a case the best interests of the child would counsel placement with another person.

Chapter 4. No Exit and Parental Autonomy

1. For economic and historical accounts of this shift, see, e.g., Burggraf (1997); Folbre (1994).
2. Nor would it necessarily be fair to require individuals to compensate for the specific losses their own parents incurred. It is true, if cliché, that we do not choose our parents, and it may be unfair to hold individual children responsible for their own parents' lives. Instead, it makes more sense to think of each person as having an obligation to help pay the *average* cost of rearing children.
3. In principle, children could pay back the previous generation through debt financing. Suppose that Generation 1 parents are raising children of Generation 2. The children obviously have no money during the time they are being reared, but we could create a National Parents' Fund that would borrow the funds needed to pay Generation 1 parents and pledge as security the earnings of Generation 2. Unless the size of generations varies substantially, however, this sort of plan amounts to the "pay forward" system I describe in the text. Generation 1 parents receive funds provided by adult members of their own generation, and the Generation 2 children eventually grow up and contribute a share of their earnings to parents of Generation 2.
4. Eva Kittay (1999) has a wonderful account of the "transparent self" that evolves when a parent cares for a dependent child.
5. See Raz (1986, p. 204).
6. See, e.g., Nedelsky (1989, pp. 221–223); Raz (1986, pp. 369–78).
7. Boswell (1988).
8. Rubenfeld (1989).
9. A philosopher might object that the autonomy burden of the No Exit obligation is not so unusual. Isn't it just an example of the well-known precommitment problem? The precommitment dilemma has motivated a classic debate among liberal theorists; a brief introduction will clarify the issues.

   In the standard case, an individual commits to a life plan at Time 1 and promises never to exit; for example, he might enter a strict monastery and sign a contract promising to remain for the rest of his life. At Time 2, he decides he would like to change his mind and leave. The question is whether the state best promotes his autonomy by permitting his exit at Time 2 or by enforcing his Time 1 promise. If we emphasize the importance of revisability of life plans, the state should not enforce the contract. If we put decisive weight, instead, on the coherence of a single life and the importance of personal accountability, the state should enforce the original promise. The question is so perplexing that some noted theorists have simply set it aside. Among those who offer an answer, some emphasize the value of revisability, although there is not a clear consensus. See Ackerman (1980, pp. 197–199); Feinberg (1986, pp. 81–87); Parfit (1984).

But the precommitment problem is a red herring in this case. The No Exit obligation does not apply only to those parents who choose to make a No Exit promise at Time 1 and then change their mind. Instead, the state properly imposes a No Exit obligation at Time 1 and enforces it at Time 2, *whether or not parents endorse the No Exit condition at either time.* The question is whether such a universally applicable regulation should be understood as a limitation on parents' autonomy. True, the No Exit obligation creates the appearance of precommitment. Every parent should understand the No Exit obligation at time 1, when he chooses to have a child. In this sense, he promises to abide by the no Exit obligation when he undertakes the task of child rearing. But the state should not be able to justify draconian restrictions on autonomy simply by giving notice ahead of time. The question is whether the social role is itself fairly defined, a question to which the precommitment issue offers no insight.

10. See Ackerman and Alstott (1999).
11. Shiffrin (2003).
12. See, e.g., Rakowski (1991, 2002).
13. See Dworkin (1981b, 2000).
14. In *Social Justice in the Liberal State*, Bruce Ackerman (1980) argues strongly that parents should post a bond to pay the cost of their children's share of social resources, but he also seems to anticipate that the state should both operate and fund the public schools.
15. U.S. Constitution, Amend. V, prohibits the taking of private property for public use without just compensation.
16. See Ackerman (1980, pp. 217–221).
17. See, e.g., Folbre (1994, 2002, esp. pp. 49–51, 109–113); George (1987).
18. See Ackerman (1980, pp. 109–111).
19. See Rakowski (1991, pp. 153–155).
20. See, e.g., Rawls (1997).
21. See, e.g., Ackerman (1980, pp. 191–193).
22. Burkett (2000).
23. See, e.g., Ackerman and Alstott (1999, pp. 129–154); Dworkin (1981b, 2000); Graetz and Mashaw (2000).

Chapter 5. Caretaker Resource Accounts

1. The program could be administered either way. Social Security and Medicare offer a model for governmental accounting and vouchering, and Individual Development Accounts and IRAs have made use of private sector resources to monitor account-holders' compliance. The tax system, with its numerous tax credit vouchers, offers a third option.

2. In any year, a caretaker could draw on the entire balance in the account. In the *first* year, by definition, the maximum would be $5,000. In a later year, caretakers could draw on a new allotment of $5,000, plus whatever deferred amounts remained from prior years.

3. In 1997, the average weekly cost of child care for *full-time employed mothers using paid care* was $80 per week. The average cost was $61 per week for one child and $88 for two. Assuming a 50-week working year, these translate into annual average costs of between $3,050 for one child and $4,400 for two (U.S. Bureau of the Census, 2002, p. 17, Table 8). The highest-cost child care is for families with children under age 5; those families spend an average of $92 per week or $4,600 per year.

4. I.R.C. sec. 21 (dependent care credit). In 1999, the federal government spent $10.6 billion on the child care and development block grant and $840 million on Temporary Assistance to Needy Families child care funds; the states spent an extra $5 billion (U.S. General Accounting Office, 2001). In 2001, the federal government made an estimated "tax expenditure" of $2.4 billion on the dependent care tax credit and $0.7 billion on tax-free dependent care assistance plans provided by employers (U.S. House of Representatives, 2000, p. 780, Table 13-2).

5. For example, the child care and development block grant serves families whose incomes fall below 85 percent of the state's median income. In practice, however, not all eligible recipients receive funds; states concentrate their resources on families receiving TANF (welfare) and those who have recently exited TANF (U.S. General Accounting Office, 2001).

6. See Giannarelli and Barsimantov (2000, Figure 1).

7. See U.S. Bureau of the Census (2002, p. 2, Table 2: employed mothers below the poverty line were more likely to use relative care and less likely to use day care for their preschoolers.

8. For an overview, see Graetz and Schenk (2001, pp. 746–768). The tax benefit is most valuable to employees in high marginal tax brackets, that is, higher-income workers.

9. See Presser (1994).

10. See Kennickell, Starr-McCluer, and Surette (2000).

11. In 1998, 18 percent of U.S. households had zero net worth, and 30 percent had net worth of less than $10,000 (Wolff, 2000, Table 1).

12. For data on child care affordability, see Helburn and Bergmann (2002, pp. 1–6, 15–32).

13. See Langbein and Wolk (2000, pp. 26–27), showing that pension coverage generally increases with income, but that 15 percent of workers earning $50,000 or more have no pension coverage. Among workers earning from $15,000 to $19,999, roughly 30 percent have no pension coverage.

14. In 2000, the average public community college charged less than $1,500 per semester for tuition, and the average public four-year college charged about $3,800 (U.S. Bureau of the Census, 2001d, p. 173, Table 278).

15. To accomplish this, the law should adopt two measures. First, caretaker resource accounts should be nontransferable; they should not be legally divisible or available to satisfy a caretaker's obligations of any kind. Second, the divorce and child support laws should be amended to prohibit judges from taking into account the caretaker resource grant when awarding alimony or child support.

16. U.S. Bureau of the Census (2001d, Table 671).

17. In opinion polls, parents express concern about abuse and neglect in day care centers, and poor parents are especially concerned. See Public Agenda Online (2000b). Ethnographic studies confirm that working-class parents have a higher degree of trust in relatives and rely on relatives to impart shared values, traditions, and language (Zinsser, 2001, pp. 123–124).

18. For older children, relative care is less prevalent; beginning with the pre-school years, more children attend school, and fewer are cared for at home. See Capizzano et al. (2000, p. 3, Table 1); see also U.S. Bureau of the Census (2002, p. 4, Table 2, and p. 10, Table 4).

19. See, e.g., Ackerman and Alstott (1999, proposing a one-time capital grant); Van Parijs (1995, proposing a basic income). A real-world example exists in the state of Alaska, which has devoted some of its oil revenue to the Permanent Fund, which pays an equal dividend, nearly $2,000, to every man, woman, and child in Alaska each year.

20. On the difficulties of distinguishing between serious and incidental volunteer jobs, see Chapter 10.

21. The program could be expanded to small-business investments, but as the text suggests, there are significant monitoring problems and a greater potential for fraud, compared to the options of child care, education, and retirement savings. It is relatively easy to determine whether, say, a semester at a technical college costs $5,000, whether day care for two children costs

$5,000, or whether a financial institution properly accepted a $5,000 retirement account contribution. It is harder to determine whether $5,000 is appropriate seed capital for, and was spent on, the startup of a real-estate business.

22. See generally Bradford and Shaviro (1999).
23. For studies of higher-education subsidies, see Bound and Turner (1999); Dynarski (1999. 2000); Kane (1995); Lemieux and Card (1998).
24. Empirical studies of IRAs reach mixed results. See Bernheim and Scholz (1993); Engen, Gale, and Scholz (1994); Poterba, Venti, and Wise (1995).
25. See Alstott (1999).
26. See Chapter 3.
27. See Witchel (2002).
28. See, e.g., Mahony (1995); Wax (1998).
29. Even tax-based programs, sometimes thought to be cheap to administer, often have difficulty with income testing; the earned income tax credit (EITC), for instance, has been plagued by high rates of taxpayter error (often involving small violations of technical rules). See Alstott (1995, pp. 564–589).
30. The 20 percent tax is implied by the numbers given: to reduce a grant of $5,000 to zero over a $25,000 income range, a caretaker must forfeit twenty cents for every additional dollar of earnings.
31. See Gokhale, Kotlikoff, and Sluchynsky (2002, p. 61, Table 4), showing *marginal* tax rates for workers in families earning in this range; their Table 1 shows that *average* tax rates are lower.

Chapter 6. A Closer Look at Caretaker Resource Accounts

1. See Moffitt (1992). Other studies found that unreported levels of employment were much higher; recipients were evading the means test. See Edin and Lein (1997).
2. See Rosen (1999, overview); Eissa (1995, studying married women). For studies of single mothers and the EITC, see Eissa and Liebman (1996); B. Meyer and Rosenbaum (1999).
3. See, e.g., Berger and Black (1992); D. Blau (2001); D. Blau and Robins (1988); Connelly (1992); Han and Waldfogel (2001)
4. See Mahony (1995); Wax (1998).
5. Kennickell et al. (2000, p. 5, Table 1).
6. The seminal work on individual development accounts is Sherraden (1991). Michael Sherraden has been tireless in promoting the idea, which now has a national demonstration project. For human capital accounts for youth, see

Haveman (1986). For a discussion of the Blair plan, see Ackerman and Alstott (2001). The Blair plan has some striking similarities to stakeholding, which Bruce Ackerman and I proposed in Ackerman and Alstott (1999).

7. For this reason, we shall see in Chapter 11 that life-planning insurance rejects the account structure; it would be ineffectual to endow all families (or all families of children with disabilities) with a set amount, when the aim of the program is to address severe inequalities of circumstance.

8. See, e.g., Fineman (1995); Folbre (1994); Pateman (1988, 2002);Van Parijs (1995).

9. Indeed, I have defended basic income against alternative proposals for wage-based subsidies. See Alstott (1999).

10. See Edin and Lein (1997).

11. See Okin (1989, pp. 142–167).

12. Okin was well aware of the facts of marital breakdown; see, e.g., Okin (1989, pp. 172–173). My claim is not that she disregarded the facts, but that it has taken some time for us to internalize the trends they embody.

13. For leave policies focusing on men, see Malin (1994); Selmi (2000).

14. See Leira (1993, Sweden); Selmi (2000, pp. 755–759, data on U.S. fathers' leave patterns).

15. Rawls makes a similar point in Rawls (1997).

16. Following Nancy Chodorow (1978), Okin (1989, pp. 131–132) worries that the gendered division of child rearing has psychological consequences for both boys and girls, as girls come to identify with the mothering role and boys to reject it. The caretaker role, or the repudiation of it, becomes part of one's own identity. But the Chodorow theory is the subject of a lively debate; critics like Groskurth (1991) and others worry that Chodorow has turned a psychoanalytic into a sociological insight without adequate evidence. See Lorber, Coser, Rossi, and Chodorow (1981). Even if the theory accurately represents the psychodynamics of the traditional family, these dynamics might change if legal institutions help redefine the caretaker role. Today, children may equate caretaking not only with femininity but with powerlessness and reduced opportunities. If new institutions grant caretakers a greater range of opportunities and people lead more diverse lives, then the transmission of gender roles may change as well. In a social context in which mothers and fathers pursue a variety of life plans, one's own mother's choices may become less freighted, less a representation of the One Road to Motherhood. Children might still make the simple equation of women with caretaking, but they might also absorb a richer message about capable *people* and flexible lives.

Chapter 7. Life-Planning Insurance

1. For example, Toth (1997, pp. 20–21) mentions a study of 19 states in which 2 percent of children in foster care were placed there because of the child's disability.

2. For evidence of stress in families with disabled children, see, e.g., Mauldon (1992).

3. See e.g., Lukemeyer, Meyers, and Smeeding (2000); Marcenko and Meyers (1994).

4. For personal accounts of care for a child with a developmental disorder, see, e.g., Bérubé (1996); Featherstone (1980); Greenfeld (1978); Kittay (1999). For a study of the extra effort required to care for children with severe disabilities compared to ordinary children, see Roberts and Lawton (2001).

5. See, e.g., Featherstone (1980); Greenfeld (1978); Samuels (2000).

6. Breslau, Salkever, and Staruch (1982). That study found that the negative effects on work effort were greatest for black and low-income families. Meyers et al. (2000) found that low-income mothers with disabled children are 20 to 30 percent less likely to be employed than similar mothers with healthier children.

7. Einem and Cuskelly (2002).

8. See Lukemeyer, Meyers, and Smeeding (2000).

9. See Graetz and Mashaw (2000).

10. See, e.g., Dworkin (1981b, 2000).

11. See Kittay (1999, pp. 147–161).

12. The distinction is Dworkin's (1981b, 2000). The distinction between option luck and brute luck is not entirely clear-cut, of course. Even rare calamities are in some sense foreseeable and might be construed as matters of option luck. Here, I am not concerned with such borderline cases.

13. This basic principle may require modification in two circumstances. First, we might properly hold adolescents responsible for some of their decisions (to drink and drive, for instance); as children near adulthood, they should be understood to have a growing capacity to make gambles and take the consequences. Second, we might hold *parents* responsible if they put their children at risk in some way, for example, by letting them play with matches or ride motor scooters without helmets. But as to the *children*, a failure of parental supervision should still be brute luck: the children did not choose their parents.

14. See Ackerman (1980), pp. 186–195.

15. Compare, e.g., Ackerman (1980) with Dworkin (1981b).

16. This is a more radical position than it may appear. Today, caretakers are excluded from mainstream social insurance programs unless they hold a paid job over a long period or (in the case of certain programs) remain married to someone who does. See Ackerman and Alstott (1999, pp. 140–154).

17. See Haveman and Wolfe (2000, pp. 1033–1035); U.S. House of Representatives (2000, pp. 251–252).

18. Kelman and Lester (1998).

19. The objective standard ensures that parents receive assistance commensurate with the child's needs, and that different parents in similar situations receive similar assistance. Put another way, the program should not provide greater assistance to caretakers with a fragile, easily disrupted life than to those with a sturdier and more flexible one. A child's illness or disability may be more or less disruptive, depending on the parents' jobs and family arrangements. For example, a parent whose job requires extensive travel might find her life more disrupted than a parent with a local job if a child requires care that precludes travel. A parent with a job that requires daily presence at the office—a receptionist, say, or a construction supervisor—may be harder-pressed than someone who has more flexible working conditions. It would be difficult, as a practical matter, and not beyond debate, as a matter of fairness, for a program to attempt to mitigate these individualized risks, which follow from the nature of the pursuits that parents choose.

20. Featherstone (1980, pp. 186–188) offers concrete suggestions for support services and notes the difficulties parents face in finding them. For the value of respite care and its scarcity relative to demand today, see U.S. General Accounting Office (1990). For the complexities of creating viable respite care for very ill children, see Robinson, Jackson, and Townsley (2001).

21. See Warfield and Hauser-Cram (1996).

22. See Robinson et al. (2001), documenting the difficulties in finding care workers to care for children who are tube-fed, even though families feed the children on their own.

23. Medical personnel now routinely discharge quite sick children to home care, expecting caretakers to learn to administer complicated treatments and monitoring devices. See, e.g., Fisher (1998); Robinson et al. (2001).

24. Home health aides, who often have very little medical training and only a high school diploma (if that), make about $18,000 per year. Licensed practical nurses, typically with two years of post–high school training, make $30,000. Registered nurses earn $45,000 or so (U.S. Bureau of Labor Statistics, 2002, pp. 267–270, 287–288, 317–320, on median earnings).

25. See Lukemeyer, Meyers, and Smeeding (2000); Meyers, Brady, and Seto (2000).

26. See Warfield and Hauser-Cram (1996).
27. Many small providers do not comply with the ADA. See Buell and McCormick (1999). Under the law, centers cannot exclude disabled children unless the child's presence would create a "direct threat" to the safety of others or would require a "fundamental alteration" of the program. See U.S. Department of Justice (2002). For case law, see, e.g., *Burriola v. Greater Toledo YMCA*, 133 F. Supp. 1034 (Dist. Ohio, 2001), holding that the ADA required YMCA afterschool program to make greater efforts to accommodate disruptive behavior by an autistic child.
28. See, e.g., Featherstone (1980, pp. 57–58).
29. Ibid., 76–80.
30. See Danish Ministry of Social Affairs (2002); Gartner, Kerzner, Lipsky, and Turnbull (1991, pp. 113–115).
31. See Gartner et al. (1991, pp. 115–120). Programs as of the early 1990s included an attendance care allowance and an invalid care allowance, with the latter targeted especially to parents who cannot work because they care for a person with a severe disability.
32. See U.S. House of Representatives (2000, pp. 16–35).
33. See Graetz and Mashaw (2000, pp. 205–206); U.S. House of Representatives (2000, pp. 279–314).
34. For a summary of programs that provide income support or educational, medical, or social services to children with disabilities, see Future of Children (1996).
35. 29 U.S.C. sec. 2601 et seq.
36. Whether the "serious health condition" language of FMLA would permit leave in such a case depends on the child's condition and course of treatment. The statutory language emphasizes inpatient care or continuing medical treatment; the model is an illness model rather than a disability model (29 U.S.C. sec. 2611).
37. See Graetz and Mashaw (2000, chapters 4 and 11).
38. In 1999, the federal SSI benefit for an individual represented an income equal to 75 percent of the poverty threshold (U.S. House of Representatives, 2000, p. 244, Table 3-9). The "last resort" language is taken from p. 225.
39. U.S. House of Representatives (2000, p. 229, Table 3.3).
40. U.S. House of Representatives (2000, p. 252).
41. For Medicaid eligibility, see U.S. House of Representatives (2000, pp. 892–903). Children may qualify because they live in poor families, because they are disabled and receive SSI, or because they are "medically needy." In 1998, more than 50 percent of children under the poverty level received Medicaid (p. 902, Table 15-12). Some children can qualify for Medicaid even if

they come from middle-class families but require extensive and expensive medical care.

42. 20 U.S.C. sec. 1400 et seq. For an overview of the expenses associated with IDEA, see Haveman and Wolfe (2000, pp. 1035–1037).

43. See Future of Children, 1996; Gartner, Lipsky, and Turnbull (1991, pp. 123, 160–161).

44. See, e.g., Oregon State Office for Services to Children and Families (1996), authorizing limited-duration housekeeping services to families if the care of ill or handicapped children precludes normal housekeeping.

45. See Gartner et al. (1991, pp. 160–161); U.S. General Accounting Office (1990, pp. 3–4).

46. See Waldfogel (1998b).

47. The 12 weeks that FMLA offers may also be about right. Job leave is better suited to short-term emergencies in children's lives than to long-term absences from work, which tend to erode the leavetaker's firm-specific human capital. In addition, if children suffer disabilities that permanently interfere with a parent's ability to hold a paid job, job retention by definition diminishes in importance as a means of mitigating damage to caretakers' lives.

Chapter 8. Parents and Paid Work

1. For thoughtful work taking a pragmatic view of paid employment for mothers, see Bergmann (1986, 1996). Joan Williams (2000) is an important proponent of workplace reforms, but she also devotes significant attention to family law reforms to improve mothers' financial position, whether or not they hold paid jobs.

2. For two thoughtful expressions of such theories, see Fraser (1996); Schultz (2000).

3. See Bergmann (1986, 1996).

4. See Graetz and Mashaw (2000) for an especially well-worked-out and comprehensive vision of a support strategy for working parents.

5. For a variety of family-friendly workplace ideas, see Crittenden (2001); Williams (2000).

6. A majority of Americans from every income class prefer to have one parent take time out of the paid workforce to care for young children. See Sylvester (2001, pp. 53–61); see also Public Agenda Online (2000a).

7. See Williams (2000). Ann Crittenden (2001) also takes a more holistic approach; she proposes a variety of reforms to assist mothers in very different circumstances.

8. Social science studies suggest that working mothers *as a group* suffer fewer episodes of depression and isolation than their at-home peers. But these studies commonly suffer from self-selection bias. The studies do not (for obvious reasons) randomly assign one group to work and the other to stay at home; instead, they study people in their chosen state. The result is an inevitable bias toward finding depression and other mental illness or efficacy problems in the at-home group, simply because depressed or ill people are more likely to be at home. See Ross and Mirowsky (1988); Waldron and Jacobs (1988). More detailed studies reveal that depression and isolation are functions as much of other factors as of one's participation in paid work; for example, working women with a supportive spouse and good child care are happier than the average, and working women with child care problems or spousal conflict suffer the highest levels of stress and depression of any group (Ross and Mirowsky, 1988). Parents' sharing of high-schedule-control and low-control tasks also matters, as does women's perception of the fairness of the division of household tasks. See Barnett and Shen (1997); Shelton and John (1996). One of the clearest contributors is the mother's own opinion of her path: whether working or at home, mothers who feel the most strain in combining (or forgoing) their dual roles report great stress, whereas mothers at peace with their roles report greater well-being Goldsmith, Veum, and Darity, 1996, report that mothers who chose to leave the workforce felt more control than unemployed mothers seeking work.

9. See Kelman (2001, pp. 841–842). It is an empirical question whether any particular policy would represent an accommodation in this sense.

10. See F. Blau et al. (1998, pp. 207–209).

11. See Cohn (2000, pp. 97–105).

12. Burkett (2000); see also Case (2001).

Chapter 9. Practical Limitations of the Family-Friendly Workplace

1. See Chapter 7.

2. 29 U.S.C. sec. 2601 et seq. Employees qualify if they have worked for the same employer for at least a year and worked at least 1,250 hours during the past year. In general, companies that employ 50 or more workers must comply with FMLA.

3. For a study arguing that the costs of parental job leave are lower than replacing a worker who quits, see Marra and Lindner (1994). They assume, however, that denial of leave means that the worker will quit and do not consider the alternative that people would otherwise stay on the job and

take shorter leaves using accrued sick days, vacation time, and individually negotiated leave.

4. See Mitchell (1990); Summers (1989).
5. See Hamermesh (1979, payroll taxes); Gruber and Krueger (1990) and Viscusi and Moore (1987, 1991, workers' compensation).
6. The classic prediction is that the minimum wage reduces employment of low-wage workers because it requires an above-market wage. Because the law by definition precludes wage cuts, employers respond by cutting employment of low-skilled workers and by substituting capital or higher-skilled (and more productive) workers. In recent years, economists have debated the magnitude of the employment losses due to the minimum wage, but the basic prediction remains standard. For the debate focusing on Card and Krueger's (1995, 1998) work, see Neumark, Schweitzer, and Wascher (2000); Neumark and Wascher (2000); see also Organisation for Economic Co-operation and Development (1998, pp. 42–45); Shaviro (1997).
7. See, e.g., Cantor et al. (2001, Appendix Table A2-2.14); a higher percentage of female workers than male workers take FMLA leave for children.
8. These graphs represent a simplification of Christine Jolls's (2000, pp. 236–251) helpful analysis. Ruhm (1997) contains a similar discussion.
9. Jolls (2000).
10. Gruber (1994).
11. See Waldfogel (1997). Jolls (2000, pp. 296–297) points out that many women were entitled to FMLA-type benefits before enactment of the law, and that it is not clear whether women's leave-taking increased after enactment of FMLA.
12. See Cantor et al. (2001, Table A2-6.12); Waldfogel (2001, p. 19, Table 2).
13. In 2000, nearly 90 percent of U.S. businesses were not subject to FMLA. Nearly 60 percent of workers worked in FMLA-covered establishments (Cantor et al., 2001, Table 3.1).
14. 29 U.S.C. sec. 2614.
15. Ruhm (1998).
16. See Chapter 7.
17. For a thoughtful proposal for social insurance for job leave, see Issacharoff and Rosenblum (1994).
18. Broder (2002) briefly describes the new legislation.
19. If the government over- or undercompensated for employers' costs, the program could create worse distortions in employment. See Alstott (1999) for a description of the difficulties involved in structuring employment subsidies.

20. Under Title VII, it is illegal to discriminate against *mothers* and potential mothers, but it may be acceptable to discriminate against *parents*. See *Phillips v. Martin-Marietta*, 400 U.S. 542 (1971); *King v. Trans World Airlines*, 738 F. 2d 255 (8th Cir. 1984); *Trezza v. The Hartford, Inc.*, 78 FEP 1826 (S.D.N.Y. 1998).

21. Jolls (2000, pp. 255–257).

22. See, e.g., Hantrais and Letablier (1996); Leira (1993).

23. See Waldfogel (2001, p. 103, Table 1).

24. See Organisation for Economic Co-operation and Development (2001, p. 45, Chart A5.1).

25. See Williams (2000, pp. 51–52).

26. See Hantrais and Letablier (1996); Leira (1993).

27. A high percentage of employers have some job leave policy. For example, a 1998 study of a representative sample of large companies found that 90 percent offered 12 weeks or more of parental leave. Although these companies are subject to FMLA, 33 percent offered more than 12 weeks of maternity leave, and 16 percent offered more than 12 weeks of paternity leave. In addition, 53 percent of companies go beyond the FMLA mandate and offer at least some replacement pay during maternity leave; 13 percent do so for paternity leave. See Families and Work Institute (1998, p. 4).

28. Ruhm (1998). Suppose that the social insurance benefit is funded by a new payroll tax $T on every worker. For young women, the group most likely to take leave, the benefit is likely to have a value greater than $T (because $T is the pro rata cost allocated to all workers, not just young women). The program thus represents a wage increase in effect.

29. See, e.g., Bravo (1991, p. 170).

30. See, e.g., Radcliffe Public Policy Center (2000, pp. 3–4, 82 percent of young men age 21–39 and 85 percent of young women agreed that having a work schedule that allows time with family is "very important"); Families and Work Institute (1997, finding that 70 percent of parents felt they did not have enough time with their children, and that 63 percent of workers would prefer to work fewer hours).

31. Radcliffe Public Policy Center (2000, p. 3): 61 percent of respondents said they wished to spend more time with their families and would sacrifice pay to do so.

32. Cantor et al. (2001, Appendix Tables A2-5.20 and A2-5.21).

33. See Galinsky, Bond, and Freeman (1996, pp. 117–118). They found that mothers were more likely than fathers to express a willingness to make trade-offs to secure part-time work, telecommuting, or flextime.

34. See Sugarman (1987).

Chapter 10. Implementing Caretaker Resource Accounts

1. In 2001, median weekly earnings for full-time male workers over age 25 were $722 (U.S. Department of Labor, 2001, Table 37). Ninety percent of that is $650, 80 percent is $578, and 70 percent is $505. Thus, the *weekly* motherhood wage gap for full-time workers is from $72 to $145, implying an annual gap (based on a 50-week year) of $3,600 to $7,250. This is, of course, a rough translation of Waldfogel's (1998a, 1998b) estimate.

2. U.S. Bureau of the Census (2001d, p. 173, Table 278).

3. Not coincidentally, current subsidies for higher education fall in the same range. The average Pell grant in 2000 was about $2,000; federal student loans averaged about $3,800 (U.S. Bureau of the Census, 2001d, p. 172, Table 276).

4. See U.S. Bureau of the Census (2001d, p. 350, Table 535): aggregate contributions of $104 billion and 31 million active participants.

5. The lower figure is for individual retirement accounts; the higher is for qualified pension plans. See Graetz and Schenk (2001, p. 763).

6. See U.S. Bureau of the Census (2002, p. 15, Table 7, and p. 17, Table 8).

7. Ibid., p. 17, Table 8.

8. U.S. Bureau of the Census (2001d, Table 671).

9. See Alstott (1996).

10. See I.R.C. sec. 21.

11. Some administrative complexities remain; for example, custody decrees may inaccurately describe the child's actual living arrangements. The law might either presume that the custody decree is correct, placing the burden on the parents to go to court and amend the decree, or else adopt a rule that turns on the child's *actual* presence in the household. The tax law takes this latter course. See I.R.C. sec. 32(c) (3), 152(e)(1).

12. The problem is most severe when parents live together, but even when they live apart and share custody, the sacrifices each caretaker makes will not always mirror the legal terms of the custody decree. For example, even in cases of joint physical custody, mothers do more of the everyday work than fathers. See Maccoby and Mnookin (1992, p. 213, Table 9.2).

13. See Deutsch (1999); Hochschild (1989, 1997).

14. See Chapter 2.

15. "Parent" should, of course, be understood in the broad sense to include any legal parent or guardian; a "parent" thus might be a biological or adoptive parent, or a grandparent, aunt, or uncle, or even a nonrelative who is the child's legal guardian.

16. To avoid gaming, the earnings measure should take into account not only cash salary but pension contributions and other deferred compensation (e.g., options). For administrability, earnings would be determined retrospectively; that is, one would look to the previous year's tax return for the earnings comparison. The retrospective method does raise a first-year question: Which parent receives the caretaker resource account in the year of a (first) child's birth? In that situation, the prior year's earnings reveal little about the caretaker role. I am inclined to favor a maternal preference, on the grounds that the biological commitment of the mother in the early months renders that year unique. Alternatively, one might defer awarding the first year's grant of $5,000 until the following year, and at that time award $10,000 based on the initial year's earnings.

17. Winkler (1998). The data include families with and without children; I have been unable to find data that focus specifically on couples with children.

18. See Rhode (1989, pp. 111–125).

19. Parents could also create administrative controversies in order to sabotage each other. For instance, suppose that parents are separated and that the father has physical custody of the children. If the mother has lower earnings, she could claim (falsely) to be resident in the same household and claim the caretaker account. Although the father could eventually prevail, the mother's claim could delay payment of the caretaker account, and she might gain leverage in divorce negotiations by threatening to do so. (Similar problems can arise in the tax law, which requires residence determinations in the EITC and the dependency rules.) Under current law, hostile spouses can plague one another with litigation, but the caretaker account opens up a new venue for infighting: some couples will, for the first time, have money to fight over.

20. For example, a primary caretaker might lose only one-third of her $5,000 allotment in the first year of a relative earnings change, two-thirds in the second year, and so on. That rule would minimize arbitrary shifting based on temporary income fluctuations but also would create an incumbency advantage for the child's first caretaker.

21. See Alstott, 1995; Yin, Scholz, Forman, and Mazur, 1994 (similar issues in the earned income tax credit).

22. See Mahony (1995); Wax (1998).

23. See, e.g., Kamo (2000).

24. See Laibson (1997, 1998).

25. See Bradford and Shaviro (1999).

26. Caretakers in school should also be able to withdraw funds for child care.

27. U.S. Bureau of the Census (2002, p. 3, Table 1).

28. Individual retirement accounts lock up funds only through a tax penalty; I may cash in my IRA at any time, if I am willing to pay income taxes and penalty taxes on the withdrawal. Employer pensions, in contrast, usually lock up funds quite effectively, using the employer as the gatekeeper. That regime is not suitable to a portable system that benefits individuals directly rather than workers at specific firms. The IRA model might, however, be adapted to the new program. Financial institutions would be permitted to accept "caretaker retirement accounts" *only* if they adopted measures to ensure no cash withdrawals (or loans) before the beneficiary provided evidence that he had reached retirement age.

29. See, e.g., Graetz and Goldberg (1999); Graetz and Mashaw (2000, pp. 292–293).

30. See generally Bradford and Shaviro (1999).

Chapter 11. Implementing Life-Planning Insurance for Parents

1. See Graetz and Mashaw (2000, pp. 70–73).

2. For a description of the SSI disability standard for children, see U.S. House of Representatives (2000, pp. 251–252).

3. See Mashaw (1983).

4. The classic book is Lipsky (1980).

5. See Graetz and Mashaw (2000, pp. 208, 264–267); Sugarman (1987).

6. Income support poses different, but more familiar, problems. The difficulty is to measure need appropriately. In principle, life-planning insurance should identify families in which the child's need for care takes up so much parental time that parents' working time is limited. There are other reasons why parents may not work, or if they do, may still be poor: parental disability, parents' earning capacity, and so on. But life-planning insurance is not intended to function as an adult disability program or as a general wage subsidy.

7. See Graetz and Mashaw (2000); Ulrich (2002).

8. Graetz and Mashaw (2000, pp. 87–91).

Conclusion

1. See Ackerman and Alstott (1999).

2. See Broder (2002).

References

Ackerman, B. (1980). *Social justice in the liberal state.* New Haven: Yale University Press.

Ackerman, B., and Alstott, A. (1999). *The stakeholder society.* New Haven: Yale University Press.

Ackerman, B., and Alstott, A. (2001, May 6). Tony Blair's big idea. *New York Times,* sec. 4, p. 15.

Alstott, A. (1995). The earned income tax credit and the limitations of tax-based welfare reform. *Harvard Law Review, 108(3),* 533–592.

Alstott, A. (1999). Work versus freedom: A liberal challenge to employment subsidies. *Yale Law Journal, 108,* 967–1058.

American Law Institute. (1998). *Principles of the law of family dissolution.* Draft.

Anderson, D., Binder, M., and Krause, K. (2001, February 6). *The motherhood wage penalty revisited: Experience, heterogeneity, work effort and work-schedule flexibility.* SSRN Working Paper. www.ssrn.com.

Angrist, J. D., and Evans, W. N. (1996, September). *Children and their parents' labor supply: Evidence from exogenous variation in family size.* NBER Working Paper No. 5778.

Arendell, T. (1995). *Fathers and divorce.* Thousand Oaks, Calif.: Sage Publications.

Arneson, R., and Shapiro, I. (1996). Democratic autonomy and religious freedom: A critique of *Wisconsin v. Yoder.* In I. Shapiro (Ed.), *Democracy's place,* pp. 137–174. Ithaca, N.Y.: Cornell University Press.

Barnett, R. C., and Shen, Y. (1997). Gender, high- and low-schedule-control housework tasks, and psychological distress. *Journal of Family Issues, 18(4)*, 403–428.

Bartholet, E. (1999). *Nobody's children.* Boston: Beacon Press.

Bartlett, K. T. (1984). Rethinking parenthood as an exclusive status: The need for legal alternatives when the premise of the nuclear family has failed. *Virginia Law Review, 70, 879–963.*

Bartlett, K. T. (1999) Child custody in the 21st century: How the American Law Institute proposes to achieve predictability and still protect the individual child's best interests. *Willamette Law Review, 35(3), 467–483.*

Bartlett, K. T., and Stack, C. (1986). Joint custody, feminism, and the dependency dilemma. *Berkeley Women's Law Journal, 9, 13–41.*

Berger, M. C., and Black, D. A. (1992). Child care subsidies, quality of care, and the labor supply of low-income, single mothers. *Review of Economics and Statistics, 74(4), 635–642.*

Bergmann, B. (1986). *The economic emergence of women.* New York: Basic Books.

Bergmann, B. (1996). *Saving our children from poverty: What the U.S. can learn from France.* New York: Russell Sage Foundation.

Bernheim, B. D., and Scholz, J. K. (1993). Private saving and public policy. In *Tax policy and the economy* (Vol. 7, pp. 73–110). Cambridge: MIT Press.

Bernstein, N. (2001). *The lost children of Wilder.* New York: Pantheon.

Bérubé, M. (1996). *Life as we know it.* New York: Pantheon.

Bianchi, S. M., Milkie, M. A., and Sayer, L. C.(2000). Is anyone doing the housework? Trends in the gender division of household labor. *Social Forces, 79(2),* 191–228.

Blank, R. (1997). *It takes a nation.* Princeton, N.J.: Princeton University Press.

Blau, D. M. (2001). *The child care problem.* New York: Russell Sage Foundation.

Blau, D., and Robins, P. (1989). Fertility, employment, and child care costs. *Demography, 26, 287–299.*

Blau, F. (1998). Trends in the well-being of American women, 1970–1995. *Journal of Economic Literature, 36(1), 112–165.*

Blau, F., Ferber, M. A., and Winkler, A. E. (1998). *The economics of women, men, and work* (3rd ed.). Upper Saddle River, N.J.: Prentice Hall.

Blustein, J. (1982). *Parents and children.* New York: Oxford University Press.

Boswell, J. (1988). *The kindness of strangers.* New York: Pantheon.

Bound, J., and Turner, S. E. (1999, December). *Going to war and going to college: Did World War II and the G.I. Bill increase educational attainment for returning veterans?* NBER Working Paper No. 7452.

Bradford, D. F., and Shaviro, D. N. (1999). *The economics of vouchers.* NBER Working Paper No. 7092.

Bravo, E. (1991). Family leave: The need for a new minimum standard. In J. S. Hyde and M. J. Essex (Eds.) *Parental leave and child care* (pp. 165–175). Philadelphia: Temple University Press.

Breslau, N., Salkever, D., and Staruch, K. S. (1982). Women's labor force activity and responsibilities for disabled dependents: A study of families with disabled children. *Journal of Health and Social Behavior, 23(1)*, 169–183.

Broder, J. M. (2002, September 24). Family leave in California now includes pay benefit. *New York Times*, sec. A, p. 20.

Bronars, S. G., and Grogger, J. (1994, December). The economic consequences of unwed motherhood: Using twin births as a natural experiment. *American Economic Review, 84(5)*, 1141–1156.

Budig, M. J., and England, P. (2001). The wage penalty for motherhood. *American Sociology Review, 66(2)*, 204–225.

Buell, M. J., McCormick, M. G., and Hallam, R. A. (1999). Inclusion in a childcare context: Experiences and attitudes of family childcare providers. *Topics in Early Childhood Special Education, 19(2)*, 217–224.

Bumpass, L., and Lu, H. (2000). Trends in cohabitation and implications for children's family contexts in the United States. *Population Studies, 54(1)*, 29–41.

Burggraf, S. P. (1997). *The feminine economy and economic man.* Reading, Mass.: Addison-Wesley.

Burkett, E. (2000). *The baby boon.* New York: Free Press.

Burrell, B. C. (1994). *A woman's place is in the House.* Ann Arbor: University of Michigan Press.

Buss, E. (2000). The parental rights of minors. *Buffalo Law Review, 48*, 785–833.

Buss, E. (2002). "Parental" rights. *Virginia Law Review, 88*, 635–683.

Cantor, D., et al. (2001). *Balancing the needs of families and employers: Family and medical leave surveys, a report submitted to the U.S. Department of Labor.* (accessed 17 September 2002).

Capizzano, J., Adams, G., and Sonenstein, F. (2000, March). *Child care arrangements for children under five: Variation across states.* The Urban Institute, No. B-7.

Card, D., and Krueger, A. B. (1995). *Myth and measurement.* Princeton, N.J.: Princeton University Press.

Card, D., and Krueger, A. B. (1998, January). *A reanalysis of the effect of the New Jersey minimum wage increase on the fast-food industry with representative payroll data.* NBER Working Paper No. 6386.

Carrieri, J. R. (1991). *Child custody, foster care, and adoptions.* New York: Lexington Books.

Case, M. A. (2001). How high the apple pie? A few troubling questions about where, why, and how the burden of care for children should be shifted. *Chicago-Kent Law Review, 76(3)*, 1753–1786.

Catalyst. (1997). *A new approach to flexibility: Managing the work/time equation.*

Chaifetz, J. (1999). Listening to foster children in accordance with the law: The failure to serve children in state care. *New York University Review of Law and Social Change, 25(1),* 1–28.

Chambers, D. L. (1984). Rethinking the substantive rules for custody disputes in divorce. *Michigan Law Review, 83,* 477–569.

Chambers, D. L. (1989). Accommodation and satisfaction: Women and men lawyers and the balance of work and family. *Law and Social Inquiry, 14,* 251–287.

Chodorow, N. (1978). *The reproduction of motherhood.* Berkeley: University of California Press.

Choudhury, S., and Leonesio, M. V. (1997). Life-cycle aspects of poverty among older women. *Social Security Bulletin, 60(2),* 17–36.

Cohn, S. (2000). *Race and gender discrimination at work.* Boulder, Colo.: Westview Press.

Cole, M., and Cole, S. R. (1993). *The development of children.* New York: Scientific American Books.

Conlin, M., Merritt, J., and Himelstein, L. (2002, November 25). Mommy is really home from work. *Business Week,* p. 101.

Connelly, R. (1992). The effect of child care costs on married women's labor force participation. *Review of Economics and Statistics, 74(1),* 83–90.

Crittenden, A. (2001). *The price of motherhood.* New York: Metropolitan Books.

Dale, M. J., et al. (2000). *Representing the child client.* Lexis Nexis.

Daniel, B., Wassell, S., and Gilligan, R. (1999). *Child development for child care and protection workers.* London: Jessica Kingsley.

Danish Ministry of Social Affairs (2002). *Social policy in Denmark.* www.sm.dk/eng/dansk_socialpolitik/index.html (accessed 1 October 2003).

Davies, D. (1999). *Child development.* New York: Guilford Press.

Demo, D. H., and Acock, A. C. (1993). Family diversity and the division of domestic labor: How much have things really changed? *Family Relations, 42(3),* 323–331.

Deutsch, F. M. (1999). *Halving it all.* Cambridge, Mass.: Harvard University Press.

Dixon, S. D., and Stein, M. T. (2000). *Encounters with children.* St. Louis: Mosby Year Book.

Dworkin, R. (1981b). What is equality? Part 2: Equality of resources. *Philosophy and Public Affairs, 10(3),* 283–345.

Dworkin, R. (2000). *Sovereign virtue.* Cambridge, Mass.: Harvard University Press.

Dynarski, S. M. (1999, November). *Does aid matter? Measuring the effect of student aid on college attendance and completion.* NBER Working Paper No. 7422.

Dynarski, S. M. (2000, June). *Hope for whom? Financial aid for the middle class and its impact on college attendance.* NBER Working Paper No. 7756.

Edin, K., and Lein, L. (1997). *Making ends meet.* New York: Russell Sage Foundation.

Einem, M., and Cuskelly, M. (2002). Paid employment of mothers and fathers of an adult child with multiple disabilities. *Journal of Intellectual Disability Research, 46(2),* 158–167.

Eissa, N. (1995). *Taxation and labor supply of married women: The Tax Reform Act of 1986 as natural experiment.* NBER Working Paper No. 5023

Eissa, N., and Liebman, J. B. (1996). Labor supply response to the Earned Income Tax Credit. *Quarterly Journal of Economics, 111(2),* 605–637.

Engen, E. M., Gale, W. G., and Scholz, J. K. (1994). Do savings incentives work? *1994 Brookings Papers on Economic Activity,* pp. 85–151.

Eyer, D. E. (1992). *Mother-infant bonding.* New Haven, Conn.: Yale University Press.

Fagenson, E. A., and Jackson, J. J. (1994). The status of women managers in the United States. In N. J. Adler and D. N. Izraeli (Eds.), *Competitive frontiers in a global economy* (pp. 388–405). Cambridge, Mass.: Blackwell.

Families and Work Institute. (1997). *1997 National Study of the Changing Workforce.* https://swww.igc.apc.org/fwi/pubs/nscw.pdf (accessed 25 April 2001).

Families and Work Institute. (1998). *1998 Business Work-Life Study.* https:/swww.igc.apc.org/fwi/pubs/worklife.pdf (accessed 17 April 2001).

Featherstone, H. (1980). *A difference in the family.* New York: Basic Books.

Federal Interagency Forum on Child and Family Statistics. (2001). *America's children: Key national indicators of well-being.* www.childstats.gov/americaschildren (accessed 15 June 2002).

Feinberg, J. (1980). The child's right to an open future. In W. Aiken and H. LaFollette (Eds.), *Whose child? Children's rights, parental authority, and state power* (pp. 124–153). Totowa, N.J.: Rowman and Littlefield.

Feinberg, J. (1986). *Harm to self.* New York: Oxford University Press.

Fineman, M. (1995). *The neutered mother.* New York: Routledge.

Fisher, I. (1998, June 7). Health care comes home. *New York Times,* sec. 1, p. 1.

Fishkin, J. (1983). *Justice, equal opportunity, and the family.* New Haven, Conn.: Yale University Press.

Folbre, N. (1994). *Who pays for the kids?* New York: Routledge.

Folbre, N. (2001). *The invisible heart.* New York: New Press.

Fonagy, P. (2001). *Attachment theory and psychoanalysis.* New York: Other Press.

Fraser, N. (1996). *Justice interruptus.* New York: Routledge.

Future of Children. (1996). Special education for students with disabilities, Appendix: Selected federal programs serving children with disabilities. *Future of*

Children, 6(1), 162–173, www.futureofchildren.org/information2826/
information_show.htm?doc_id=72518 (accessed 30 September 2002).

Galinsky, E., Bond, J. T., and Friedman, D. E. (1996). The role of employers in
addressing the needs of employed parents. *Journal of Social Issues, 52,* 111–136.

Gangadharan, J., and Rosenbloom, J. L. (1996, July). *The effects of child-bearing on
married women's labor supply and earnings: Using twin births as a natural
experiment.* NBER Working Paper No. 5647.

Gartner, A., Lipsky, D. K., and Turnbull, A. P. (1991). *Supporting families with a
child with a disability.* Baltimore: Brookes Publishing.

George, R. (1987). Who should bear the cost of children? *Public Affairs Quarterly,
1,* 1–33.

Giannarelli, L., and Barsimantov, J. (2000, December). *Child care expenses of
America's families.* Urban Institute, Assessing the New Federalism Project,
http://www.urban.org/Template.cfm?Section=ByAuthor&Nav-
MenuID=63&template=/TaggedContent/ViewPublication.cfm&Publica-
tionID=7496 (accessed 8 October 2003).

Gokhale, J., Kotlikoff, L. J., and Sluchynsky, A. (2002, August). *Does it pay to work?*
NBER Working Paper No. w9096.

Goldin, C. (1997). Career and family: College women look to the past. In F. D.
Blau and R. G. Ehrenberg (Eds.), *Gender and family issues in the workplace*
(pp. 20–58). New York: Russell Sage.

Goldsmith, A. H., Veum, J. R., and Darity, W., Jr. (1996). The psychological impact
of unemployment and joblessness. *Journal of Sociology and Economics, 25*(3),
333–58.

Goldstein, J. (1984). In whose best interest? In J. Folberg (Ed.), *Joint custody and
shared parenting* (pp. 47–55). Washington, D.C.: Bureau of National Affairs.

Goldstein, J., Freud, A., and Solnit, A. J. (1973). *Beyond the best interests of the
child.* New York: Free Press.

Goldstein, J., Freud, A., and Solnit, A. J. (1979a). *Before the best interests of the
child.* New York: Free Press.

Goldstein, J., Freud, A., and Solnit, A. J. (1979b). *Beyond the best interests of the
child* (2nd ed.). New York: Free Press.

Goldstein, J., Freud, A., and Solnit, A. J. (1996). *The best interests of the child.* New
York: Free Press.

Goldstein, J., Freud, A., Solnit, A. J., and Goldstein, S. (1985). *In the best interests of
the child.* New York: Free Press.

Graetz, M. J., and Goldberg, F. (1999, February). *Reforming Social Security: A practical and workable system of personal retirement accounts.* NBER Working
Paper No. 6970.

Graetz, M. J., and Mashaw, J. (2000). *True security.* New Haven, Conn.: Yale University Press.

Graetz, M. J., and Schenk, D. H. (2001). *Federal income taxation* (4th ed.). New York: Foundation Press.

Grant, L., Simpson, L. A., Rong, X. L., and Peters-Golden, H. (1990). Gender, parenthood, and work hours of physicians. *Journal of Marriage and the Family, 52(1),* 39–49.

Greenfeld, J. (1978). *A place for Noah.* New York: Holt, Rinehart and Winston.

Grosskurth, P. (1991, October 24). The new psychology of women. *New York Review of Books, 38,* 25–32.

Gruber, J. (1994). The incidence of mandated maternity benefits. *American Economic Review, 84(3),* 622–641.

Gruber, J., and Krueger, A. B. (1991). The incidence of mandated employer-provided insurance: Lessons from workers' compensation insurance. In D. Bradford (Ed.), *Tax policy and the economy* (pp. 111–144). Cambridge, Mass.: MIT Press.

Gutmann, A. (1987). *Democratic education.* Princteon, N.J.: Princeton University Press.

Hamermesh, D. S. (1979). New estimates of the incidence of the payroll tax. *Southern Economic Journal, 45(4),* 1208–1219.

Han, J., and Waldfogel, W. (2001). Child care costs and women's employment: A comparison of single and married mothers with pre-school-aged children. *Social Science Quarterly, 82(3),* 552–568.

Hantrais, L., and Letablier, M. (1996). *Families and family policies in Europe.* London: Longman.

Haralambie, A. M. (1993). *Handling child custody, abuse, and adoption cases.* Colorado Springs, Colo.: Shepard's/McGraw-Hill.

Haveman, R. H. (1986). *Starting even.* New York: Simon and Schuster.

Haveman, R. H., and Wolfe, B. (2000). The economics of disability and disability policy. In A. J. Culyer and J. P. Newhouse (Eds.), *Handbook of health economics* (pp. 995–1051). Amsterdam: Elsevier Science, North-Holland.

Helburn, S. W., and Bergmann, B. R. (2002). *America's childcare problem.* New York: Palgrave.

Hewlett, S. A. (2002). *Creating a life.* New York: Talk Miramax Books.

Hochschild, A. R. (1989). *The second shift.* New York: Penguin.

Hochschild, A. R. (1997). *The time bind.* New York: Metropolitan.

Hundley, G. (2000). Male/female earnings differences in self-employment: The effects of marriage, children, and the household division of labor. *Industrial and Labor Relations Review, 54(1),* 95–114.

Issacharoff, S., and Rosenblum, E. (1994). Women and the workplace: Accommodating the demands of pregnancy. *Columbia Law Review, 94,* 2154–2221.

Jolls, C. (2000). Accommodation mandates. *Stanford Law Review, 53(2),* 223–306.

Kamo, Y. (2000). "He said, she said": Assessing discrepancies in husbands' and wives' reports on the division of household labor. *Social Science Research, 29(4),* 459–476.

Kane, T. J. (1995, July). *Rising public college tuition and college entry: How well do public subsidies promote access to college?* NBER Working Paper No. 5164.

Kelly, J. B., and Lamb, M. E. (2000). Using child development research to make appropriate custody and access decisions for young children. *Family and Conciliation Courts Review, 38(2),* 297–311.

Kelly, R. F., and Ward, S. L. (2002). Allocating custodial responsibilities at divorce: Social science research and the American Law Institute's approximation rule. *Family Court Review, 40(3),* 350–365.

Kelman, M. (2001). Market discrimination and groups. *Stanford Law Review, 53(4),* 833–896.

Kelman, M., and Lester, G. (1998). *Jumping the queue.* Cambridge, Mass.: Harvard University Press.

Kennickell, A. B., Starr-McCluer, M., and Surette, B. J. (2000). Recent changes in U.S. family finances: Results from the 1998 Survey of Consumer Finances, (accessed 10 July 2002).

Kittay, E. F. (1999). *Love's labor.* New York: Routledge.

Klerman, J. A., and Leibowitz, A. (1999, May). Job continuity among new mothers. *Demography, 36(1),* 145–155.

Laibson, D. (1997). Golden eggs and hyperbolic discounting. *Quarterly Journal of Economics, 112(2),* 443–477.

Laibson, D. (1998). Life-cycle consumption and hyperbolic discount functions. *European Economic Review, 42(3–5),* 861–871.

Langbein, J. H. (1988). The twentieth-century revolution in family wealth transmission. *Michigan Law Review, 86,* 722–751.

Langbein, J. H., and Wolk, B. A. (2000). *Pension and employee benefit law.* New York: Foundation Press.

Leira, A. (1993). The "woman-friendly" welfare state? The case of Norway and Sweden. In J. Lewis (Ed.), *Women and social policies in Europe* (pp. 49–71). Aldershot, England: Edward Elgar.

Lemieux, T., and Card, D. (1998, September). *Education, earnings and the "Canadian G.I. Bill."* NBER Working Paper No. 5718.

Lipsky, M. (1980). *Street-level bureaucracy.* New York: Russell Sage.

Lorber, J., Coser, R. L., Rossi, A. L., and Chodorow, N. (1981). On the reproduction of mothering: A methodological debate. *Signs, 6,* 482–514.

Lukemeyer, A., Meyers, M. K., and Smeeding, T. (2000). Expensive children in poor families: Out-of-pocket expenditures for the care of disabled and chronically ill children in welfare families. *Journal of Marriage and Family, 62(2),* 399–415.

Maccoby, E. E., and Mnookin, R. H. (1992). *Dividing the child.* Cambridge, Mass.: Harvard University Press.

Mahony, R. (1995). *Kidding ourselves.* New York: Basic Books.

Malin, M. (1994). Fathers and parental leave. *Texas Law Review, 72,* 1047–1095.

Marcenko, M. O., and Meyers, J. C. (1994). How families of children with severe disabilities choose to allocate a cash subsidy. *Journal of Mental Health Administration, 21(3),* 253–262.

Marra, R., and Lindner, J. (1994). The true cost of parental leave: The parental leave cost model. In Families and Work Institute, D. E. Friedman, E. Galinsky, and V. Plowden (Eds.), *Parental leave and productivity* (pp. 55–78). New York: Families and Work Institute.

Mashaw, J. L. (1983). *Bureaucratic justice.* New Haven, Conn.: Yale University Press.

Mason, M. A. (1999). *The custody wars.* New York: Basic Books.

Mauldon, J. (1992). Children's risks of experiencing divorce and remarriage: Do disabled children destabilize marriages? *Population Studies, 46(2),* 349–362.

Melli, M. S., Brown, P. R., and Cancian, M. (1997). Child custody in a changing world: A study of postdivorce arrangements in Wisconsin. *1997 University of Illinois Law Review,* 773–800.

Meyer, B. D., and Rosenbaum, D. T. (1999). *Welfare, the Earned Income Tax Credit, and the labor supply of single mothers.* NBER Working Paper No. 7363.

Meyers, M. K., Brady, H. E., and Seto, E. Y. (2000). *Expensive children in poor families: The intersection of childhood disabilities and welfare.* San Francisco: Public Policy Institute of California.

Mitchell, O. (1990). The effects of mandating benefits packages. In L. J. Bassi and D. L. Crawford (Eds.), *Research in labor economics* (Vol. 11, pp. 297–320). Greenwich, Conn.: JAI Press.

Moen, P., Downey, G., and Bolger, N. (1990). Labor-force reentry among U.S. homemakers in midlife: A life-course analysis. *Gender and Society, 4(2),* 230–243.

Moffitt, R. (1992). Incentive effects of the U.S. welfare system: A review. *Journal of Economic Literature, 30(1),* 1–61.

Morris, B. (2002, October 14). Trophy husbands. *Fortune,* p. 78.

Nedelsky, J. (1989). Reconceiving autonomy: Sources, thoughts, and possibilities. *Yale Journal of Law and Feminism, 1,* 7–36.

Neumark, D., Schweitzer, M., and Wascher, W. (2000, February). *The effects of minimum wages throughout the wage distribution.* NBER Working Paper No. 7519.

Neumark, D., and Wascher, W. (2000). Minimum wages and employment: A case study of the fast-food industry in New Jersey and Pennsylvania. *American Economic Review, 90(5),* 1362–1396.

Okin, S. M. (1989). *Justice, gender, and the family.* New York: Basic Books.

Oregon State Office for Services to Children and Families. (1996, January 2). Client services manual I, section C: Supportive services. (accessed 10 September 2002).

Organisation for Economic Co-operation and Development. (1998). *Employment outlook.* Paris: OECD.

Organisation for Economic Co-operation and Development. (2001). *Society at a glance.* Paris: OECD.

Orrange, R. M. (1999). *Women as household managers in dual-earner couples.* BLCC Working Paper No. 99-05, Cornell Employment and Family Careers Institute.

Parfit, D. (1984). *Reasons and persons.* Oxford: Clarendon Press.

Pateman, C. (1988). The patriarchal welfare state. In A. Gutmann (Ed.), *Democracy and the welfare state* (pp. 231–260). Princeton, N.J.: Princeton University Press.

Pateman, C. (2002, May). *Democratizing citizenship: Some advantages to basic income.* Paper presented at the Rethinking Redistribution Conference, University of Wisconsin-Madison, http://www.ssc.wisc.edu/havenscenter/ruprr.htm (accessed 14 June 2002).

Poterba, J. M., Venti, S. F., and Wise, D. A. (1995). Do 401(k) contributions crowd out other personal saving? *Journal of Public Economics, 58(1),* 1–32.

Presser, H. (1994). Employment schedules among dual-earner spouses and the division of household labor by gender. *American Sociological Review, 59(3),* 348–364.

Public Agenda Online. (2000a). Child care: A nation divided? www.publicagenda.org/issues/nation_divided_detail.cfm?issue_type=childcare&list=2 (accessed October 2001).

Public Agenda Online. (2000b). Necessary compromises: How parents, employers, and children's advocates view childcare today. www.publicagenda.org/specials/childcare/childcare.htm (accessed 10 July 10 2002).

Radcliffe Public Policy Center. (2000). *Life's work: Generational attitudes toward work and life integration.* Cambridge, Mass.: Radcliffe Public Policy Center.

Rakowski, E. (1991). *Equal justice*. New York: Oxford University Press.

Rakowski, E. (2002). Who should pay for bad genes? *California Law Review, 90(5)*, 1345–1414.

Rawls, J. (1971). *A theory of justice*. Cambridge, Mass.: Belknap Press.

Rawls, J. (1997). The idea of public reason revisited. *University of Chicago Law Review, 64,* 765–807.

Raz, J. (1986). *The morality of freedom*. Oxford: Clarendon Press and New York: Oxford University Press.

Rhode, D. L. (1989). *Justice and gender*. Cambridge, Mass.: Harvard University Press.

Roberts, K., and Lawton, D. (2001). Acknowledging the extra care parents give their disabled children. *Child: Care, Health, and Development, 27(4)*, 307–319.

Robinson, C., Jackson, P., and Townsley, R. (2001). Short breaks for families caring for a disabled child with complex health needs. *Child and Family Social Work, 6(1)*, 67–78.

Roman, M., and Haddad, W. (1978). *The disposable parent: The case for joint custody*. New York: Penguin.

Rosen, H. S. (1999). *Public finance* (5th ed.). Boston: Irwin/McGraw-Hill.

Ross, C. E., and Mirowsky, J. (1988). Child care and emotional adjustment to wives' employment. *Journal of Health and Social Behavior, 29(1)*, 127–138.

Rubenfeld, J. (1989). The right of privacy. *Harvard Law Review, 102(4)*, 737–807.

Ruhm, C. (1997, summer). Policy watch: The Family and Medical Leave Act. *Journal of Economic Perspectives, 11(3)*, 175–186.

Ruhm, C. (1998). The economic consequences of parental leave mandates: Lessons from Europe. *Quarterly Journal of Economics, 113(1)*, 285–317.

Samuels, C. A. (2000, October 9). Day care scarce for disabled children. *Washington Post*, Metro sec., p. B03.

Sanger, C. (1996). Separating from children. *Columbia Law Review, 96(2)*, 375–517.

Schneider, C. E., and Brinig, M. F. (2000). An invitation to family law (2nd ed.). St. Paul, Minn.: West Group.

Schultz, V. (2000). A life's work. *Columbia Law Review, 100(7)*, 1881–1964.

Scott, E. S. (1992). Pluralism, parental preferences, and child custody. *California Law Review, 80(3)*, 615–672.

Scott, E. S. (2001). Divorce, children's welfare, and the culture wars. *Virginia Journal of Social Policy and Law, 9(1)*, 95–115.

Scott, E. S., and Scott, R. E. (1995). Parents as fiduciaries. *Virginia Law Review, 81,* 2401–2476.

Selmi, M. (2000). Family leave and the gender wage gap. *North Carolina Law Review, 78(3)*, 707–782.

Shaviro, D. (1997). The minimum wage, the Earned Income Tax Credit, and optimal subsidy policy. *University of Chicago Law Review, 64,* 405–481.

Shelton, B. A., and John, D. (1996). The division of household labor. *Annual Review of Sociology, 22,* 299–322.

Sherraden, M. (1991). *Assets and the poor.* Armonk, N.Y.: M. E. Sharpe.

Shiffrin, S. V. (2004). Egalitarianism, choice-sensitivity, and accommodation. In S. Scheffler (Ed.), *Reasons and values: Themes from the work of Joseph Raz.* Oxford: Oxford University Press.

Social Security Administration. (2000). *Annual statistical supplement to the Social Security Bulletin.*

Sugarman, S. (1987). Short term paid leave: A new approach to social insurance and employee benefits. *California Law Review, 75(2),* 465–494.

Summers, L. H. (1989). What can economics contribute to social policy? Some simple economics of mandated benefits. *American Economic Review, Papers and Proceedings 79(2),* 177–183.

Sylvester, K. (2001). Caring for our youngest: Public attitudes in the United States. *The Future of Children, 11(1),* 53–61.

Toth, J. (1997). *Orphans of the living.* New York: Simon and Schuster.

Ulrich, K. E. (2002). Insuring family risks: Suggestions for a national family policy and wage replacement. *Yale Journal of Law and Feminism, 14(1),* 1–68.

U.S. Bureau of the Census. (2000c). *Statistical abstract of the United States: 2000.*

U.S. Bureau of the Census. (2001a). *Fertility of American women: June 2000.*

U.S. Bureau of the Census. (2001b). *Living arrangements of children: 1996.*

U.S. Bureau of the Census. (2001c). *Reasons people do not work: 1996.*

U.S. Bureau of the Census. (2001d). *Statistical abstract of the United States: 2001.*

U.S. Bureau of the Census. (2002, July). *Who's minding the kids? Child care arrangements: Spring 1997.*

U.S. Bureau of Labor Statistics. (2000). Families with own children: Employment status of parents by age of youngest child and family type, www.bls.gov/news.release/famee.to4.htm, famee/to5.htm, and /famee.to6.htm (accessed 29 September 2002).

U.S. Bureau of Labor Statistics. (2002). Occupational outlook handbook, www.bls.gov/oco/home.htm (accessed 8 July 2002).

U.S. Department of Health and Human Services, Administration for Children and Families, Children's Bureau. (1994). Analysis of state child welfare data: VCIS survey data from 1990 through 1994, www.acf.hss.gov/programs/cbthisisanoldcb/dis/vcis/preface.htm (accessed 8 July 2002).

U.S. Department of Health and Human Services, Administration for Children and Families, Children's Bureau. (2001, June). The AFCARS report, interim

FY 1999 estimates as of June 2001, www.acf.dhhs.gov/programs/cb (accessed 8 July 2002).

U.S. Department of Justice, Civil Rights Division, Disability Rights Section. (2002). Commonly asked questions about child care centers and the Americans with Disabilities Act, www.usdoj.gov/crt/ada/childq&a.htm (accessed 29 September 2002).

U.S. Department of Labor, Bureau of Labor Statistics. (2001). Median weekly earnings of full-time workers, ftp://ftp.bls.gov/pub/special.requests/lf/aat37.txt (accessed 21 October 2003).

U.S. General Accounting Office. (1990, September). *Respite care: An overview of federal, selected state, and private programs.* GAO/HRD-90-125.

U.S. General Accounting Office. (2001, February). *Child care: States increased spending on low-income families.* GAO-01-293.

U.S. House of Representatives. (2000). *2000 green book.*

Van Parijs, P. (1995). *Real freedom for all.* Oxford: Clarendon Press and New York: Oxford University Press.

Viscusi, W. K., and Moore, M. J. (1987). Workers' compensation: Wage effects, benefit inadequacies, and the value of health losses. *Review of Economics and Statistics, 69(2),* 249–261.

Viscusi, W. K., and Moore, M. J. (1991). Worker learning and compensating differentials. *Industrial and Labor Relations Review, 45(1),* 80–96.

Waldfogel, J. (1997). The effect of children on women's wages. *American Sociological Review, 62,* 209–217.

Waldfogel, J. (1998a). The family gap for young women in the United States and Britain: Can maternity leave make a difference? *Journal of Labor Economics, 16(3),* 505–545.

Waldfogel, J. (1998b). Understanding the "family gap" in pay for women with children. *Journal of Economic Perspectives, 12(1),* 137–156.

Waldfogel, J. (2001). International policies toward parental leave and child care. *The Future of Children, 11(1),* 99–111.

Waldron, I., and Jacobs, J. (1988). Effects of labor force participation on women's health: New evidence from a longitudinal study. *Journal of Occupational Medicine, 30(12),* 977–983.

Warfield, M. E., and Hauser-Cram, P. (1996, October). Child care needs, arrangements, and satisfaction of mothers of children with developmental disabilities. *Mental Retardation, 34,* 294–302.

Waters, E., and Noyes, D. M. (1983–1984). Psychological parenting vs. attachment theory: The child's best interest and the risks in doing the right things for the wrong reasons. *New York University Review of Law and Social Change, 12,* 505–515.

Wax, A. L. (1998). Bargaining in the shadow of the market: Is there a future for egalitarian marriage? *Virginia Law Review, 84(4)*, 509–672.

Williams, J. (2000). *Unbending gender.* Oxford: Oxford University Press.

Winkler, A. E. (1998). Earnings of husbands and wives in dual-earner families. *Monthly Labor Review, 121*, reprinted at http://www.bls.gov/opub/mlr/1998/04/art4abs (accessed 22 October 2003).

Witchel, A. (2002, February 7). At home with Candice Olson. *New York Times*, sec. F, p. 1.

Wolff, E. N. (2000, April). *Recent trends in wealth ownership, 1983–1998.* Jerome Levy Economics Institute, Working Paper No. 300.

Woodhouse, B. B. (1993). Hatching the egg: A child-centered perspective on parents' rights. *Cardozo Law Review, 14*, 1747–1865.

Woodhouse, B. B. (1995). Of babies, bonding, and burning buildings: Discerning parenthood in irrational action. *Virginia Law Review, 81*, 2493–2521.

Yeung, W. J., et al. (2001). Children's time with fathers in intact families. *Journal of Marriage and Family, 63(1)*, 136–154.

Yin, G. K., Scholz, J. K., Forman, J. B., and Mazur, M. J. (1994). Improving the delivery of benefits to the working poor: Proposals to reform the Earned Income Tax Credit program. *American Journal of Tax Policy, 11*, 225–298.

Zinsser, C. (2001, spring/summer). Child care within the family. *The Future of Children, 11(1)*, 123–127.

Index

Printed in the United States
137937LV00001B/11/A